CW00660609

Transgender Athletes in Competitive Sport

While efforts to include gay and lesbian athletes in competitive sport have received significant attention, it is only recently that we have begun examining the experiences of transgender athletes in competitive sport. This book represents the first comprehensive study of the challenges that transgender athletes face in competitive sport; and the challenges they pose for this sex-segregated institution. Beginning with a discussion of the historical role that sport has played in preserving sex as a binary, the book examines how gender has been policed by policymakers within competitive athletics. It also considers how transgender athletes are treated by a system predicated on separating males from females, consequently forcing transgender athletes to negotiate the system in coercive ways. The book not only exposes our culture's binary thinking in terms of both sex and gender, but also offers a series of thought-provoking and sometimes contradictory recommendations for how to make sport more hospitable, inclusive and equitable.

Transgender Athletes in Competitive Sport is important reading for all students and scholars of the sociology of sport with an interest in the relationship between sport and gender, politics, identity and ethics.

Eric Anderson is Professor of Sport, Masculinities and Sexualities at the University of Winchester, UK. He holds four degrees, has published 17 books, over 60 peer-reviewed articles, and is regularly featured in international television, print and digital media. Professor Anderson is recognized for research excellence by the British Academy of Social Sciences and is a fellow of the International Academy of Sex Research. His work shows a decline in cultural homohysteria and promotes inclusive attitudes toward openly gay, lesbian and bisexual athletes as well as a softening of heterosexual masculinities.

Ann Travers is Associate Professor of Sociology at Simon Fraser University, Canada. She has published two books, 13 peer-reviewed articles, and is a regular presenter at conferences relating to sport, embodiment and sociology more generally. She has received over $200,000 in funding for her research relating to sport and gender and transgender issues in sport.

Routledge Research in Sport, Culture and Society

Transgender Athletes in Competitive Sport

Edited by Eric Anderson and Ann Travers

Routledge
Taylor & Francis Group

LONDON AND NEW YORK

First published 2017
by Routledge
2 Park Square, Milton Park, Abingdon, Oxon OX14 4RN

and by Routledge
711 Third Avenue, New York, NY 10017

Routledge is an imprint of the Taylor & Francis Group, an informa business

© 2017 Eric Anderson and Ann Travers

The right of Eric Anderson and Ann Travers to be identified as
the authors of the editorial matter, and of the authors for their
individual chapters, has been asserted in accordance with sections
77 and 78 of the Copyright, Designs and Patents Act 1988.

All rights reserved. No part of this book may be reprinted or
reproduced or utilised in any form or by any electronic,
mechanical, or other means, now known or hereafter invented,
including photocopying and recording, or in any information
storage or retrieval system, without permission in writing from
the publishers.

Trademark notice: Product or corporate names may be trademarks
or registered trademarks, and are used only for identification and
explanation without intent to infringe.

British Library Cataloguing in Publication Data
A catalogue record for this book is available from the British
Library

Library of Congress Cataloging in Publication Data
Names: Anderson, Eric, editor. | Travers, Ann, editor.
Title: Transgender athletes in competitive sport / edited by Eric
Anderson and Ann Travers.
Description: Abingdon, Oxon ; New York, NY : Routledge, 2017. |
Series: Routledge research in sport, culture and society | Includes
bibliographical references and index.
Identifiers: LCCN 2016056045| ISBN 9781138235632 (hardback) |
ISBN 9781315304274 (ebook)
Subjects: LCSH: Transgender athletes. | Gender identity in sports.
| Sex differences in sports. | Sports–Rules–Social aspects.
Classification: LCC GV708.8 .T73 2017 | DDC 796.086/64–dc23
LC record available at https://lccn.loc.gov/2016056045

ISBN: 978-1-138-23563-2 (hbk)
ISBN: 978-1-315-30427-4 (ebk)

Typeset in Sabon
by Wearset Ltd, Boldon, Tyne and Wear

MIX
Paper from
responsible sources
FSC
www.fsc.org   FSC® C013056

Printed and bound in Great Britain by
TJ International Ltd, Padstow, Cornwall

Contents

Illustrations

Figures

Tables

Contributors

Jay Anonymous

Jonathan Ospina Betancurt, The Technical University of Madrid, Spain.

Nereida Bueno-Guerra, University of Barcelona, Spain.

Helen J. Carroll, National Center for Lesbian Rights, USA.

José Devís-Devís, University of Valencia, Spain.

Agnes Elling, Mulier Instituut, Netherlands.

Kiki Collot d'Escury, Mulier Instituut, Netherlands.

Maylon Hanold, Seattle University, USA.

Vanessa Heggie, Birmingham University, UK.

Elena Lopez-Cañada, University of Valencia, Spain.

Adam Love, Mississippi State University, USA.

Kinnon MacKinnon, University of Toronto, Canada.

Rory Magrath, Southampton Solent University, UK.

Maria Jose Martinez-Patiño, University of Vigo, Spain.

Riley McCormack, Seattle University, USA.

Mark F. Ogilvie, Durham University, UK.

Sofía Pereira-García, University of Valencia, Spain.

Lindsay Parks Pieper, Lynchburg College, USA.

Karen R. Rosenberg, University of Delaware, USA.

Victor Manuel Perez Samaniego, University of Valencia, Spain.

Michelle A. B. Sutherland, Georgetown University, USA.

Brendon Tagg, University of Queensland, Australia.

Claudio Tamburrini, Stockholm University, Sweden.

Sarah Teetzel, Manitoba University, Canada.

Eric Vilain, University of California Los Angeles, USA.

Introduction

Eric Anderson and Ann Travers

In September of 2015, eight of the Iranian national women's football squad were described in the press as actually "being men" awaiting sexual reassignment surgery. This declaration came on the heels of the country's football governing body revealing that four national team players were DMAB (designated male at birth) who had not completed sex-change operations, the year prior. Also in that year came former Olympic decathlon gold medal winner Bruce Jenner's announced of her gender transition to Caitlin. Perhaps more important to the governance of sport, that same year 19-year-old Indian runner, Dutee Chand, appealed her ban by the Athletics Federation of India (AFI) because her testosterone levels were deemed to be "too high" to be naturally occurring in a "woman." Her appeal, to the International Association of Athletics Federation (IAAF)'s Court of Appeal for Sport (CAS) was successful. These cases indicate just how complex ideas and practices relating to sex, gender and athletic performance really are; and that business as usual around sex, gender and sport are being subject to unprecedented challenge and criticism.

Despite this complexity, the common sense assumption that sports are a neutral institution for deriving and demonstrating athletic excellence remains relatively intact (McDonagh and Pappano 2007). This assumption, however, fails to account for the impact of economic dis/advantage and various forms of doping/cheating on athletic achievement or the standard of 'fairness' assumed to be achieved by dividing sport into two groups: males and females (Mitra 2014). Yet sporting discourse concerning fairness almost exclusively revolves around the second of these, drugs and cheating in sport. It takes sex segregation as a natural fundamental, from community level of play, right up through to the professional ranks. Thus, we compete not according to ability categories, nor weight/size categories, but rather according to our assignment to one of only two sex categories. Even when other characteristics are accounted for, such as age categories, or ability/disability categories, sport continues to be divided by sex. In segregating athletes into two neat, yet wholly incomplete, categories, sport remains one of the most important institutions in reproducing the sex/gender binary (Joseph and Anderson, forthcoming).

In most societies, the sex/gender binary has been socially constructed in accordance with commonsense interpretations of biological sex difference (Cancian 1987). We are influenced in all aspects of our lives by the sex – male or female – to which we are socially assigned at birth. Because of the strength of the association between the male and masculinity and the female and femininity, even though 'gender' (a cultural category) and 'sex' (a biological category) are not synonymous, in commonsense discourse they are used interchangeably. Together, they have produced dominant ideas of males and females, masculinity and femininity; ideas that were cemented into sport during its early history and subsequent spread from the West to other countries throughout the world (Dong 2014). Queer/feminist science studies have revealed that sex is not naturally restricted to only two categories. And gender is not innately connected to one's physical anatomy, but, more accurately, to the interconnections between sex and gender, and to one's sense of biological self and personal identity (both of which may vary from what is socially ascribed).

Transgender, transsexual, gender queer, gender nonconforming ...

Since the 1950s, transgender and gender nonconforming individuals have emerged as polemic and sensationalized figures in Western media accounts. Some of the controversy has centered on their participation in sex-divided sporting spaces since Rene Richards groundbreaking appearance on the Women's Tennis Association tour in 1977. Richards, a transsexual woman, set an important precedent in 1977 when she successfully sued the Women's Tennis Association for barring her participation (Birrell and Cole 1990). Since then, more recent cases at both amateur and professional levels of sport have challenged simplistic notions of binary-based biological sex difference (Griffin and Carroll 2010; Travers and Deri 2010). Other ground-breaking trans athletes in elite amateur and professional sports include Canada's Michelle Dumaresq (women's mountain biking); Denmark's Lana Lawless; Indian Runner Shanti Soundarajan; the USA's Miane Bagger (Ladies Professional Golf Association); Kai Allums (NCAA women's basketball); Keelin Godsey (two-time NCAA women's hammer throw champion); Fallon Fox (Mixed Martial Arts); Chris Mosier (triathlon) and Caitlyn Jenner (1976 Olympic gold medal winner decathlon).

Sport in the West, and much of the world is organized in terms of taken-for-granted assumptions of binary and hierarchical sex difference by virtue of sex segregated sporting spaces and grossly unequal cultural and economic spaces. More broadly, sport also normalizes white leadership, heterosexual masculinity and class privilege (Douglas and Jamieson 2006).

The exploration of issues relating to transgender participation in sport in this volume therefore needs to have an intersectional footprint (Banet-Weiser 1999; Crenshaw 1998; Hill Collins 2005) as race, class, sexuality, gender and nation constitute assemblages of power and privilege (Puar 2007) working in and through sport that are far from simplistic (Douglas 2013). Assumptions of unfair male advantage, for example, lean heavily on a Western image of white, middle- and upper-class female frailty. The ways in which women of color who compete in sport are read through this lens reveals the extent to which the sex/gender binary is racialized at a fundamental level.

Also, how we define transgender is a challenging and yet important starting point. We acknowledge the considerable debate about transgender and transsexual definitions, and the often-difficult relationships between transsexuals who are seeking medical and legal re-assignment to 'opposite' sex identities, and transgender persons who resist full transition according to the gender binary. There is, at times, considerable tension and overlap among and between transgender and transsexual persons and self-definitions rarely conform to hard and fast categorical distinctions. We address these tensions throughout the book but take as our starting point Susan Stryker's definition in that transgender does not:

> refer to one particular identity or way of being embodied but rather as an umbrella term for a wider variety of bodily effects that disrupt or denaturalize heteronormatively constructed linkages between an individual's anatomy at birth, a nonconsensually assigned gender category, psychical identifications with the sexed body images and/or gendered subject positions, and the performance of specifically gendered, social, sexual, or kinship functions.
>
> (1998: 149)

In other words, there are many ways to be transgender. That said we hold to two central principles in this volume: first, a focus on athletes who challenge simplistic binary sex/gender systems, and second, that the last word on their sex/gender identity is self-defined.

Concerns about transgender participation in sport tend to crystallize around assumptions about exposure to testosterone – either prior to or as part of transitioning – as conferring an unfair advantage. Assumptions about male athletic superiority that characterize and structure mainstream sporting policies (Sykes 2006) are pervasive, in spite of documented overlaps between male and female athletic performance (Fausto-Sterling 2000; Kane 1995; Travers 2008). We are not arguing that there is not a mean difference between 'the sexes' but that the overlap, depending upon the sport, is significant and socially unrecognized. We tend to consider all men as stronger, faster, or better than all women. Similarly, testosterone is coded as a male hormone despite its presence in varying degrees in all of our bodies (Fausto-Sterling 2000), Teetzel (2006) successfully uncouples concerns about testosterone as a performance-enhancing substance from concerns about steroid use in sport by establishing that the performance-enhancement effect resulting from doping is far greater than any advantage from past or present levels of testosterone predating or resulting from gender transition. Indeed, Teetzel (2006) regards the latter as negligible. Authors in this volume will, however, challenge that assumption.

Athletes challenging the gender binary

The history of sport is characterized by male domination (Anderson 2005, 2014). Accordingly, it has famously been described by Dunning (1986, p. 79) as a "male preserve," an institution by and for men. It has been through competitive, often violent, team sports, such as American football or rugby, that boys and men have traditionally been able to demonstrate an acceptable form of masculinity (Pronger 1990). This masculine domain has, however, weathered several challenges. The first came in the form of female participation, albeit mostly in segregated sporting spaces, which began in earnest in the late 1970s and dramatically expanded in proceeding decades. The next challenge came from gay men, who, as recently as the 1990s were thought to be pariahs in the world of men's sports. Yet, research on gay men in competitive, organized team sport shows that they are mostly accepted into ostensibly heterosexual team sports; often times with heart-warming reception (Anderson *et al.* 2016). What both of these categories of challenges to the homosocial world of twentieth-century men's sport have in common, however, is that they – even if inadvertently – promoted dualistic thinking about sex. Gay men, for, example, who were once so socially stigmatized that they were thought akin to women, were accepted as males, and welcomed into gender-segregated sport.

Accordingly, a genuinely radical challenge to the sex/gender binary is advanced by athletes who refuse to participate in it, those that we might perhaps describe as a third wave of threat to the business as usual operations of sport: female to male transsexuals who continue to identify as "dykes" or transmen and play in lesbian leagues, or athletes who once competed for men's teams but now compete for women's teams. Others may have no particular desire to identify as male or female at all. These athletes are, by definition, outside the norm of the sex/gender binary. They not only defy cultural understandings of sex and gender, but they press for a cultural re-examination of what it means to be a man or a woman, and (perhaps most significantly), call for institutional action in the making of laws and rules that govern the rules of sport, bathroom and locker rooms, and other public arenas.

There is now a patchwork of policies regarding transgender athletes across the West. For example, in the United States, the National Collegiate Athletic Association (NCAA) has policies that vary compared to the International Olympic Committee (IOC), which might vary compared to other countries in that they differ with respect to the extent an athlete must have 'transitioned' in order to be eligible (Teetzel 2014).

In this book we explore the impact – contemporary and potential – of transsexual, transgender, intersexual, and gender queer athletes on the social structure and practices of organized sport. But we also provide the most comprehensive set of data concerning the actual experiences of these athletes to date. The different chapters of this book explore the complexities of both sex and gender in different sports and varied social contexts. If the reader fails to find something to disagree with, we will consider ourselves to have failed in this endeavor.

Our efforts highlight that sport remains a largely unexamined bastion of sex segregation in Western cultures. This is to say that our culture predominantly believes in the rightfulness of men's and women's segregation via athletic teams; even when it comes at the expense of women's participation and cultural and economic equality. Culture nominally justifies this segregation as a result of 'ability', yet do not structure most sporting leagues by ability. This gender exclusion is, to most, so ordinary that it escapes notice, and certainly critical scrutiny – although a small body of work in critical sport studies has challenged the appropriateness of sex segregation, connecting it not to natural differences in ability but rather a patriarchal gender order (see, for example, Anderson 2009; Kane 1995; McDonagh and Pappano 2008; Travers 2008, 2013). If, for example, one were to walk onto various university playing surfaces and see to the left a team comprised of black men playing another team of black men, and on the right, a team of white men playing another team of white men, we propose that the average person would recognize that as racial segregation – and hopefully be alarmed by such. Yet, very few would see sex segregation. Opposite sex integration in most Western sporting contexts is "unthinkable" (Travers 2013) and therefore, unseen. By highlighting individuals who don't fit the sex/gender system, and who operate within the epitome of that system, we hope to illustrate the fallacy upon which we maintain our culture's binary thinking and social organization.

To do this, we have recruited authors invested in social and scientific understandings of sport. They approach the issues from different theoretical paradigms to complement and complicate the challenge to the role of organized sport in constructing and reinforcing traditional notions of sex and gender difference. However, we have requested that our authors write in an accessible manner. We desire this book to be accessible to those not invested in academic language, while retaining critical, and data driven ideas.

In the book, we argue that trans athletes, people who refuse and refute traditional categorization, reveal the limitations of the biologically determined sex/gender system, and that they make salient that there is a continuum within which men and women often have more in common than not – a fact upon which social scientists and biologists agree (Connell 2009), but which rarely sees the light of day in terms of its impact on common sense understandings and cultural systems.

This terrain is exciting to us for a number of reasons, as academics who believe that power inequalities across intersecting categories of sex, gender, race, class, and sexual orientation, we are encouraged by the increasing emergence of transsexual and transgender athletes and their champions. This is exciting, but not unexpected.

Research on the experience of gay and lesbians in sport shows that there has been tremendous social progress over the last few decades. Gay men are coming out in increasingly rapid numbers in professional sport, and research into their lives, as well as those who play at the university and community levels of play, show that for-the-most-part they are having outstanding sporting experiences, attenuated by social acceptance and even the promotion of social cohesion within teammates (Anderson 2011; Anderson *et al.* 2016).

This has been a result of a major cultural shift in the West from viewing homosexuality as deviant and immoral to instead viewing sexual plurality as normal and homophobia as unacceptable. For readers interested in this aspect of sport and social inclusion, we suggest you read *Out in Sport: The Experiences of Gay and Lesbian Athletes*, published with Routledge (Anderson *et al.* 2016).

While gay/lesbian/bisexual identities refer to a different category of classification than trans and non-gender binary people (the former is about sexuality and the latter about gender), they rely on each other for meaning. In Western contexts since the turn of the millennia, the transgender community has had a growing presence in the LGBT rights movement (this, in spite of the catalytic and yet historically suppressed roles of gender nonconformers at Stonewall in 1969). This is evidenced in a myriad of ways, from increasing legal equality for those who transition, to major expansion of gay and lesbian organizational mandates, such as the Human Rights Campaign in the United States and Stonewall in the United Kingdom to (now) fight for transgender rights as well (we recognize that there is a body of literature critiquing a rights-based approach) and some progress is also being made in sport (Travers and Deri 2011).

However, whereas gay and lesbian athletes challenge heteronormativity within sport, they typically do so with homonormativity (Duggan 2003; Forte 2014), doing little to challenge broader social hierarchies or the sex segregation of sport. In this manner, transsexual and transgender athletes offer more hope for cultural change around binary sex/gender systems than do gay and lesbian athletes. In the process of challenging and changing these rules, facilities, and institutions, we hope that they will also facilitate a transformation of attitudes regarding not only transgender and gender nonconforming people, but the way we look at sex and gender in Western culture as a whole.

About this edited volume

When Routledge asked us to write a book about transgender athletes, we jumped at the opportunity to produce – in a single publication – a powerful resource for academics and an informative and interesting book for sport professionals and general readers. The result is a book that is wide-ranging across different historical periods, different sports, and different local and global contexts, although predominantly focused on sport in the West. It incorporates personal, ideological and political narratives; varied conceptual, methodological, and theoretical approaches; and examples of complexities and nuanced ways of understanding the gendered and sexualized dynamics of sport.

To accomplish our task, we sought chapters from established scholars who have made important contributions to the field, as well as from emerging scholars who are breaking new ground. We also looked outside the field of sports studies to those from other disciplines and to some outside academe. We wanted to reflect the growing interest in sports studies in countries outside the West, but found difficulty securing enough contributions to give a truly global feel to our work. The lack of literature in the global south in the specific field of sport, gender and sexuality, and the problem of writing in English for non-English speakers, were major barriers.

We are also pleased that our book is comprised of a variety of authors. We have both cis and trans authors, and some who don't identify as having a particular gender at all. We also have authors who represent a spectrum of sexualities. We recognize that these categories of analysis are not however, the only categories that are important. Intersectionality with issues of race, age, and other variables are also important. Accordingly, while our authorship is mostly white, it is not exclusively; and our authors range from established professors, to those still working on their doctoral degrees.

References

Anderson, E. "In the game." *Gay Athletes and the Cult of Masculinity*. Albany, NY: SUNY (2005).

Anderson, E. "The maintenance of masculinity among the stakeholders of sport." *Sport Management Review* 12, no. 1 (2009): 3–14.

Anderson, E. "Updating the outcome gay athletes, straight teams, and coming out in educationally based sport teams." *Gender & Society* 25, no. 2 (2011): 250–268.

Anderson, E. *21st Century Jocks: Sporting Men and Contemporary Heterosexuality*. Palgrave Macmillan (2014).

Anderson, E., Magrath, R. and Bullingham, R. *Out in Spot: The Experiences of Openly Gay Male Athletes*. London: Routledge (2016).

Banet-Weiser, S. and Portwood-Stacer, L. " 'I just want to be me again!' Beauty pageants, reality television and post-feminism." *Feminist Theory* 7, no. 2 (2006): 255–272.

Birrell, S. and Cole, C. "Double fault: Renée Richards and the construction and naturalization of difference." In P. Creedon (ed.), *Women, Media and Sport: Challenging Gender Values*. (pp. 207–238). Thousand Oaks, CA: SAGE Publications, Inc. (1994).

Cancian, F. "Love in America." In *Gender and Self-development*. Cambridge: Cambridge University Press (1987).

Connell, R. W. and Pearse, R. *Gender: In World Perspectives*, London: John Wiley & Sons (2009).

Crenshaw, W. K. "The intersectionality of race and gender discrimination." In *Background Paper, Expert Group Meeting on Gender and Race Discrimination*, November, pp. 1331–1387 (1998).

Dong, J. "Revolution, resistance and resilience." In J. Harhreaves and E. Anderson (eds.), *Routledge Handbook of Sport, Gender and Sexuality* (p. 87). London: Routledge (2014).

Douglas, D. D. "Forget me … not: Marion Jones and the politics of punishment." *Journal of Sport and Social Issues* (2013).

Douglas, D. D. and Jamieson, K. M. "A farewell to remember: interrogating the Nancy Lopez farewell tour." *Sociology of Sport Journal* 23, no. 2 (2006): 117.

Duggan, L. *The Twilight of Equality?: Neoliberalism, Cultural Politics, and the Attack On Democracy*. Boston: Beacon Press (2003).

Fausto-Sterling, A. *Sexing the Body: Gender Politics and the Construction of Sexuality*. New York: Basic Books (2000).

Forte, M. *Good Intentions*. Vol. 4. Lulu.com (2014).

Griffin, P. and Carroll, H. J. *On the Team: Equal Opportunity for Transgender Student Athletes*. NCLR, National Center for Lesbian Rights (2010).

Hill Collins, P. "Prisons for our bodies, closets for our minds: racism, heterosexism, and black sexuality." *Sex, Gender, and Sexuality* (2005): 115–137.

Ikeda, K. "Ryōsai-kembo, liberal education and maternal feminism under fascism: women and sport in modern Japan." *The International Journal of the History of Sport* 27, no. 3 (2010): 537–552.

Kane, M. J. "Resistance/transformation of the oppositional binary: exposing sport as a continuum." *Journal of Sport and Social Issues* 19, no. 2 (1995): 191–218.

McDonagh, E. and Pappano, L. *Playing with the Boys: Why Separate is Not Equal in Sports*. Oxford: Oxford University Press (2008).

Mitra, P. "The untold stories of female athletes with intersex variations in India." *Routledge Handbook of Sport, Gender and Sexuality* (p. 384). London: Routledge (2014).

Pronger, B. *The Arena of Masculinity: Sports, Homosexuality, and the Meaning of Sex*. Macmillan (1990).

Puar, J. K. "Queer times, queer assemblages." *Social Text* 23, no. 3–4, 84–85 (2005): 121–139.

Stryker, S. "Kaming Mga Talyada (we who are sexy): the transsexual whiteness of Christine Jorgensen in the (Post) colonial Philippines." *The Transgender Studies Reader* 2 (2013): 352.

Sykes, H. "Transsexual and transgender policies in sport." *Women in Sport and Physical Activity Journal* 15, no. 1 (2006): 3–13.

Teetzel, S. "On transgendered athletes, fairness and doping: an international challenge." *Sport in Society* 9, no. 2 (2006): 227–251.

Teetzel, S. "The onus of inclusivity: sport policies and the enforcement of the women's category in sport." *Journal of the Philosophy of Sport* 41, no. 1 (2014): 113–127.

Travers, A. "The sport nexus and gender injustice." *Studies in Social Justice Journal* 2, no. 1 (2008): 79–101.

Travers, A. "Thinking the unthinkable: imagining an 'un-American,' girl-friendly, women- and trans-inclusive alternative for baseball." *Journal of Sport & Social Issue* 37, no. 1 (2013): 78–96.

Travers, A. and Deri, J. "Transgender inclusion and the changing face of lesbian softball leagues." *International Review for the Sociology of Sport* 46, no. 4 (2010): 488–507.

Part I

Individual stories of transgender sporting experiences

Chapter 1

Advantage Renée?

Renée Richards and women's tennis

Lindsay Parks Pieper

Newcomer Renee Clarke cruised by top-seeded Robin Harris, 6–1, 6–1, in the finals of the 1976 La Jolla tennis tournament. Clarke's precise baseline shots and powerful serves proved too much for Harrison. While her 6'2" frame awed the crowd, it particularly impressed San Diego reporter, Dick Carlson. He originally researched her for background information to produce a feel-good story about a remarkable local athlete. Instead, Carlson aired an expose that pushed the new star into the spotlight. He identified Renee Clarke as Renée Richards, the former male professional tennis player Richard Raskind. The discovery of a male-to-female trans athlete in women's tennis immediately raised eligibility questions and sparked protest.

Moreover, when Richards announced her intention to compete in the 1976 US Open, she challenged the classification structure of tennis. Like most sport organisations, the United States Tennis Association (USTA) and Women's Tennis Association (WTA) divided participants into male and female categories. Richards's very presence complicated these rules. She also surfaced just as women's tennis was making significant strides in both professional opportunities and payments. Viewing her as a threat to sex-segregated contests, and a menace to the newly popular women's tour, the USTA and WTA barred her by instituting a chromosomal check for all female participants. Richards consequently sued. A victory in the New York Supreme Court paved the way for her inclusion on the women's tennis circuit; however, the ruling extended only to Richards, and did not provide blanket acceptance for trans athletes in sport (DeMartini 2014). She participated in the 1977 US Open, lost in the first round, and retired from sport four years later.

Richards's athletic career demonstrates the importance of gender norms in the determination of sex in women's tennis. She overtly challenged biological conceptions of sex but also performed stereotypical understandings of femininity. Significantly, Richards repeatedly downplayed her athleticism – to diminish concerns of her supposed biological edge – and highlighted her weakened physique. Journalists similarly responded to accusations of advantage by focusing on her feminine appearance, while the reaction from female tennis players largely centred on questions of fairness. Although many argued that trans athletes threatened the sex-segregated blueprint of sport, an overview of Richards's time on the women's circuit instead illustrates a reaffirmation of binary understandings of both sex and gender.

Two sides of the net: a sex divide on the court

Before appearing in the women's division of the local California tournament, Richards participated in men's matches. She enrolled at Yale University and captained the tennis team. As a Yale Bulldog, Richards won the 1953 Men's Eastern Junior Indoor Championship. She later graduated from the University of Rochester Medical School in 1959, started an ophthalmology practice, and continued to compete. In 1964, she won the New York State men's clay-court title and, in 1972, ranked sixth nationally in the men's 35-and-over division. Despite finding success in medicine and athletics, Richards remained discontent. "My feeling for appropriate masculine behaviour came from more observation and impersonation than it did from any internal mechanism", she wrote in her 1983 autobiography *Second Serve: The Renée Richards Story*. "A lot of times I was like a man from a foreign country trying to blend in with the population" (111). Richards underwent sex reassignment surgery in 1975 and moved to California for a fresh start. Her success in the La Jolla Junior Veteran's Championship the following year ended her anonymity. The press immediately picked up the story and headlines appeared around the world.

Her decision to continue competing not only ensured more news coverage, but it also caused policy changes. When Richards announced her plans to participate in the 1976 US Open, the USTA and WTA banned her by enacting the Barr body test. This method, also known as the buccal smear test, checked competitors' chromosomes. The International Association of Athletics Federation (IAAF) and the International Olympic Committee (IOC) had already instituted the technique, purportedly to detect male imposters in elite sport.[1] Sport officials incorrectly argued that all women possessed XX chromosomes and all men possessed XY chromosomes.[2] In 1967, the IAAF introduced the Barr body test as a requirement for all female track and field athletes; the IOC followed suit the next year for all female Olympians (Pieper 2016).

Tennis officials thus had the Barr body test at their disposal in 1967. The USTA and WTA did not mandate the check until Richards appeared on the tennis scene nine years later. Disregarding warnings from scientists who argued that chromosomes did not unequivocally identify sex, the organisations used the precedent established by the IAAF and IOC. They instituted sex testing for the 1976 US Open to eliminate "persons not genetically female" from competition. Although worded broadly, the policy was aimed at Richards. Richards (1983) argued that "they knew in all likelihood I could never pass such a test, though it is not infallible proof of sexual identity" (343).

The USTA and WTA's decision to bar Richards from women's tennis stemmed from two false assumptions: that sports are fair and men possess a biological advantage in all athletic events. In a 1976 USTA press release explaining the new practice, the organisation suggested that "entry into women's events at the U.S. Open, the leading international tennis tournament, of persons not genetically female would introduce an element of inequality and unhappiness into the championships". The WTA echoed this idea. *New York Times* reporter Neil Amdur summarised the organisation's position as "it's damn unfair to a woman who has devoted her whole life to tennis to lose a sport in a draw to a man" (15 August 1976, 147). The new regulation, and the USTA's and WTA's defence of it, illustrates what sport scholar Heather Sykes (2006) refers to as the "unfair advantage discourse". This discourse falsely assumes that relatively higher levels of testosterone guarantee athletic success, that all male competitors are better than all female competitors in all sporting activities, and that men will undergo sex changes to reap the benefits of women's sport. Research on testosterone is inconclusive regarding the likelihood of gains in strength, and muscularity is not the only attribute necessary for sporting success. Plus, no man has ever changed sex for the sake of sporting victory.[3]

Despite evidence proving the unfair advantage discourse erroneous, the USTA and WTA held firm. "If I was allowed to play", Richards recalled (1983), the tennis organisations believed "the floodgates would be opened and through them would come tumbling an endless stream of made-over Neanderthals who would brutalize Chris Evert and Evonne Goolagong. Of course, this was sheer nonsense" (345). Nonsense or not, Richards needed to fight for entrance to the women's tour. One way she sought to dispel assumptions of her supposed advantage was to perform stereotypical femininity.

Richards's performance of femininity

The USTA and WTA believed that Richards's biology gave her an unfair advantage in tennis. "They think of me as bionic woman", she explained in a 1976 *New York Times* interview. So Richards regularly resisted such sentiments. "I'm not the world-beater they think I am", she argued (18 August 1976, 61). To help quell any misnomers about her athleticism, she displayed conventional femininity and highlighted her weakened physique, in line with Judith Butler's notion of gender performativity (1990). According to Butler, gender is constructed through the performance of acts that mirror social ideals. Richards's repetitive performances of femininity were important for her eventual inclusion on the women's circuit.

To prove her womanhood, Richards made herself the epitome of femininity in three ways. First, she outwardly upheld gender norms with makeup, nail polish, jewellery, and dresses. At a press conference following the La Jolla tournament, Richards appeared in "distinctly female" clothing, complemented by matching peach nail polish and "graceful gold pierced earrings". Second, she readily enacted stereotypes of female behaviour. For instance, Richards described herself as a newly emotional person. She claimed that hormone treatments had lifted her mood, but also left her off balance. "The hormones seemed to induce in me an uncharacteristic sense of well-being, even though my emotional swings increased markedly", she explained (2007). "I had laughing fits and crying jags, but they seemed natural and even therapeutic" (235). Her use of "natural" is striking. It suggests an essentialist notion of gender that reaffirms the belief that women as a group are more sensitive and irrational than men.

Third, and more significant in the realm of sport, Richards downplayed her athleticism and emphasised her weakness. She did so to abide by social protocol that views female athletes as inferior to male athletes. Thus, to prove to the USTA, WTA, and her competitors that she did not have an unfair advantage, Richards highlighted her weaknesses. She repeatedly described her reduced muscle mass, increased tiredness, and weight loss as signifiers of her womanhood. Even more overtly, Richards publicly equated losing with being a woman. Writing in *Second Serve*, she (1983) described playing tennis with male friends. "They were amazed at my skills ... but, when I missed a ball, they were quick to blame it on my being a woman", she wrote. But Richards's male competitors were not alone in labelling her mistakes as feminine. "I didn't mind these jibes because they affirmed my womanliness", Richards wrote. "Even the putdowns were welcomed reinforcements" (238). This behaviour, of course, upheld the idea that femininity and athleticism are oxymoronic. As sport philosopher Knutte Jonsson (2007) explains, these biological arguments of difference help "legitimate the gender hierarchy ... by seeing women's (inferior) gender roles as something that is natural" (245). Richards's enactment of stereotypical femininity therefore not only upheld society's ideals about gender, but also reinforced cultural practices that mark sport as a male space.

Journalists also regularly made note of Richards's outward appearance. Reports discussed her "high cheekbones", "sharply defined eyebrows", "shapely legs", and general attractiveness. *New York Times* writer Charles Friedman described Richards as "stylish and statuesque in a light blue tennis dress with a flared skirt and large loop earrings" (20 July 1977, 34). Although the presence of a trans athlete threatened to upend society's beliefs about the division between men and women, reporters largely covered Richards in the same (pejorative) way as they did other female athletes. As sport scholars Susan Birrell and Cheryl Cole (1990) explain, this type of coverage reproduced, rather than challenged, dominant understandings of sex and gender. They argue that the media upheld the "assumption that there are two and only two, obviously universal, natural, bipolar, mutually exclusive sexes that necessarily correspond to stable gender identity and gendered behavior" (3). Although many positively commented on Richards's carefully constructed appearance, not everyone was happy to include her in women's tennis.

Richards and the women's liberation movement

Richards may have viewed her lesser capabilities as justification for entrance to the women's tour, but her opponents on the court largely disagreed. When director of Tennis Week Open, Gene Scott, invited her to participate in an August 1976 tournament, twenty-five of the thirty-two women scheduled to compete dropped out in protest. The number two seed Ann Kiyomura told reporters that the reason for the mass exodus was because "We all feel she's still a man and it's just not fair" (*Chicago Tribune*, 21 August 1976, 4). Similarly, Wimbledon runner-up Janet Newberry argued that "We are not prepared to commit ourselves to a women's tournament in which a man is playing" (*Los Angeles Times*, 21 August 1976, C2). The WTA also revoked its sanction of Tennis Week Open on the premise that "there is a man in our tournament" (*Los Angeles Times*, 20 August 1976, E1). Presumptions of an unfair advantage again underlined these concerns. Some people also thought that including Richards diminished the gains women's tennis had only recently earned. In connection with the women's liberation movement, professional female players had established a professional tour for women in 1970 and continued to fight for equal purses to the men. Richards thus not only raised questions of fairness and advantage, but also highlighted the precarious nature of women's professional sport.

With the implementation of Title IX, and with support from the women's liberation movement, women's sport grew. Title IX stipulated equal sporting opportunities for men and women, increasing female participation at the high school and collegiate level. In professional tennis, Richards appeared on the scene just as Billie Jean King and other tennis players were advancing women's events. King was among the first to embrace the cause of women's tennis. The vocal advocate led the fight for equality and convinced eight of the top tennis competitors to start the Virginia Slims Tour in 1970. Shortly thereafter, King earned $117,000, becoming the first female athlete to breach the 100-grand mark. Her easy defeat of Bobby Riggs in the 1973 match billed as "The Battle of the Sexes", also provided justification for the expansion of women's sport. King's on-court efforts buttressed the women's movement and provided a strong symbol of successful female entrance into traditionally male realms (Ware 2011).

Consequently, some feared male-to-female trans athletes diminished the achievements of women's athletics and belittled the goals of the women's liberation movement. Gloria Steinem (1983), for example, embraced the unfair advantage thesis and wondered "if Richards had changed identity only to prove that any man, even a former one, could beat any woman" (227–228). Similarly, self-identified radical feminist Janice Raymond (1979) expressed even more hostile opposition to the possibility of trans inclusion in sport. She argued that "transsexuals" were men reconstructed in the guise of femininity in order to subvert women's progress. Raymond argued that Richards's campaign for inclusion was an attempt to dismantle the recent achievements of women's tennis. Raymond claimed that Richards had "succeeded in hitting the benefits of sex discrimination back into the male half of the court. The public recognition and success that it took Billie Jean King and women's tennis years to get, Renée Richards has achieved in one set" (xiii).

Richards continued to gain public recognition. When the Tennis Week Open tournament rolled around, only seven of the original thirty-two enlisted athletes participated. Richards defeated Cathy Beene, 6–0, 6–2, Caroline Stoll, 6–2, 0–6, 6–1, and Kathy Harter, 6–4, 7–6. Then, in front of a sell-out crowd of 36,000, she lost to seventeen-year-old Lea Antonoplis, 7–6, 3–6, 0–6, in the semi-finals. Her performance left many unimpressed. As *New York Times* reporter Amdur succinctly put it, "So what was all the fuss about" (29 August 1976, 141)? Beene commented that "I thought she would be a much stronger player than she was" and "she's not as strong or powerful as I anticipated" (*Chicago Tribune*, 22 August 1976, B3). When Richards failed to demolish other female competitors as initially expected, those opposed to her started to ease up on their protests. She continued to compete in tournaments – those not sanctioned by the USTA or the WTA – and many athletes came to a similar conclusion. As Richards (1983) recalled in *Second Serve*, "most of the women [the USTA and WTA] were supposedly protecting didn't want to be protected. In fact, they were on my side" (346). But because the tennis organisations remained unmoved, Richards sued for access.

Renee Richards vs. United States Tennis Association

In 1977, Richards filed suit against the USTA, WTA, and the US Open Committee. She argued that their refusal to allow her entrance to the women's tour was discriminatory and a deprivation of her civil rights. The case focused on three issues: the reliability of the Barr body test in the determination of sex, how to define sex, and the reaction of female athletes. When the New York Supreme Court ruled in Richards's favour on 16 August 1977, the decision opened the door for her to compete on the women's tennis circuit.

The court first heard arguments regarding the use of chromosomes as a prerequisite for competitions. Richards's lawyer argued that the Barr body test was "insufficient, grossly unfair, inaccurate, faulty and inequitable" in the determination of sex (*Richards v. United States Tennis Assn.*, 2). The doctors who testified on her behalf argued that a phenotype test was more accurate. Phenotype tests take into consideration an assortment of characteristics, such as anatomy and bodily appearance. The USTA refuted the argument by pointing to the IOC's use of the buccal smear test. Furthermore, the tennis organisation speculated that by removing the control method, a torrent of male imposters would flood women's tennis.

Next, Richards and the USTA attempted to provide a definition of sex. Famed sexologist John Money testified on behalf of Richards. He argued that a person's sex depended upon a variety of factors, including internal anatomy, external genital appearance, endocrine balance, somatic structure, psychology, and chromosomes. For the USTA, chair of the Department of Medicine at Stanford Medical School, Daniel Federman, prioritised the Y chromosome in the identification of sex. According to Federman, chromosomes are the most important factor when considering one's sex.

Finally, female athletes submitted affidavits for both sides. King supported Richards, arguing that she did "not enjoy physical superiority or strength so as to have an advantage over women competitors in the sport of tennis". Contrastingly, Françoise Dürr, Newberry, Kristien K. Shaw, and Vicki Berner claimed that trans athletes possessed a biological edge and pointed to Richards's height, strength, and wingspan as proof.

After taking all the arguments into consideration, Judge Ascione ruled in Richards's favour. He mandated that the USTA and WTA accept her in the women's category for all future tournaments. According to the decision, the singular use of the Barr body test in the determination of sex was "grossly unfair, discriminatory and inequitable, and violative of plaintiff's rights" (*Richards v. United States Tennis Assn.*, 6). To use the chromosomal control in conjunction with other measures, such as anatomical, legal, physical, and social features would suffice, he noted. And on those counts, Richards was a woman:

> In that her external genital appearance is that of a female, her internal sex is that of a female ..., she is psychologically a woman, and, as the result of the administration of female hormones, she has the muscular and fat composition of a female.
>
> (*Richards v. United States Tennis Assn.*, 1)

As with the media coverage of Richards, the decision upheld – rather than challenged – dominant understandings of sex and gender. Rather than question the sex-segregated, binary-gender-dependent nature of sport, Ascione merely modified the boundaries of womanhood to uphold a binary. Instead of questioning sex and gender barriers, the New York Supreme Court simply readjusted the criterion for women participants. Furthermore, the ruling pertained to Richards alone. Without setting a direct precedent, Ascione essentially guaranteed that all future questions would be considered on a case-by-case basis. Richards was permitted because she reaffirmed, not dismantled, the sport structure.

With the legal victory, Richards competed in the 1977 US Open. She lost in the first round, 1–6, 4–6, to Virginia Wade. While Richards never dominated the competition as many feared she would – and we can speculate that issues relating to her inclusion would have played out differently had she demolished her opponents as expected – she did find minimal success in doubles events. In the 1977 US Open, she and partner Betty Ann Grubb Stuart reached the finals. Richards also reached the semi-finals in mixed doubles at the US Open with partner, Ilie Năstase. After only four years playing professional women's tennis, Richards retired in 1981.

Her name mostly remained out of the headlines for three decades. Then, in 2007, she reappeared in the spotlight. In a series of interviews, Richards vigorously opposed trans inclusion in sport. She called the IOC's 2004 Stockholm Consensus – which permitted trans athletes access if sex reassignment surgery, legal recognition, and hormone therapy had been completed – "a particularly stupid decision" (*New York Times*, 1 February 2007, F1). Citing a natural masculine advantage in elite competition, she further suggested that the decision "is going to come back and haunt them" (*The Advocate*, 27 March 2007). Richards's protests shocked many who pointed out that such policies would have allowed her to compete. Yet, her opposition seemed to stem from her beliefs about gender: sporting prowess is a male achievement.

Conclusion

Richards's short stint in women's tennis illustrates the importance of gender expression in the identification of sex. At first, fears of a male biological advantage in sport led the USTA and WTA to enact the Barr body test. To counteract her supposed threat to the gender status quo, Richards highlighted her femininity and undermined her skills. Her endorsement of stereotypical gender norms worried leaders of the women's liberation movement, as did her fight for inclusion at the exact moment when women's tennis was on the rise. Yet, Richards's performance of conventional femininity helped her in the courtroom. The New York Supreme Court ruled her legally a woman, but stopped short of setting an influential precedent.

As shown in Richards's career, masculinity and femininity played a significant role in the determination of manhood and womanhood. On the surface, Richards's fight for inclusion in women's tennis appeared to challenge society's conception of sex; however, her outward appearance, performance of stereotypical femininity, press coverage, and legal victory all served to uphold a sex and gender divide. The reaffirmation of dichotomous sex and gender, in turn, further cast sport as an activity for men. It was only when Richards showcased her femininity and highlighted her weakness that people agreed she should play on the women's tour.

Notes

1 Neither the IAAF nor the IOC ever discovered a male imposter via the gender verification of women participants in elite sport. Rather, several women who learned they had intersex characteristics from the testing had their athletic careers and many aspects of their lives ruined.
2 Different chromosomal constitutions undermined this belief. For example, people with Androgen Insensitivity Syndrome (AIS), chromosomal mosaicism, Klinefelter Syndrome, and Turner Syndrome all disprove the idea that men and women can be separated into XY and XX. The Centre for Genetics Education, "Genes and chromosomes: the genome", *Genetics.edu*, www.genetics.edu.au.
3 For more information on the limitations of testosterone research, see Katrina Karkazis, Rebecca Jordan-Young, Georgiann Davis, and Silvia Camporesi, "Out of bounds? A critique of the new policies on hyperandrogenism in elite female athletes", *The American Journal of Bioethics* 12, no. 7 (2012): 3–16. For information on biological advantages of women as a group in sport, see Eileen McDonagh and Laura Pappano, *Playing with the Boys: Why Separate is Not Equal in Sports* (Oxford: Oxford University Press, 2009).

References

Birrell, Susan and Cheryl L. Cole. Double fault: Renee Richards and the construction and naturalization of difference. *Sociology of Sport* 7 (1990): 1–21.

Butler, Judith. *Gender Trouble: Feminism and the Subversion of Identity*. New York: Routledge, 1990.

DeMartini, Anne L. Thirty-five years after *Richards v. USTA*: the continued significance of transgender athletes' participation in sport. In *Sport and the Law: Historical and Cultural Intersections*, edited by Samuel O. Regalado and Sarah K. Fields, 97–114. Fayetteville: The University of Arkansas Press, 2014.

Jonsson, Knutte. Whose afraid of Stella Walsh? On gender, "gene cheaters", and the promises of cyborg athletes. *Sports, Ethnics and Philosophy* 1, no. 2 (2007): 121–144.

Karkazis, Katrina, Rebecca Jordan-Young, Georgiann Davis and Silvia Camporesi. Out of bounds? A critique of the new policies on hyperandrogenism in elite female athletes. *The American Journal of Bioethics* 12, no. 7 (2012): 3–16.

McDonagh Eileen and Laura Pappano. *Playing with the Boys: Why Separate is Not Equal in Sports*. Oxford: Oxford University Press, 2009.

Pieper, Lindsay Parks. *Sex Testing: Gender Policing in Women's Sports*. University of Illinois Press, 2016.

Raymond, Janice. *The Transsexual Empire: The Making of the She-Male*. Boston: Beacon Press, 1979.

Richards, Renée. *No Way Renée: The Second Half of My Notorious Life*. New York: Simon & Schuster, 2007.

Richards, Renée. *Second Serve: The Renée Richards Story*. New York: Stein and Day, 1983.

Steinem, Gloria. *Outrageous Acts and Everyday Rebellion*. New York: Holt, Rinehart and Winston, 1983.

Sykes, Heather. Transsexual and transgender policies in sport. *Women in Sport & Physical Activity Journal* 15, no. 1 (2006): 3–13.

Ware, Susan. *Game, Set, Match: Billie Jean King and the Revolution in Women's Sports*. Chapel Hill: The University of North Carolina Press, 2011.

Chapter 2

My name is Jay, I transitioned and I'm a disabled young athlete

Jay Anonymous

My name is Jay and I am 21 years old.

I haven't always had this name, but, for as long as I can remember, I have always *been* male. I wasn't necessarily seen as male by others, and was assigned female at birth, but this did not stop me from achieving my male identity. I am using an alias to write this chapter, as I am currently completely stealth and intend to maintain this way.

I am currently in my final year of my undergraduate degree, at a small University in London; and I am proud to say that nobody is aware of my gender history. I often enter intimate relations with others without disclosing my history and I love being comfortable being naked in front of my partners, without feeling the need to tell them something that I feel is irrelevant to my life now. I spent a lot time ensuring that I would be able to lead this life; and looking at me now, it is easy to see how I am able to be stealth – but it hasn't always been this way.

Loving boy sports

My transition has only been physical. I have always been male. My sense of male identity can be linked back to as early as age five, when I asked my mother 'when will I grow a willy?' I was upset and confused when she informed me that this would not happen. I always assumed that I would grow up to be male, so I continued to play with my friends as normal and participate in typically male activities, like rugby and judo. Looking back at pictures from this period, I am clearly a young boy playing sport, however due to my mother's resistance, I was unable to cut my hair as short as I desired. I was frustrated with my longer hair and its inconvenience as I attempted to throw people around the judo mat at my local school club.

Sports lessons in school were always a confusing time for me as, although I loved sport in general, I hated having to partake in 'girly' sports such as netball (a British sport similar to basketball) and dancing. I remember watching and being jealous that the other boys were able to play football or show their aggression through rugby. Around the age of 10, in a particularly warm sports lesson, the other boys were able to remove their shirts to play football. I immediately removed my shirt and saw the shock that the teacher had as I ran around topless.

Despite my hatred for most other female sports, I enjoyed rounders (a sport similar to baseball) and represented the school for many matches. From a young age, my physical disability meant that I was not able to run particularly well. I would be in immense pain when any pressure was placed on my foot and these problems continued to worsen as I matured. Despite this, I loved lobbing a ball as far as possible, and this was evident when the athletics season started, and I was able to throw heavy items.

Throwing individuals in judo was also another love and I thrived in the male-driven environment. Judo gave me permission to show my aggression in a controlled manner and it was clear that I had a talent for it. I was selected to compete in many regional and national competitions. I participated in these events as female and after achieving multiple gold medals at national level, I felt as though it was not fair for others to compete with a male in their section, so I decided to take a break. It felt very strange competing as female, as it never truly felt right. At that age, I did not fully comprehend my male gender; I was often told that I would grow out of my 'tom boy' stage and thought that my male traits were normal at that age.

Aged 11 my mother sent me to an all-female boarding school. I failed to make friends, and had particular trouble with swimming. Before puberty had hit, I really enjoyed swimming. I did so wearing only shorts. For boarding school, however, I had to shop for a suit with a top. I felt dysphoric towards my body as my mother picked one out and urged me to try it on. At my previous school, and after weeks of fighting, I was permitted to wear a t-shirt, however the boarding school was not as lenient. I initially completely refused to participate in swimming and would often sit on the side cuddled up in a ball, or would attempt to jump in the pool before anybody caught sight of my body. I was quite overweight, so I tried to blame my discomfort on my size. However, I was always trying to hide how I really felt.

I found some relief in lacrosse. My preferred position was goalie, as it did not require a skirt due to the various pads. I enjoyed building a team and competing with the girls, however I still couldn't help feeling so weird compared to the other players.

My awkwardness extended outside of sport, too. For example, we were permitted to go into the local town to do our shopping and my teammates would spend copious amounts of time on their makeup and appearance whilst looking at me in disgust, as I threw on my trackies. They always seemed to know something was different about me and continued to direct their negative thoughts towards my differences. I would attempt to fit in by lying about certain aspects of my life. I remember one occasion, when I was with six girls in a circle, and they were sharing their experiences with boys. They had all disclosed to me that they had some form of sexual experience with boys and wondered if I had the same. At this stage, I was 12 years old and had never even looked at boys in that respect. However, I did have, what I thought at the time were 'strange feelings', towards my sports teacher. Years later, I can now endorse my attraction towards her and also confirm my good taste as a young man!

Sexuality, gender and sex were all marvellous discoveries that I made whilst at the boarding school. I was not fully aware of the term transgender, however. I was able to confirm that I had an attraction to women, and that my gender identity was definitely not female. I realised how different I was from the girls at school, however I also learnt a lot about a young female's perspective on sex. After struggling to fit in, I began to become deeply depressed and started to miss the interaction with my male friends. I would soon be reunited with them, however: the headmistress determined that I was not mentally stable enough to be at the school. For the remaining three months of the school year, I settled back into my hometown and started judo again.

Learning to fight for boyhood

The first person I told I was male was my grandmother. I was happy to learn that she supported me, and would keep it to herself. Her support was important, because I had other growing issues, too. First, I was very overweight, and gaining yet more weight. Second, my anxiety had increased due to the onset of puberty, and I started to develop further problems with one foot. Ostensibly, my physical problems should have contributed to my overall anxiety, but I took advantage of the discussions regarding my foot and decided to take the opportunity to also explore my gender, through asking for a referral to a gender specialist. I was able to do this without my parent's knowledge.

I also opted to take courses focusing in sports studies in school. Here, I experienced competition between other boys and began to understand my hesitation in entering the changing room as a girl. As I was assumed to be a lesbian, the girls would shy their bodies away from me. Their discomfort always meant that I would wait until the toilet was free to change into my sports clothes. I failed to make friends at this school, too. This was not helped when I was first advised to use a wheelchair full-time due to my progressive condition with my foot.

It was also in these times that I began to learn to stand up for myself. If my parents, teachers and coaches would not protect me: I learned to advocate for myself. The school tried to prevent me from studying sport, but I demanded equal access. I even remember once participating in a basketball lesson in my wheelchair, when a senior staff member entered the court and insisted that I leave the lesson as my participation was again against 'health and safety'.

School uniform has always raised an issue for me and concerns were continued when I was asked to represent the school for athletics. The girls were asked to wear sports skirts and I made my position very clear – that I was not going to represent the school unless I was able to wear a tracksuit. At a particular competition, I vividly remember another student asking his mother 'why has that boy got long hair and standing with girls to throw?' My mannerisms at this age were similar to my male peers, so I could completely understand where the boy's comments were coming from. Being seen as male was very strange for me as a child as I was often told by my family that I should try to 'behave like a girl'. Although being referred to as male felt right, I could not help but feel as though my attempt to act female had failed. I remember also feeling extremely uncomfortable as I stood next to the females competing. I couldn't help but laugh at the ways in which they were throwing the javelin, discus and shot put. Contrary to my throwing, the females seemed to lack aggression. I continued to excel at representing the school in a variety of sports, within the realms of my disability, and my performance remained constant as I joined a large youth organisation.

From the age of 14, I was a member of the Army Cadet Force (ACF) and participated in many sports through the organisation. I was determined to be a team player, so I participated in swimming, despite my apprehension. I competed wearing my typical shorts and t-shirt at the local level and was soon invited to represent the county at regional level. However, I was told that I would have to wear a woman's bathing suit. My discomfort levels at this age were already particularly high, as I stopped shaving my legs, so I decided against further swimming competitions as I would receive strange looks entering the pool.

At this stage, I had not informed anybody of my male identity, as I felt comfortable being 'one of the guys'. With a beret, short hair and a stocky figure, it was assumed by others that I was male and I was comfortable with this. Still, my health was deteriorating, and I found myself back in my wheelchair. I would attempt to partake in physical activities, however, I would struggle to change after exercise, as I would have to enter the female block to change etc. I ensured that I was the last person to enter the building or would wait until the last moment to change. Despite the blocks often being open-plan, the female cadets respected my privacy and were able to appreciate that I was a bit different. It was very strange competing against women within cadets, however, with my disability, it gave me an opportunity to be slower than the other males. I assumed that when I transitioned, I would be treated the same as the other males – unfortunately this was not the case.

Physically becoming a boy

Shortly after my seventeenth birthday, I had learnt that my grandmother had passed. With us being so close, I was struck with the reality of the shortness of life and I began to appreciate that I should start to live my life for my own happiness. This was the moment that I took the decision to transition. Upon reflection, I did not take a lot of time to make a decision, however, it felt completely right and I was determined to finish the process as soon as possible.

I shortly changed my name by deed poll and started the process of coming out to people who were not already aware. I started raising money for surgery and hormones. Unfortunately, my mother did not take my transition particularly well, so I spent a few months between homes, often sleeping in my car and spending Christmas by myself. I was determined to still become physically male. My friends helped me raise money for my transition, which lead me to making a private appointment for surgery. I was informed that treatment for gender dysphoria was not available for individuals under the age of 18, so I waited until my birthday to ensure that the referral was processed.

An appointment was made with a psychiatrist, who was able to diagnose that I had gender identity disorder from the age of five. I was adamant that I wanted to start hormones (testosterone) as soon as possible, however my complex history meant that it was necessary to confirm a correct diagnosis. After two psychiatric visits and one endocrinology appointment, I was able to rapidly start testosterone (T) treatment after my eighteenth birthday. At this stage, I was living at home with my mother and father and I was reluctant to tell my family that I had started the treatment. After my first injection, I had placed the packaging in the bin and unfortunately, my mother discovered the evidence. She stated that she could not stand to be in the same house as me as I undergo my physical changes and consequently walked out on my father and I. Despite my father's acceptance, my mother and I failed to reconcile our differences, which resulted in us having no contact.

My coming out to cadets was a difficult transition, as they failed to follow the necessary legal procedures. After changing my name, I contacted the officer in command and explained the situation. I was reassured that it would be dealt with sensitively, however this was not the case. I initially stated that I wanted everyone to be using male pronouns, yet after a few weeks of coming out, it was apparent that this would not be possible. The adult instructors were extremely disrespectful and often made derogatory comments aimed at me, which lead to me insisting to go back in the closet. As I was at the beginning stages of hormone treatment, a very difficult decision was made as to whether I'd be able to compete with females. It was decided that I was to remain as a female for competitions, despite the imminent physical changes. As the organisation failed to accept me as male, I was determined to achieve national level standards. With only nine months left in the organisation, I set aside my worries about competing with women and concentrated on my own individual performance.

Testosterone initially made me feel so amazing! I could feel it running round my body as I started to experience physical and emotional changes. I became extremely motivated to get myself back in shape and attempt to gain some muscle by attending the gym regularly. It gave me a newfound confidence, and I was able to go into the male changing room at the gym and feel more and more comfortable every day.

As I entered the small, local gym, I would often receive negative comments, as the town was aware of my transition. I started an evening personal training course at the same time as my college courses and started to build a client base, whilst attempting to raise more money for future surgery. With my exercise intensity increasing, binding (the process in which pressure is placed on the chest with a special garment, to give the appearance of a male chest) became a serious issue and I became more motivated to have a flat chest. Nevertheless, I was achieving promotions within the cadets and was invited to complete a week in Bavaria full of adventurous activities.

Army Cadets signified both the best and the worse parts of my life. At this stage, I had achieved the highest qualifications possible, regardless of gender, and held the highest rank in the whole of the company. I was supposed to receive one further promotion, but was informed that I did not because of 'my situation'. I protested, and was suspended. Extremely upset, I left the organisation and prepared for top-surgery.

My chest surgery represented a huge step for my transition as my confidence increased, and I felt more comfortable in my body. I took a gap year between college and university to ensure that I would be able to join university without disclosing my gender history. I continued to visit the gym after my recovery and I noticed a vast increase in my strength while my physical state continued to develop. After a few months of hard fighting, I was given the all clear for the first stage of genital surgery and I could begin to see an end to my transition.

Genital (bottom) surgery is completed in many stages and often over many years. I was able to get my other health problems in check and develop physically so that I could pass better, before starting university in the September. With the first stage of bottom surgery under my belt (excuse the pun), I decided to return to judo as I moved away from my hometown.

Being a Paralympic male

Moving to London for university was a brilliant decision, as I was able to move away from my previous life and start my new, stealth life as Jay. In order to be stealth, I could not let the club know that I had previously competed in judo, so I began at the beginning – a white belt. My sensei could tell that I had previous experience, but allowed me to continue. I remember the amazing feeling of putting my judogi on without a shirt, and automatically being paired to train with the other males. Now, as unquestionably male, I bloomed as an individual. I loved being in the communal showers, feeling comfortable in my own body. I progressed through the judo grades again, however further complications to my foot, resulted in me not being able to place any pressure on one foot and having to rely on crutches or my wheelchair.

My disability had always been particularly difficult; however, I had never truly realised the effect that it had on me. Having been in and out of my wheelchair since the age of 15, I tried to ignore its presence, but it reached a point where it was impossible to overlook. At the same time, I was being operated on every three months to complete my physical transition, which ultimately caused great difficulty with my degree and sport. I caught myself waking up in the middle of the night in pain and taking the strongest painkillers available by prescription. My physical state deteriorated, and I began to become extremely unfit again. Despite this, I was determined to get back into shape and again boost my confidence. I found an advertisement for a Paralympic event that promoted various sports and attended.

The hall was filled with an assortment of sports and I endeavoured to try as many as possible. My gender was never questioned.

At this stage, I had a full beard and nobody would ever query that I had transitioned. I thoroughly enjoyed a lot of the sports, however took a specific liking to powerlifting, wheelchair racing and the field sports. The event organisers saw my potential and I was invited to attend the local clubs for all three sports.

Powerlifting was the first para sport that I tried. The team were great, and I remember attending my first session, watching individuals that didn't look particularly strong, lift over twice their weight. I never disclosed my transition, as I didn't feel it necessary. As para powerlifting requires competitors to lie on an alternative bench, I was initially conscious that my body would look slightly different to other males in the team. However, I was fully transitioned at this stage, with full male body composition so I did not worry for too long. With bench press being the only lift, I thought that I would be mindful of my chest however, it never crossed my mind and I never thought about my gender until I was asked to compete later on in the year.

I felt it necessary to disclose my transition to my coach as I was technically prescribed a performance-enhancing drug (testosterone). Although it did not give me any advantage over other competitors, I was scared of being banned from the sport, through a drug test, and realised that I would need a Therapeutic Use Exemption (TUE) form. This form allows an athlete to compete, whilst using a banned substance. I expressed the importance of keeping my history between the two of us and he respected that. Typical of a coach, he even suggested that I time my testosterone shots with competitions to achieve the maximum performance!

The TUI form was initially problematic as I was unsure how much information I wanted to disclose. I needed to guarantee that the form was accurate, without disclosing unnecessary information that could be problematic in the wrong hands. Luckily, there was a problem with my GP practice and I was unable to fill in the form before the competition. I anticipate that I will have to complete a TUI in the future, however I will accept the help of an individual that is aware of both gender disclosure and sport laws. By disclosing my history, I am no longer stealth to a number of officials however I am being truthful: I imagine that this will also make me feel uncomfortable, as I no longer identify as transgender. Although the disclosure of my powerlifting coach was recent, I have not yet disclosed to my athletics coach.

Field athletics are a recent discovery of mine, and I am still in the beginning stages of these throwing sports. As there are only a number of individuals that participate in throwing events, my coach anticipates that I will be competing in the Tokyo 2020 Paralympics. It's extremely strange to look back on my passion as a child for athletics and how it has transitioned through my life into adulthood. It has always been my ambition to be a professional athlete, however, I do worry about the disclosure of my history. I feel as though I could be a great ambassador for trans athletes, however as I do not currently identify as transgender, I feel it would not be appropriate to take on this role. I also feel a great embarrassment for my previous gender and awkward if anybody is aware of my birth name. I fear that as I progress within Paralympic sport, my 'story' may come to light and will be sensationalised by the media. I imagine that I will disclose my history to my athletics coach, as I believe it is an issue that we can tackle together.

As my disability mainly affects one foot and doctors are determined to give up on my treatment, I am a serious candidate for an elective, below-knee amputation. This will enable my pain to be significantly reduced, while allowing me the opportunity to walk again (with help of a prosthetic). The battle with doctors to allow for an elective amputation is an on-going struggle and I am hopeful for a future where I can participate in amputee sport, without my transition holding me back.

My gender and transition has never really held me back from achieving in sport, however, I feel as though my discomfort and the actions of others ultimately have. I feel positive for the future of other trans athletes and hope for there to be a platform for trans people to compete against each other. Nevertheless, I am relatively happy that coaches are not aware of trans situations, as this allows me to be stealth until/if I decide to disclose. I hope to achieve my potential and compete in the Paralympics, however I am open to the idea that my views on my stealth identity might change. I am currently delighted with my physical and mental state and confident that other trans athletes are able to achieve, as I have, despite difficult a background.

Chapter 3

Becoming me

Transitioning, training and surgery

Riley McCormack and Maylon Hanold

This chapter consists of selected excerpts from a female to male (FTM) transgender recreational athlete (Riley) and his advisor (Maylon) during the time period that Riley completed his master's thesis in a sport management program. As part of his qualitative study on the lived experiences of recreational transgender athletes, Riley wrote about his own experiences of transitioning and training for running. Maylon, Riley's advisor, worked closely with Riley on his project and also kept a journal on her experiences in the advisor role over a period of nine months (September 2015 to May 2016). At the beginning of the study, Riley was pre-surgery and had been on testosterone for one year and four months. During the 9-month period of the study, Riley trained for a 10k, underwent top surgery, and resumed running post-surgery. In order to reflect our Collaborative Autoethnography (CAE) process, we juxtapose our different narratives so that neither voice is lost for the sake of consensus (Geist-Martin *et al.* 2010). What follows is the co-telling of our stories through excerpts from our writing that highlight three significant experiences: silencing past sport experiences, ongoing efforts to give enough 'gender cues,' and post-surgery and running.

Maylon

I glance down at the list of names of students in my class. I quickly survey the room. Hmm ... I should have five women and ten men. It's not easy to tell. For a moment I feel stuck, destabilized – my 'blink' response. I feel a wave of embarrassment. Why am I assuming gender based on name? I know about gender fluidity, the power of the gender binary, the social construction of gender. I teach this stuff! "Professor Hanold, I just wanted to let you know that I go by 'Riley.' I haven't officially changed my name, yet." My felt sense of 'order' falls into place. I attribute it to what I know. However, I'm frustrated that my education, my scholarship, my own history of working to 'break' the strength of the gender binary didn't keep me from warding off that initial tendency to sort ... by gender.

Riley

At five years old, I did not feel comfortable saying, 'I'm a girl.' I have rejected every notion, every behavior – everything about what it means to 'be feminine.' Twenty years later, I still despise these words. Every day, I live in a body that was assigned female sex at birth. I live in a body that is not mine.

Even when I had socially transitioned, sometimes in the heat of the moment during a softball game, the other players on the field would call me by my birth name. It became harder and harder to focus on just playing. I felt uneasy, not right. I've learned to call this sense of unease 'dysphoria' – I struggled to play sport as a transgender athlete – whenever "she" or "birth name" were ever accidentally used, I understood, but little by little sport, often a happy space for me, became a frustrating, angry space."

Collaborative autoethnography

Griffin and Caroll (2010) point out how the gender binary leaves little space for transgender and gender fluid athletes to participate in sport. Indeed, the landscape for transgender athletes can be characterized as "turbulent terrain" (Lucas-Carr and Krane 2011: 533) in which it is almost impossible to "be me and be an athlete all at the same time" (532). Notably, Hargie *et al.* (2015: 4) note that overall, "the experiences, emotions, needs and difficulties of transgender people in sport remain poorly understood."

One of the most significant decisions a transgender athlete makes is when and how to transition. Transitioning is the process by which one's gender expression comes in line with how one identifies on the gender spectrum. Krane *et al.* (2012: 18) remind us that transitioning can take numerous forms, including:

> …altering appearance (e.g., hair style, clothing), changing name and pronoun use, and making changes to the body via hormone therapy and/or surgery. There is not a monolithic path for transitioning; individuals consider what changes are comfortable, correspond with their gender identity, and fit into their life situations.

Reeser (2005) emphasizes that transitioning is not to gain any cultural reward or personal athletic advantage, it is about seeking personal harmony between body and mind. However, the history of exclusion and stigmatization of transgender athletes also points to the importance of the social and cultural context in which transitioning athletes participate. Simply put, transitioning and being an athlete is not only an internal experience, but also takes place *with and among* others. With these understandings, we employed collaborative autoethnography (CAE) to explore more fully what it means to be a transgender recreational athlete. Chang *et al.* (2013: 18) point out that CAE, "has potential to engender a deeper understanding of self and others in the social and cultural context than is possible from a solo analysis." CAE uses the traditional methods of autoethnography, which involves

> telling a story, weaving intricate connections among life and art, experience and theory, evocation and explanation ... and then letting go, hoping for readers who will bring the same careful attention to your words in the context of their own lives.
>
> (Holman Jones 2005: 765)

In CAE, "autoethnographers work together, building on each other's stories" (Chang *et al.* 2013: 23).

Silencing the past: (dys)appearing in sport

Riley

While riding home in a Lyft (a taxi summoned by a mobile phone app), the driver and I got on the topic of sports. We talked about what professional sports teams we loved (Chicago Cubs!), then he asked what sports did/do I play? I hesitated for a moment ... deciding whether to bend the truth or come out as trans. I was scared and worried that the driver would be unfriendly, even aggressive toward me or ignorant of the trans community, and I'd have to explain. I told him I played volleyball, basketball, and baseball in high school. In reality, I played softball. I lied. In our society, boys play baseball, girls play softball. The Lyft driver mentioned he didn't know high schools had men's volleyball teams. I simply mumbled 'yeah' and let it go for fear of continuing that line of conversation. We went right back to professional sports. I took a breath, relieved. I felt sad in the moment. I didn't like having to go against my values and be dishonest, but I was afraid.

Today, I ran jamming to my music, running with the beat, thinking how I used to run around the track in high school before volleyball or softball practice. I miss running to train for something. I can't play on the girls' team anymore because I started T (testosterone) over a year ago. I can't play on the guys' team because I still have a chest that bounces up and down. So where do I go? I pick up my pace a little and run harder.

Today my friend told me she found a gay softball league to play in. I'm happy for her, but I can't help feeling sad also. I don't belong to the lesbian/dyke community anymore. I'm passing more and more each day as I progress in my transition. I can't help but feel loss about a community that once made me feel accepted. I think back to my experiences of playing sports in high school, playing intramurals in college, and how much fun they were. I wish I could join a lesbian softball league because I would feel most comfortable playing there. I can't join now because I'm seen as 'not female' due to the T. I worry that people will think I'm "cheating" because I have some sort of physical advantage due to the T. I listened to my friend talk about softball and kept silent. I can't play a team sport in the middle of transitioning unless I were to find an all queer/trans team, but I want to play with all different types of people, not just queer people.

Running frees my mind and body from the trapped feelings of dysphoria. It provides the space where I don't have time to tear myself down or wonder how everyone else reads me. At times I can feel the T pumping through my veins. I feel powerful and more connected to my body. With each run I can feel my muscles becoming more defined. I can feel my muscles work harder. I feel my body becoming me with each run.

Maylon

Riley reported today on the progress of his study. He wants to run a 10k. I think that's awesome. I started asking him if he's run before and what sports he's done. He was hesitant. I learn he played team sports, and that he didn't like having to deal with it when coaches would yell, "Come on, ladies!" I follow his train of thought. I don't want to pry or push and our conversation moved into how he's really appreciated being able to run with a classmate, and how much he values that friendship. Sometimes I think our interactions are awkward as we talk about his study and his experiences. I don't want to make Riley feel like he's speaking for all transgender athletes. I want to be respectful, but I stumble. I reflect too much on what I should say, what I should ask. I think I should grow comfortable with fumbling.

The art and pain of gender clues

Riley

Getting ready for my run today, I put on a men's XXL long sleeve shirt and basketball shorts that go past my knees. I make sure that the shirt I'm wearing isn't too tight for fear that my chest will be noticeable while running. I check myself in the mirror to confirm that the clues I'm putting forth are read as masculine. Going through all this, I thought about when I had to dress for volleyball. The uniforms were female. They were meant for skinny girls. I was neither skinny nor comfortable in my body. I suffocated between the jersey and the spandex booty shorts. But, I made sure to do my hair perfectly. I wore the same frilly ponytail that matched the other girls along with pre-wrap in my hair. Back then, it was about me conforming to my volleyball uniform, when in reality it should be the uniform fitting my body. I feel like what Butler says, "we act as if this 'being' of a man or 'being' of a woman is an internal reality, when rather it is a phenomenon that we produce and reproduce all the time" (Butler 2011, 191). Today, I fit the uniform to my body, but I still have to be careful. I make sure the t-shirt doesn't reference a past sport I played such as 'girls' basketball.' I do this to avoid the stares that go from my chest to my eyes and to prevent the sinking feeling of nostalgia as a team player. In my mind, I can picture myself running with a flat chest one day. I can envision myself 'being' a man with a chest that better suits me.

I'm still wearing sports bras these days to run. I wear two sports bras to hold my chest down. This ritual often reminds me of the day in high school when I woke up late and forgot to wear even one sports bra. I felt humiliated, embarrassed, and angry at myself. I felt my skin crawling all over for the first half of the day. I could not focus on anything else but the fact that I did not wear the most essential clothing that helped me feel in control of my body on a daily basis. How was I going to participate in gym class that day? How was I going to go to practice for basketball later and play without a sports bra on? It wasn't possible! I faked being sick and asked to go to the school nurse so that I could go home. I felt a wave of embarrassment and pain. A pain inside that didn't ever settle, but rather lingered and eventually festered into an unbearable feeling that made continuing to live in a female body impossible.

I ran my 10k today. That part was good, but I had to go to the restroom before the run. I've been going into men's restrooms for over a year now. I wore my usual two sports bras to hold my chest down. When I left, an older man walked in and without hesitation looked at my chest and then we made eye contact. In that moment, I felt shame, humiliation, and anger for entering a space where, according to society, my body did not belong. I felt shame and humiliation for not wearing a looser shirt so that my chest was not noticeable. I felt anger because it has been over a year on testosterone and I'm still getting 'ma'amed' and stared at for going into spaces where I feel comfortable. I used my frustration and anger toward society to push me through my first 10k.

Maylon

It's always made sense to me that a transgender person doesn't feel at home in the body they were born into. Yeah, I got that. That's the definition … but, it never occurred to me to really think about what it 'feels like' to not feel at 'home' in your body. Hearing Riley talk about his working out, I realize the unproblematic ways I get to be an athlete. I've always felt comfortable in my female athletic body. I listened intently today to Riley talk more about his transitioning and running. The feelings of discomfort being in a 'girls' locker room and not feeling right even while still being in a female body. It's like despite everything aligning on the outside – female body, female locker room – that experience is painfully awkward for a transgender person. But even during the transition, his body still betrays him, so locker rooms, restrooms and any gender specific space is awkward, uncomfortable, and painful. What also becomes clear is the effort that Riley has to put forth to 'pass' as male. As I write these words, I think that what I've realized is obvious, has been talked about, and something I knew intellectually and in theory. I can talk about these struggles, but what I became conscious of today was my own visceral shift, my own emotional, 'felt' connection to Riley's experiences by connecting to his stories.

I've been reading John Shotter's (2011: 38) work on 'withness thinking,' and I'm reminded, "we are always having to act in relation to all the others (and othernesses) around us." I am acutely aware that I'll never be able to walk in Riley's shoes, I'll never really 'get it,' but I feel like I walked beside him today- and it really hit home. "Intimate speech is imbued with a deep confidence in the addressee, in his sympathy, in his sensitivity and good will of his responsive understanding" (Bakhtin 1986: 97). I'm realizing that, indeed, "It takes two, at least two ... for us to be fully ourselves to ourselves" (Shotter 2011: 52).

Surgery, running and becoming 'me'

Riley

I love my new chest! I can't wait for the scars to heal and my nipples to grow in because all I want to do is run! I want to run past that second mile into the 'sweet zone' where that rush of adrenaline enters. Running is the one physical activity that I enjoy doing with a passion. The past eight weeks have been filled with excruciating anticipation. I just want to run. I want to run in a body that finally aligns with how I feel internally, that finally is more me. I have this tension building up inside of me with each testosterone injection I take as the weeks' progress and my scars heal. I want to know what it's like to run with my new chest. I want to feel the freedom. I want to shape my body and work out because now my body truly belongs to me.

I lace up my shoes and check to make sure I'm all set to go. I look at my outfit in the mirror, tuck in my shirt, and smile at the fact that I do not have to wear a sports bra ever again. I do not have to be reminded by people's stares that I'm in a female body. I'm only partially in a female body now, but I'm happy with my new chest.

I feel the fresh air hit my face, my lungs burning, and my legs carrying me one step further and further. I feel the tension release inside as I my breathing evens out. With each person I pass, I make eye contact with them, the best part is their eyes don't fall to my chest. I grin from ear to ear. My heart racing and my breathing begins to even out. It's my first day running post-surgery, I'm out on a trail run with a friend as the rain turns from mist to downpour. I smell the evergreens, the smell of the rain is intoxicating, and I love every minute running in the rain. I feel free, comfortable, and finally I can run as me, as Riley.

Getting soaked by the rain, running with my new chest brings about a sense of feeling re-born into the 'male' body I was meant to be in. With top surgery, I am accepting that this alignment between my body and mind is as good as it is going to get. I still feel the disconnect with my bottom area, however, I now pass according society's view of what 'being' male looks like. I have the right clues to portray my masculinity and with it comes a new type of privilege, one I need to be very careful about. My friend checks in with me during the run, asks how I am doing? She does a great job of providing a safe space. I feel more confident in my body, in who I am as a person, all due to surgery and being able to be more me.

Maylon

When Riley walked into my office today, I was struck by how 'Riley' seemed. I couldn't place it. Was it his full beard? Lower voice? Way of walking. I couldn't help but smile – there was so much more 'at ease' in his manner and his presence. In these later stages of transition, I keep thinking about Riley's thesis when he quotes Butler (1990: 191) from *Gender Trouble*. Butler describes the construction of gender as "a stylized repetition of acts … in which bodily gestures, movements, and styles of various kinds constitute the illusion of an abiding gendered self." For Riley, his abiding gendered self-growing up were both acts. His body itself was an illusion, to which he acted in accordance just enough to make it work socially. It seems as though the most significant 'bodily gesture' that signified 'female' was his body. Nothing about being in a female body constituted 'real' for Riley. Transitioning has been this process of creating a materiality that is 'real' for him. A big part of that 'real' has also been reconnecting with sport in a new way – the old ways don't work because it's not easy to fit in – from his own and others' views – they only bring up anger and sadness. When running, Riley feels a greater alignment between his inner felt sense of gender and outer materiality. It's also his outlet. He still has to pay attention to bodily gestures, styles, and ways of being so that he can pass as 'male.' In other words, the body can't do the work alone. He still has to 'act' and give enough clues to pass as male.

References

Bakhtin, Mikael, M. *Speech Genres and Other Late Essays*, translated by V. W. McGee, edited by Caryl Emerson and Michael Holquist. Austin: University of Texas Press (1986).

Butler, Judith. *Gender Trouble: Feminism and the Subversion of Identity.* Routledge (2011).

Chang, Heewon, Faith Wambura Ngunjiri and Kathy-Ann C. Hernandez. *Collaborative Autoethnography.* Vol. 8. Walnut Creek, CA: Left Coast Press (2012).

Geist-Martin, Patricia, Lisa Gates, Liesbeth Wiering, Erika Kirby, Renee Houston, Anne Lilly and Juan Moreno. "Exemplifying collaborative autoethnographic practice via shared stories of mothering," *Journal of Research Practice* 6, no. 1 (2010): 8.

Griffin, Pat and Helen Carroll. "The transgender athlete." *Inside Higher Education* (2010).

Hargie, Owen D. W., David H. Mitchell and Ian J. A. Somerville. " 'People have a knack of making you feel excluded if they catch on to your difference': transgender experiences of exclusion in sport," *International Review for the Sociology of Sport* (2015): 1012690215583283.

Krane, Vikki, Katie Sullivan Barak and Mallory E. Mann. "Broken binaries and transgender athletes: challenging sex and gender in sports," *Sexual Orientation and Gender Identity in Sport: Essays From Activists, Coaches, and Scholars* (2012): 13–22.

Lucas-Carr, Cathryn B. and Vikki Krane. "What is the T in LGBT? Supporting transgender athletes through sport psychology," *Sport Psychologist* 25, no. 4 (2011): 532.

Reeser, Jonathon C. "Gender identity and sport: is the playing field level?" *British Journal of Sports Medicine* 39, no. 10 (2005): 695–699.

Shotter, John. *Getting It: Withness-thinking and the Dialogical–in Practice.* New York: Hampton Press (2011).

Part II

Research into transgender sporting experiences

Chapter 4

An introduction to five exceptional trans athletes from around the world

Kinnon MacKinnon

Trans people and sport

Despite the advancement of explicit legal protections for transgender/ transsexual/transitioned (hereon referred to as "trans") people in many Western nations around the world, sport remains a contentious domain for trans and other gender-variant people. Even in light of increasing exposure to positive representations of trans people in international media, the sporting world is confounded by athletes whose bodies, identities, and hormonal profiles do not fit neatly into binary sex-segregated competition categories.

Perhaps partly as a result of these barriers, we see very high rates of trans people avoiding sport and physical activity. For instance, the Trans Pulse Project conducted in Ontario, Canada found that 44 percent of trans people avoid going to the gym out of fear of being outed, harassed, or being read as trans (Scheim *et al.* 2014). Similarly, 58 percent of trans people in Victoria, Australia reported avoiding some sports due to their gender identity (Symons *et al.* 2010). And in a United States-based study that compared rates of physical activity and participation on team sports between sexual minority and heterosexual youth, gender non-conformity and athletic self-esteem was cited as a significant reason for low levels of sporting participation in sexual minority young people (Calzo *et al.* 2014). For trans people who already experience significant social isolation and health inequities, inclusion in sport may be an important facilitator to improving community connectedness, self-esteem, and long-term health outcomes.

Some of the factors for low turnout rate in sport may be related to homophobia and/or trans-related discrimination in sports, sparse trans role models in professional and other organized sporting leagues, and the absence of affirmative trans-inclusion policies. Or, conversely, explicit trans-inclusion policies that instead work toward including only gender-conforming trans athletes, while excluding others (e.g., stipulating mandatory genital reassignment surgery and/or hormone replacement therapy, or no allowance for non-binary or gender non-conforming persons). While these issues relating to trans inclusion in sport are outside the scope of this particular chapter, they are an important foreground. T is why, in part, elite-level athletes who come out as trans are absolutely exceptional. Whether that be following a successful career, like Olympian Caitlyn Jenner, or perhaps even more remarkably – while triumphantly trailblazing their sports like out triathlete Chris Mosier and mixed-martial artist, Fallon Fox.

Gender identity, sex, and sport

When I write about trans people, I am specifically thinking about individuals who identify as a gender that is different than their birth-assigned sex. For example, people who identify as transgender, transsexual, transitioned, bigender, genderqueer, agender, genderfluid, and any other noncisgender identity. Importantly, the Western concept "trans" has been linked to additional identities held by non-Western people, such as Indigenous two-spirit and Polynesian *fa'afafine*. But trans does not always neatly apply to these non-Western identities, and thus must be cautiously applied, especially by Western writers who are writing about non-Western gender diverse athletes, such as Jaiyah Saelua.

This chapter examines five exceptional athletes, from around the world, who are breaking gender boundaries in their sports. Before detailing their stories, however, I first share mine.

My experiences as an out trans powerlifter

> It was an incredible experience winning a gold medal for the men's 75 kilogram weight class. I had been dreaming of competing at the Gay Games since I began entering local powerlifting competitions…
>
> (MacKinnon, as quoted in Kellaway 2014)

After two years of local competitions in my province of Ontario, Canada, I was fortunate to have the opportunity to lift at the Gay Games in Cleveland Ohio. I took home a gold medal in the 165 pound men's weight class in August 2014. Weighing 158 pounds, I squatted 352 pounds, bench pressed 225 pounds, and pulled an all-time deadlift personal record of 441 pounds. Some time has passed, and as a result of a disc herniation I am limited to the bench press, hitting my best bench press of 260 pounds in the fall of 2015.

Like many other trans people, though, my story includes the instance of quitting all competitive sport and exercise around the time I came out. As a young person, I excelled at a number of sports and confidently identified myself as a "jock." But it was first freestyle skiing, and then snowboarding, from ages 16 to 19, that formed the basis of my national-level competition experiences. Like most athletes chasing an Olympic dream, I lived and breathed my sport. But throughout my later teen years, I began feeling uneasy with myself. As I came into my identity as a queer person, I couldn't conceive of a place for me in sport. At the time, I was struggling with my sexuality and gender and was not able to dedicate the time or resources to staying competitive. This, I believe, is something that many sexually diverse, but especially gender diverse, athletes must contend with. I thus sought out comfort from the LGBTQ community, and left my dreams of elite-level athletic success in the halfpipe. It was after a five-year hiatus from all sports and physical activity that I found my passion for lifting weights and began strength training seriously, and then competitively.

Notable trans athletes – past and present

For various and complex reasons, some of the athletes discussed in this chapter decided not to transition until after their professional careers were over. Others, like Fallon Fox who was coercively outed, continue to be aggressively bullied out of their sports due to transphobia. Regardless, each of the five athletes highlighted within this chapter have gone through great lengths to live authentically – both as athletes and advocates for equity, justice, and human rights in sport. Their stories are diverse and filled with as much adversity as personal success. While there are so many more trans athletes around the world breaking barriers for gender diverse athletes, I specifically selected the following individuals to represent a wide range of sports, nuanced stories, and voices that are able to challenge dominant trans narratives that are ever so present and dominant in the public domain.

Jaiyah Saelua

> [In fact, she laughs at the very notion when asked if she had ever suf-fered discrimination prior to leaving American Samoa.] No, none at all, there are lots of fa'afafine in American Samoa that play soccer, and other sports, and even in other national teams in other sports. We are all given an equal opportunity to play sport.
>
> (Saelua, as quoted in Smith, 2014)

Jaiyah Saelua (born July 19, 1998) is a force to be reckoned with – beauti-ful, intelligent, and athletically gifted. Born and raised in American Samoa, a small nation of five islands in the South Pacific, Saelua was the first trans person to play in a FIFA World Cup qualifier (Lamport, 2014). She was a talented player from when she took up the sport at age 11 and joined the American Samoa national team just a few short years later at age 14 (Smith, 2014). In 2011, she assisted with the winning goal decision against

Tonga – breaking their thirty-year losing streak (Montague, 2011). Saelua grew up as a *fa'afafine* and also identifies as a trans woman today. To date, she is the only internationally recognized *fa'afafine* footballer who played for a men's team while also holding a feminine gender identity.

Fa'afafine is a feminine gender identity held by a small minority of people born male in Polynesia. The role of *fa'afafine* is an embraced third gender engrained in Samoan culture. Saelula insists that many *fa'afafine* play sports in American Samoan, from the recreational to the national team level in many sports. Unlike in Western nations, however, Saelula says that "we are all given an equal opportunity to play sport" (Smith, 2014). In fact, Saelua reports that she never encountered transphobia until she left her home country and began studies at the University of Hawaii. She tried out for the men's team, and before the first practice began the coach asked her to leave to avoid making anyone uncomfortable. "The world can learn a lot from the culture. We might not be developed as a country, or in the sports realm, but as a culture, I think we're ahead" (Saelua, as quoted in Roberts, 2014).

Today Ms. Saelula is featured in the documentary *Next Goal Wins* and spends her time speaking publicly about including trans people in sports. She has been invited to give presentations all over the world. Saelula says that:

> I feel like being the first transgender professional footballer in the world means I have a strong voice and a chance that can open up possibilities for other transgender athletes.
>
> (Saelula, as quoted in Roberts, 2014)

Fallon Fox

> They don't ask me, 'Were you a physically strong person when you were male?' They ask, 'Did you learn technique as a man? Because if you did, that's prank.' What are they really saying? They're saying that men are smarter than women, that's what. If you were male-bodied, that makes you learn better. That's incredibly misogynistic; it's mind-boggling how they get away with it.
>
> (Fox, as quoted in Truitt, 2015)

Media sensation Fallon Fox (born November 29, 1975) is a talented American featherweight Mixed-Martial Arts (MMA) fighter who was coherced into publicly disclosing her identity as a trans woman in March 2013 (Zeigler, 2013). She is the co-star of an award-winning 2014 documentary, Game Face.

Since coming out, her career as an MMA fighter has been fraught with transphobia and painful interactions, yet very few matches. While actively fighting, Fox had a highly respected 5–1 record. But, as of the current date, Fox has not fought since 2014 and many other female athletes refuse to fight her. For example, Ronda Rousey has said in reference to Fox "She can try hormones, chop her pecker off, but it's still the same bone structure a man has … I don't think it's fair" (Koonce and Schorn, 2015). Famous American sports commentator, Joe Rogan, has spoken equally harmful words regarding Fox on his talk show, *The Joe Rogan Experience*. This is in spite of the International Olympic Committee (IOC)'s and the Associations of Boxing Commission's trans inclusion rules, and countless medical expert recommendations that argue trans women do not have an advantage (IOC, 2015; Koonce and Schorn, 2015; Tannehill, 2014). Perhaps the only positive outcome of the discrimination that Fox has faced is that she has become a rallying point behind making sports more inclusive for trans people. After being forced to come out by a reporter who knew her history, Fox has become an expert on topics related to sex, gender, hormones, and the inclusion of trans women in sport. An outspoken advocate for ending trans discrimination, she was inducted into the National Gay and Lesbian Sports Hall of Fame in 2014 (Zeigler, 2014).

Unfortunately for Fox and the MMA world, the Ultimate Fighting Championship organization has yet to sign her, and other fighters have refused her matches. As a result, Fox has not had the opportunity to succeed or fail, according to her abilities, in her sport.

Andreas Krieger

> The question is, what kind of sport do you want to see? The type where there are the normal ups-and-downs, with tears and the rest? Or do you want to see a freak show, where it is all a pure fake? In this scandal, it is mostly forgotten that the person who pays for everything is the athlete
>
> (Krieger, as quoted in Brown, 2015)

Andreas Krieger (born July 20, 1966) is a decorated German shot-putter and dedicated advocate for the anti-doping movement. Known as Heidi through his athletic career, Krieger won gold for East Germany in the women's shot put at the 1986 European Athletics Championships in Stuttgart with a 21.10 meter shot – the world record for over a decade.

Krieger's story, however, is a complicated one, providing an interesting example of the complexity of gender identity development, hormones, and competitive sport. Although he expressed that he always felt different and may have experienced gender dysphoria, it was after his athletic career was over that Krieger learned he had been fed a regimen of anabolic steroids by his coaches and doctors during the height of his success. He was among the thousands of East German athletes, including his wife the swimmer,

Uta Krause, to be victims of the Eastern bloc regime's orchestrated plans to dominate Olympic sporting events (Brown, 2015). But years after transitioning to male, Krieger still finds himself wondering about the hormones' effects on his gender identity, as he received these performance-enhancing drugs during his teen years (Vinton, 2013).

Krieger now champions the anti-doping movement in sport, and Germans who work to end doping are given the annual "Heidi Krieger Medal" (Lawton, 2012).

Erik Schinegger

> The borderline between male and female is very thin. During the 1966 World Championships, Shinegger functioned as a woman.
>
> (Hodler, as quoted in Fry, 2006, p. 132)

Handsome, charming, and popular, Erik Schinegger (born June 19, 1948) is a well-known Austrian skier and self-proclaimed "man who became a female world champion" (Schinegger, 1988). Raised as Erika in a small farming village, Schinegger went on to win the 1966 women's world championship in Chile at the age of 18. But Schinegger's dream of Olympic gold was soon crushed – at the age of 20 he learned that he was, in fact, an intersex male. Mandatory IOC-initiated sex testing for female athletes leading up to the 1968 Grenoble Olympic Games indicated that Schinegger was biologically male with an internal penis and testes (Nell Warren, 2014). Given the contentions surrounding the sex testing of Olympic athletes and researchers who question its practices and negative social effects (for example see Sykes, 2006), this was an incredibly unfortunate turn of events. Despite being an expected Olympic gold medallist in 1968, Schinegger's career as a women's downhill skier was over in 1967.

In a progressive decision with important implications for trans inclusion in sport today, Schinegger's 1966 win was not revoked, and International Ski Federation (FIS) President Marc Hodler stated that "the borderline between male and female is very thin. During the 1966 World Championships, Shinegger functioned as a woman" (Hodler as quoted in Fry, 2006, p. 132). At the same time, The Canadian Academy of Sports Medicine also offered that "individuals raised as females ... should be eligible to compete in women's competition regardless of their chromosomal, gonadal and hormonal sex" (Academy as quoted in Fry, 2006, pp. 132–133).

Schinegger made the decision to transition to male but he was not ready to walk away from the slopes or his Olympic goals. Vying for the 1972 Sapporo Games, he went on to compete in the men's European tour, keeping pace with leading male Austrian skiers (Roberts, 2014). Schinegger's stint in the men's division was frustratingly short, however; despite having transitioned to male and having the same chromosomal profile as the other male skiers, he was denied a spot on the Austrian National Ski Team. At the time, Schinegger's coaches felt he caused too much controversy.

Following his athletic career Schinegger has guest starred on Austria's "Dancing with the Stars," and has been featured in a documentary about his life, titled *ERIK(A) – Der Mann, der Weltmeisterin wurde*. This 2005 documentary by Kurt Mayer interviews Erik and many people who are closest to him.

Lana Lawless

> I am, in all respects, legally, and physically female. The state of California recognizes me as such and the LPGA should not be permitted to come into California and blatantly violate my rights. I just want to have the same opportunity to play professional golf as any other woman.
>
> (Lawless as quoted in Pohln, 2010)

Thanks to Lana Lawless, on November 30, 2010 trans female golfers were given the right to play with the Ladies Professional Golf Association (LPGA) (Zeigler, 2011). In 2008, Lawless grabbed the title of women's world long-drive golf champion with a 254-yard drive against 30 mile-per-hour gusts, but by the 2009 competition, the association adopted the LGPA's anachronistic "female at birth" policy (Pohn, 2010; Thomas, 2010).

After first requesting permission to apply for LPGA qualifying tournaments, Lawless and her lawyer, Christopher Dolan, launched a lawsuit against the LPGA and Long Drivers of America in 2010 (Gonzalez, 2010; Thomas, 2010). At the time, Lawless and Dolan cited that the IOC, the Ladies European Golf Tour, the United States Golf Association, and the Ladies Golf Union in Britain all had trans-inclusion policies in effect that allowed trans women who had genital-reassignment surgery and hormone replacement therapy to compete. Although trans inclusion policies that stipulate mandatory surgeries and hormone therapies are now recognized as human rights violations (CCES, 2016), a "female-at-birth" policy was exponentially more unjust. This is, in part, why Lawless and her lawyer argued that "female-at-birth" is a civil rights violation, and why the LPGA went on to change their policy: " 'When an organization like the (International Olympic Committee) decides to accept those changes, there's no reason for the LPGA not to. So for my point of view, it was the natural way to go,' " stated professional golfer Suzann Petterse (FoxSports, 2010).

Although the LGPA's move toward trans inclusion was seen as a win for civil rights, trans golfers, and trans athletes more broadly, Mianne Bagger, the first trans woman to qualify for the Ladies European Tour in 2004 (BBC Sport, 2014), publicly expressed her frustrations with Lawless.

Although Bagger reported that she had been working on educating golf associations from the inside since 2003 (*Daily Mail*, 2011), she bristled at the media coverage surrounding the Lawless case. In an interview with the *Daily Mail*, Bagger expressed that there really is a lack of education on trans issues in sport, and that the media needs a "major shift" in its coverage because it is "sad and frustrating to see misinformation in the media" (*Daily Mail*, 2011). Whereas Lawless' approach to making change for trans women golfers included much media exposure and public discussion, Bagger ostensibly sided with a quieter approach, building collaborations and educational opportunities directly with golf associations.

Trans athletes approaching the finish line

Much has changed since 1967 when Erik Schinegger was forced to walk away from a promising athletic career as a female downhill skier, and yet again just a few short years later as a male in the same sport. Although FIS President Hodler poignantly identified the thin line between male and female with respect to sports (Fry, 2006), today there is an abundance of information available on how to make athletic spaces inclusive for trans people – and the subsequent individual-level and collective harms against human rights and health for failing to do so.

In the contemporary context, we also have access to medical experts and scientific research that clearly states trans athletes do not have an unfair advantage in competitive sport (CCES, 2016). The Canadian Centre for Equity in Sport (CCES) has made guidance documents (CCES, 2012; 2016) publicly available to encourage sporting organizations at all levels to adopt trans inclusive practices, as have similar organizations internationally. The CCES writes: "sport is today again a mirror and a magnifying glass for society, this time as it deals with the exclusions and harms that have all too often impeded athletes with variations of sex development" (CCES, 2012, p. 3). With this abundance of knowledge based in scientific expertise, the question as to why so some trans athletes today face similar prejudice as Erik Schinegger did fifty years ago, is salient.

As the CCES highlights, sport continues to reflect certain normative social beliefs such as the idea that males are more athletic than females, and that testosterone is the single most defining factor of success in sports. These ideas affect transmasculine and transfeminine athletes differently. While transmasculine (trans men, for example) athletes are often assumed to have less innate strength and talent in sports, and thus are seen to have a competitive disadvantage against cisgender males. Transfeminine athletes are viewed conversely. So generally speaking, trans women tend to confront more stigma and discrimination in sport, entrenched in the idea that they have a biological advantage over cisgender female opponents. This is particularly true of strength sports, such as MMA, where these ideas seem to be disproportionately magnified.

Overwhelmingly, though, trans athletes are making much advancement in sporting inclusion policies, most notably at the Olympic level. With the IOC recently removing the requirement for trans athletes to have completed genital reassignment surgery, many more trans athletes, disproportionately those with access to resources, will be able to imagine themselves in high-level competition. Athletes like American triathlete Chris Mosier are now eligible to compete in the Olympics, and stand as a role model for trans and other gender variant youth who may not be able to visualize themselves in athletic spaces. The IOC's trans inclusion policies over the years have served as a catalyst, and have been cited in the development of policies to protect trans athletes in various sports at multiple levels. This is, in part, why we have observed the development of formal trans inclusion in sports from Hockey Canada to Women's Flat Track Roller Derby. Of course, trans inclusion policy is just one step of making sports and athletic culture more welcoming and respectful toward gender diverse people, but these policies act as an important communicator – authoritatively stating that yes, trans people do belong in all sports and athletic organizations.

References

BBC Sport. "Transsexual Golfer Wins Tour Spot," *BBC Sport*, November 3, 2004, http://news.bbc.co.uk/sport2/hi/golf/3980131.stm

Brown, Oliver. "The Person Who Pays for Everything is the Athlete," *Telegraph*, November 14, 2015, www.telegraph.co.uk/sport/othersports/athletics/11996319/The-person-who-pays-for-everything-is-the-athlete.html

Calzo, Jeral, P., Roberts, Andrea, L., Corliss, Heather, L., Blood, Emily, Kroshus, Emily, and S. Bryn Austin. "Physical Activity Disparities in Heterosexual and Sexual Minority Youth Ages 12–22 Years Old: Roles of Childhood Gender Nonconformity and Athletic Self-Esteem." *Annals of Behavioural Medicine* 47, no. 1 (2014): 17–27.

Canadian Centre for Equity in Sport. "Creating Inclusive Environments for Trans Participants in Canadian Sport" (trans inclusion in sport expert working group, guidelines, Ottawa, ON, 2016).

Canadian Centre for Equity in Sport. "Sport in Transition: Making Sport in Canada More Responsible for Gender Inclusivity" (guidelines, Ottawa, ON, 2012).

FoxSports. "LPGA Drops the 'Female at Birth' Clause," *Fox Sports*, December 1, 2010, www.foxsports.com/golf/story/lpga-drops-femals-at-birth-clause-allows-transgenders-120110

Fry, John. "The World of Alpine Racing," in *The Story of Modern Skiing*. London: University Press of New England, 2006, 127–149.

Gonzalez, Antonio. (2010, December 2). "Lana Lawless Gets Chance to Compete on LPGA Tour with Gender Requirement Change," *The Christian Science Monitor*, December 2, 2010, www.csmonitor.com/USA/Sports/2010/1202/Lana-Lawless-gets-chance-to-compete-on-LPGA-Tour-with-gender-requirement-change

International Olympic Committee. *"IOC Consensus Meeting on Sex Reassignment and Hyperandrogenism"* (meeting, Switzerland, 2015), www.olympic.org/Documents/Commissions_PDFfiles/Medical_commission/2015-11_ioc_consensus_meeting_on_sex_reassignment_and_hyperandrogenism-en.pdf

Kellaway, Mitch. "Photos: Meet the First Out Trans Man to Win a Gay Games Gold in Powerlifting," *The Advocate*, September 17, 2014, www.advocate.com/politics/transgender/2014/09/17/photos-meet-first-trans-man-win-gay-games-gold-powerlifting

Koonce, Katy and Susan Schorn. " 'Fuck Moving On': Talking to Fallon Fox About Fair Fights, Ronda Rousey," *Jezebel*, July 29, 2015, http://jezebel.com/fuck-moving-on-talking-to-fallon-fox-about-fair-fights-1720469599

Lamport, Joe. "Meet the First Transgender Person to Play in a World Cup Qualifier," *Vice News*, April 27, 2014, https://news.vice.com/article/meet-the-first-transgender-person-to-play-in-a-world-cup-qualifier

Lawton, Matt. "How Athletics Is Still Scarred By the Reign of the Chemical Sisters," *The Daily Mail*, August 6, 2012, www.dailymail.co.uk/sport/olympics/article-2184608/How-athletics-scarred-reign-chemical-sisters.html

Montague, James. "A First in a Cup Qualifying for a Player and a Team," *New York Times*, November 25, 2011, www.nytimes.com/2011/11/26/sports/soccer/jonny-saelua-transgender-player-helps-american-samoa-to-first-international-soccer-win.html?_r=0

Muser, Dominic. *Andreas Krieger: Heidi's Farthest Throw Short Film*. Directed by Sven Schwartz. 2015. Germany: A New Western Star.

Nell Warren, Patricia. "Russia, Sport and Transgender & Intersex Issues," *Outsports*, February 12, 2014, www.outsports.com/2014/2/12/5404842/russia-sport-transgender-intersex-issues

Pohnl, Elliott. "Lana Lawless: The Story Behind Transgender Trying to Play on LPGA Tour," October 13, 2010, http://bleacherreport.com/articles/490657-lana-lawless-the-story-behind-transgender-trying-to-play-on-lpga-tour

Reporter, Daily Mail. "Fore! Transgender Golfers Get Into Catfight Over 'Female at Birth' Rules," *The Daily Mail*, February 8, 2011, www.dailymail.co.uk/news/article-1354617/Transsexual-golfer-Mianne-Bagger-blasts-Lana-Lawless-female-birth-rules.html#ixzz46C7FTNvz

Roberts, Monica. "Olympic Gender Drama-Erik Schinegger," *Transgriot* (blog), January 7, 2014, http://transgriot.blogspot.ca/2014/01/olympic-gender-drama-erik-schinegger.html

Roberts, Scott. "Interview: Jaiyah Saelua – The World's First Professional Transgender Footballer," *Pink News*, May 7, 2014, www.pinknews.co.uk/2014/05/07/interview-jaiyah-saelua-the-worlds-first-professional-transgender-footballer/

Scheim, Ayden, Bauer, Greta and Jake Pyne. "Avoidance of Public Spaces by Trans Ontarians: The Impact of Transphobia on Daily Life." *Trans PULSE e-Bulletin* 44, no. 1 (2014): 1–3.

Schinegger, Erik. *Mein Sieg über mich: der Mann, der Weltmeisterin wurde*, edited by M. Echenz. Germany: Herbig, 1988.

Smith, Pete. "Jaiyah Saelua: If I Experience Transphobia I Just Tackle Harder," *Guardian*, August 28, 2014, www.theguardian.com/football/2014/aug/29/jaiyah-saelua-transgender-footballer-interview

Sykes, Heather. "Transsexual and Transgender policies in Sport." *Women in Sport & Physical Activity* 15, no. 1 (2006): 3.

Symons, Caroline, Sbaraglia, Melissa, Hillier, Lynne and Anne Mitchell. "Come Out to Play: The Sports Experiences of Lesbian, Gay, Bisexual, and Transgender People in Victoria." (Institute of Sport, Exercise, and Active Living, report, Victoria, AUS, 2010).

Tannehill, Brynn. "Fallon Fox and the Legacy of Satchel Paige," *Huffington Post*, December 16, 2016, www.huffingtonpost.com/brynn-tannehill/fallon-fox-and-the-legacy_b_6327072.html

Thomas, Katie. "Transgender Woman Sues L.P.G.A. Over Policy," *New York Times*, October 12, 2010, www.nytimes.com/2010/10/13/sports/golf/13lawsuit.html?_r=0

Truitt, Jos. "Fallon Fox on Life as a Trans Athlete: 'The Scope of Vitriol and Anger Was Mind-Blowing,'" *Guardian*, February 16, 2015, www.theguardian.com/sport/2015/feb/16/fallon-fox-trans-mma-athlete-interview

Vinton, Nathaniel. "German Shot Put Champion Heidi Krieger Gets Sex-Change Operation After Being Unwittingly Doped with PEDS in 1970s," *New York Daily News*, May 21, 2013, www.nydailynews.com/sports/i-team/olympian-sex-change-dson-doped-pods-article-1.1349901

Zeigler, Cyd. "Moment #42: Lana Lawless Wins Right to Play on LPGA Tour," *Outsports*. August 24, 2011, www.outsports.com/2011/8/24/4051722/moment-42-lana-lawless-wins-right-to-play-on-lpga-tour

Zeigler, Cyd. "Fallon Fox Comes Out as Trans Pro MMA Fighter," *Outsports*, March 5, 2013, www.outsports.com/2013/3/5/4068840/fallon-fox-trans-pro-mma-fighter

Zeigler, Cyd. "Gay and Lesbian Sports Hall of Fame Welcomes 15 New Inductees this Week," *Outsports*, July 9, 2014, www.outsports.com/2014/7/9/5883239/gay-and-lesbian-sports-hall-of-fame-2014

Chapter 5

Between stigmatization and empowerment

Meanings of physical activity and sport in the lives of transgender people

Agnes Elling and Kiki Collot d'Escury

Physical activity and sport are generally regarded as important social prac-tices that not only contribute to one's health, but also to personal empow-erment and social connectedness for both people belonging to hegemonic social status groups and minority groups. Critical scholars have acknow-ledged these potentials of sport, but also argued and convincingly illus-trated how especially mainstream competitive sport simultaneously plays a broader societal role in constructing and reproducing social inequalities, including those relating to gender and sexuality (e.g. Anderson 2014; Connell 2005; Hargreaves 1994; Travers 2008). This leads to often-complex dynamics of personal embodied meanings and mechanisms of social in- and exclusion in the world of recreational physical activity and sport (e.g. Bridel and Rail 2007; Wellard 2016). For transgender people, taking part in sport with its binary gender structures (e.g. competitions, changing rooms) and dominant gender/sexuality discourses therefore pro-vides extra challenges (Travers 2008).

Although we recognize there is a small, but growing group of non-binary transgender people, in this chapter we mainly focus on those persons with an ambivalent or incongruent gender identity combined with unease about their body and the wish or intense need to (partially) change their gender of birth through hormone treatment and/or surgery (Cohen-Kettenis 2013; Kuyper, 2012).[1] In medical terms such people are referred to as experiencing 'gender dysphoria' (DSM-V) or a gender identity dis-order (DSM-III). In colloquial language, they are regarded as having been 'born inside the wrong body'. One of the world's leading clinics in offering medical and social support for people – including adolescents – in the process of gender transitioning, the Center of Expertise for Gender Dys-phoria, Free University Medical Centre, is based in Amsterdam.

As in other Western countries, positive developments have occurred in the Netherlands regarding the legislation, visibility and emancipation of trans-gender people (e.g. Balzar and Hutta 2012; Cohen-Kettenis 2013; Whittle *et al.* 2008). Simultaneously, studies identified that transgender people are still very vulnerable to prejudice, stigmatization and discrimination, since they live outside the hegemonic sex/gender binary (see also FRA 2013). Next to equal treatment in employment, education, and health care, the Transgender Network Netherlands (TNN) recognizes participation and acceptance in leisure activities like physical activity and sports as important aspects of societal inclusion. Following international legislation aimed at the recognition of human rights for transgender people, in 2003 the International Olympic Committee (IOC) adopted regulations for the conditioned inclusion of 'fully transitioned' transgender people in elite competitive sport (UK Sport, 2009).[2] To regulate 'gender trouble' and promote further inclusion of transgender people at lower competitive levels and in recreational sport, adjusted guidelines have been adopted by national sport federations. In 2015 the Dutch Sports Federation (NOC*NSF) produced an advisory document for sports federations and clubs, in cooperation with TNN.[3]

In this chapter, we present the findings of two explorative, qualitative studies about the experiences in physical activities and sports among trans men and trans women. These expand the existing body of knowledge around transgender participation in sport. To date, this has mainly consisted of critical – post-structuralist/feminist/queer – theoretical perspectives focused on the disciplinary and exclusionary processes and experienced limitations for transgender people in (mainstream) competitive sports (for example, Caudwell 2012; Tagg 2012; Travers 2006; Travers and Deri 2011). Although we identify with such a critical approach, we also acknowledge other 'enfleshed' lived body-self experiences (Sparkes 1999) relating to agency, identity development and empowerment of transgender people in relation to physical activity and sports.

Critical scholars like Connell (1995) and Hargreaves (1994) argued that mainstream competitive sports are not very inclusive spaces, due to the centrality of the performative body, binary gendered structures, and hegemonic gendered/heterosexual ideologies. Although more recent research by Anderson (2014) shows that hegemonic gendered ideologies are changing, non-hegemonic or 'different' gendered bodies – like transgender bodies – are still often objectified, disciplined, or excluded. Intersex and transgender women especially face protest – mostly based on arguments of fairness – from competitors and/or the public when they participate in women's competitions (e.g. Sykes 2006). Like 'pioneer' Renee Richards, who participated – legally sanctioned – in the professional women's tennis circuit from 1977 to 1981 (see Birrell and Cole 1990), transgender female athletes are still regarded as not being 'real women' or as being 'essentially men'.[4] We acknowledge that such 'unfair advantage discourse' (Sykes 2006) is partly based on the fear for challenges to the gender binary and doesn't recognize the social construction of both sport and the gender binary. However, we simultaneously regard the existing gender categories in current competitive sport as 'logical' categories to create a more level playing field, based on 'real' competitive advantages for the category of biological men over women (cf. Travers 2006). Even in sport spaces with inclusive transgender policies, for example in some North American lesbian softball leagues (Travers and Deri 2011) and mixed netball in New Zealand (Tagg 2012), trans women may face protest.

Based on our research, we argue that alongside conflicts and exclusionary processes, physical activity and sport spaces also have more positive meanings for transgender people, relating to negotiating gender identity and (re)claiming embodied subjectivity (Johnson 2007, 55). What are the (changed) meanings of and body-self experiences in physical activities and sport among transgender people and in what ways are these different for trans men and trans women, and for young and adult transgender people?

Methodology

Our results are based on biographical narrative interviews with a total of thirty transgender people, varying from 12 to 51 years of age. Respondents were approached through distributed calls in (digital) transgender networks and through personal contacts. We acknowledge that our personal social characteristics as white, higher-educated cisgender women (one lesbian and one heterosexual) with competitive sporting experiences may have influenced the process of data collection. Although we may share several experiences relating to normative gender expectations in sport, we are not transgender and we are aware that we are in a position of power with regard to interpreting our subjects' experiences of gender transitioning.

At the time of their interviews, our respondents were in different phases of gender transition and had different socio-demographic backgrounds and sporting biographies. Some (mainly young people) had only just started the diagnostic route or begun taking puberty blockers, others had started hormone treatment, but not undergone surgery (yet) and some had undergone complete transitions, including genital surgery (recently or for many years). They also differed with respect to socio-demographic positions and experiences in mainstream, competitive sport before or during/after transitioning. The – mainly ethnically Euro-Dutch – interviewees lived in villages or more urban environments in different parts of the country and had different educational levels, with the adult respondents in the midst of relatively unsettled occupational careers. Many respondents, especially trans women, identified as lesbian/homosexual. Most of the younger transgender people still lived with their parents, who often played an important (and mostly positive) role in their decision to start transitioning at a younger age. One older trans man still lived with his mother and two trans men lived together with their male partners from before their transition. Three respondents had children from a former marriage.

We asked interviewees to tell us their life story, focusing particularly on their experiences with their body, gender identity, and physical activities and sports. The conversations with adult respondents lasted one to one and a half hours on average. Interviews were recorded, and fully transcribed. Interviewing younger transgender people, between the ages of 12 and 24 years old, however, often involved multiple shorter conversations, in different environments and in different ways, alternating 'face to face' interaction with conversations through e-mail, Facebook or WhatsApp. Interaction and communication often involved a mixture of talking and observing as well as participating in sporting activities together.

In line with Driessen's (2013, 252) concept of 'small talk', these different forms of communication and interaction made it easier to establish a relationship and talk about difficult and sensitive topics like gender identities, 'fleshy physicality' and feelings of confusion, shame or exclusion. Short stories, including literal citations, were constructed and sent back to the interviewees for informed consent concerning facts and (multivocal or layered) interpretations. Analysis of these stories took place through a multiple process of encoding and constant (interpersonal) comparison. We selected three central stories (Sam, Sandra, Patrick) and included the outcomes of other respondents in the analyses of central themes in their narratives of (dis)embodiment, gender (re)identification and sport.

Three body-self sporting narratives

Sam

Sam (17) is very fond of playing sports, namely, hockey, soccer and basketball. He started playing hockey with a girls' team when he was six years old. At that time, he already dressed as a boy: "I only wore jeans and a t-shirt, never a dress or a skirt or anything that was too tight and my hair was always short." At the age of eight Sam was diagnosed with 'gender dyshporia'. In the summer break between primary and high school he and his family decided he would attend high school as a 'boy'. Although he started to present himself as a boy when he went to high school, he continued to play hockey on a girls' team:

> I still felt very comfortable in my hockey team. They let me wear shorts, instead of a skirt, I was really happy about that. Other kids or parents sometimes said things like "hey that's not fair, they have a boy on their team!" But I didn't really mind.

Although Sam enjoyed playing hockey, he was even better at soccer, and when he turned 12 he decided to only play soccer, where he played on a regional selection team of the national football federation. During those years his 'trans feelings' started to become a bigger part of his life. He recalled his 'odd feelings', being present in the girls' changing room and showering together (which was compulsory): "…I felt guilty towards the other girls. Although my body wasn't different, I knew I felt different and I even preferred girls." He decided to quit playing soccer and start with basketball, "as a guy".

When he told his new basketball team about his transgender identity they all reacted very well. He changed with the other guys, felt accepted by his team and really enjoyed being able to play basketball as a boy. But at the same time, he was constantly afraid of not fitting in. He felt like he was physically lagging behind. He had just started taking puberty blockers but could not yet start with cross-sex hormones (testosterone), since the standards of care eligibility requirements in the Netherlands includes a minimum age of 16 years (WPATH 2011). So while all the other boys were physically growing his body was literally frozen in time.

> I remember being pushed by an opponent and falling on the ground. My teammates immediately stood up for me but I felt so ashamed. I was afraid everyone would think I was a sissy or worse … that I was a girl…

Sam eventually quit playing basketball because he felt so physically overmatched as he is "just very small for a guy".

Analysis: Sam's experience in hockey, soccer and basketball illustrate how young trans boys/men face several challenges in (competitive) sport participation during a phase in which they are physically, socially and emotionally 'migrating' to a 'new gender' (cf. Johnson 2007; Schleifer 2006). Although different from trans women, who often experience being excluded by others due to 'fairness' after transition, trans boys and men also experience issues related to fairness. Job (14) still plays soccer on a girls' team with his friends, where they all 'know'. But more and more often at games opponents and parents 'accuse' him of 'being a boy'. Although such references may be partly experienced as a compliment, since he is recognized in his 'right' gender, they may be hurtful at the same time. On the one hand, transgender boys who just started transitioning, like Sam and Job, may feel socially excluded from competitive sport participation in their gender category of birth due to their boyish looks. Similar to cisgender women who challenge norms of gender appropriate appearance, they are confronted with the unfairness discourse (Sykes 2006), even though they do not benefit from gender category related biological advantages. On the other hand, these young trans men feel excluded from participating in the boy's/men's competition, since their 'wrong' female body does not yet allow them an embodied masculinity. Simon (33) and Eric (43) recalled similar ambivalent experiences about their participation in mainstream women's football teams before/during transitioning. After transition, trans men often feel they have physical disadvantages compared to cis-men their age, as was recalled by Sander (23), Eric (43) and Jeroen (47). After having had positive experiences in his women's football team during his (first phase of) transition Simon also looked forward to playing on a lower-level amateur men's team ('the 6th team') in the same club. His positive antici-pation, like Coen's (16) first experiences on a boys' team, seem to mirror developments of inclusive masculinity in men's team sports (Anderson 2008). This is different from the elsewhere found fear of being confronted with a non-inclusive, gender- and heteronormative climate (eg trans man Finn in Caudwell 2012 or gay men who refrain from football and other men's team sports, Elling and Janssens 2009), although we do acknow-ledge that such forms of perceived stigma may still be similar 'real'. The sporting narratives of trans men especially illustrate the often-paradoxical experiences of inclusiveness and belonging as well as exclusionary pro-cesses of binary sex/gender structures and norms. Many have felt safe and a sense of belonging within their women's team or felt accepted in boys' teams, but simultaneously didn't completely fit due to either a too 'masculine' presence or a physical practice that couldn't keep up with 'real boys/men'.

Anne (19) identifies most as a trans woman although the way she presents herself differs. She participates in the transgender inclusive sport of Quidditch,[5] including some non-binary transgender people. Similar to Sam, however, most of our interviewees strive not to deconstruct sex/ gender binaries, but to achieve a clear public 'either-or' identity as a recog-nizable man or woman after transitioning, even though some may be partly critical of the binary system (cf. Roen 2001; Wilson 2002). Since most rather 'migrate' from one gender to another they could be regarded as more "conforming" instead of "transforming" transgender people (Travers 2006), although we rather acknowledge that all transgender nar-ratives in some way are challenging the gender/sex binaries in sport. Sam's story also illustrated that the wish to be 'passable' enough is related to fear. Similar, Anne stated that she only presents herself with more womanly characteristics (e.g. clothing) when she feels comfortable enough. These examples illustrate the stigma around transgender people, since being able to pass as a man or woman lessens the likelihood of experi-encing "micro-aggressions" related to gender policing that negatively impact visible transgender people (Spade 2011). Sandra's story also shows how being acknowledged and accepted as their new gender identity by others is an important condition for feelings of safety as well as pride.

Sandra

According to Sandra (41), she had lived a 'reasonably normal boys' youth', including playing football on the top boys' team of the local football club until age 18.

> In those days, I did not really see that I was in the wrong body and that I wanted to do girls' things ... Before, I was really a normal boy who liked to put on girls' clothes as a kind of hobby.

At age five she started cross-dressing, but felt comfortable in her boys' body and, for example, did not mind showering with the other boys on her football team. She changed to badminton and became a member of a club, where her brother played. At the age of 35, she "started experimenting with doing things as a woman" and living a double life, with "no space left for sports". Then she decided that she did not want to live her life as a woman in secret any longer and started the official transitioning trajectory.

Sandra moved and changed jobs, although she continued singing as a tenor – "voices cannot undergo gender transition" – in a mixed choir, where she felt at home: "With singing you just wear clothes and can hide everything ... It's a safe group although it was pretty scary to tell them about it, since they were among the first few people."

Sandra's first sport activity as a woman involved joining a women's running group, which was a positive experience, similar to other work related 'experiments' relating to living as a woman.

> I could join them without the hassle of dressing rooms, just in the car in my jogging suit; although I had to think about what is suitable to wear in sports as a woman ... The other runners were positive. They all called me a she and I didn't notice whether they knew or whether they had difficulties with it.

Nevertheless, she quit after several months, partially because she got a girl-friend. When this relationship ended, she decided to take up badminton again. Sandra joined another club, where some of the members had known her as a man. Since she had not undergone surgery at the time of interview, she didn't play competitively. This was because Sandra is apprehensive about possible resistance from other women athletes regarding issues related to fairness. She tends to be understanding when people who have known her as a man, sometimes still refer to her as 'he'. Probably due to the fact that Sandra is not very tall and of slender build, strangers never address her as a man. She notes that with respect to her relative 'feminine' posture, she profits from her Asian ethic descent among the majority of people from Euro-Dutch descent. Sandra enjoys the fact that her brother called her new car a real woman's car and experiences it as a compliment when men whistle at her on the street. At some moment in the interview, she stated that her penis doesn't really bother her. But she is also looking forward to the moment when she is legally a woman and able to fully participate in sport as such, including taking a shower and maybe also taking part in the women's competition in badminton.

Analysis: Sandra's sports biography is in a way a counter narrative, compared to several other trans women who not participated in hegemonic masculinity (Connell, 1995) via sport while living as men. Some of them had hardly voluntarily participated in sports as boys/young men before transitioning, although they often did have educational and job trajectories fitting normative gender patterns. Dorien (39), for example said: "Before my transition, I never participated in sports. You need some kind of self-respect, which I absolutely didn't have." Many of the adolescents and adults we interviewed – both trans men and trans women – recalled changing rooms, swimming pools or the beach as places to avoid because they evoked particular unease about their 'wrong' naked bodies. When they were unable to avoid them, they coped by concealing their naked bodies or body contours by wearing long, oversized clothes. Others did not experience this need to hide their bodies since they were unable to register their embodied selves; they only seemed to have material (objectified) bodies that they were unable to identify with. Peter (34), for example, said: "I denied my body so unbelievably much that I had very little shame about my own body and things in general. If something isn't there, you can't be ashamed about it either."

For others, prior to transitioning, sport was an important way of shaping/controlling their (wrong) bodies and gender identities. Sport helped them in coping with their 'forbidden feelings'. This was the case for Patrick (42, see last synopsis) and for Evelien (38), who repeatedly mentioned that she trained 'like crazy' before coming out and underscored the importance of sports in her life. At the end of the interview, just before the interviewer was about to leave the place, Evelien made a powerful 'door-knob statement' about the importance of sport in her life: "Had it not been for sports, I wouldn't be here today." Both the practices of body-denial and -disciplining are related to objectified bodies and less to being embodied subjects (cf. Schrock et al. 2005).

Since transitioning is such a profound emotional and social process (Gagné et al., 1997; Johnson 2007), similar to Sandra, most interviewees that were still active in competitive club sports (temporarily) withdrew from their familiar sports environments, even when they experienced these environments as 'safe'. Other interviewees also anticipated the potential for painful situations regarding dissonance between their gender identities and or presentations in the particular sporting environment and try to prevent them. Their cautious and attentive sensitivity regarding their (trans)gender expressions in specific spaces and among people in known and unknown social environments may explain why most respondents did not experience discrimination. One of the interviewees was less 'careful' about navigating sport during her transition. This was likely a factor in her experience of discrimination in a (psychiatric) patient volleyball group and a local recreational badminton group she joined during her period of real-life testing and hormone treatment. She noted: "they kept saying 'he' and denied my womanhood. My first name was not said anymore either ... I noticed that I was a kind of freak" (Patricia, 46).

The constant process of negotiation and acting cautiously many trans people engage in during different phases of transition (FRA 2013; Lewis and Johnson 2011) was also evident in Patrick's story.

Patrick

Born as a girl in a strict religious family, Patrick (42) was not allowed to play outside on Sundays, watch sports on television, or join a football club, despite desperately wanting to do all these things. Instead, he cycled a lot. He knew "something was wrong, physically" since he was four years old and started using a boy's name in primary school. Patrick recalls disliking physical education and finding excuses to avoid participating, especially when gymnastics were on the programme.

During his studies in the country capital, he met his male partner. At that time, he also met a trans woman for the first time, for whom he then felt pity. Although he was troubled by his own body, he decided he was strong enough to deal with it. This led him to start bodybuilding to better shape the parts he is proud of. "My body consisted of a head, arms and legs. I didn't register what was in between." Fitness also fitted his obsession with numbers, "12 repetitions, 45 seconds break, another 12 repetitions, very tightly planned." Patrick strives to be as strong as the other men in the gym.

> I think for me it was a combination of wanting to be just as strong as those other people and being so angry at your body if it doesn't function the way you like it to, that you train yourself to death. That you think 'just torture it, because that's the only thing you can do with it ... inflicting hurt on the self, like "stupid body!"'

For Patrick, the process of registration for gender transition started when surgery was deemed necessary for a neglected uterus cyst. Having formerly lived in denial of and disassociated from his female body, he finally decided to confront himself:

> In a hotel room I undressed and watched my own body in a mirror and thought, 'this isn't right'. It was the first time in my life that I

looked at my whole body. So I had to puke, I was literally sick, because you hate that body.

During the time he had to wait before he received a 'green light' to officially start the transition process with hormone treatment, sport remained important. "I was already able to pass and sport became even more a way to shape my body the way I wanted it." He was already living publicly as a man, except in the gym, where using the women's changing room and the mixed sauna was becoming more difficult. About that period, he noted: "women step in and say, 'ooooh', and go out because they think they are in the wrong room and then re-enter, blushing". He changed to the men's room when he started hormone treatment, after having informed the gym owner. Before he had surgery, he bound his breasts in the toilet or wore a vest and he took a shower at home or in an individual shower cabin. He is impressed by the effect of the hormone treatments: "I went to the dunes to walk, but I just started to run and that felt like crazy. I ran twenty kilometres and back again, that's a marathon! I had never run before in mountain shoes!"

After transitioning Patrick felt liberated and now lives his life in a more embodied way. He has become more of a body-subject – feeling 'at home' in and identifying with his (new) body – instead of controlling his body-object. And yet, Patrick is not completely satisfied with his male body, especially his small penis. He says, "All men see it and say, 'gee, that's a small one!'" He is also aware of the clear scars on his chest, and that people might ask uncomfortable questions about them. Nonetheless, it appears he is under much less pressure to identify with masculinity through sports, since he *is* a (gay) man. He continues to visit the same gym on a frequent basis, but he trains less obsessively and now feels comfortable to participate in physical activities that are considered more feminine, such as group classes for aerobics and yoga.

Analysis: Unlike many respondents, who start anew after transitioning, Patrick continued his job, stayed with his (male) partner and remained active at his fitness centre. But the training regimen he engaged in to build a masculine body and embody a masculine identity (cf. Connell 1995; Schleifer 2006), in combination with hormone treatments, was echoed by several other trans boys and men.

As particularly present in Patrick's narrative, many other interviewees also expressed feeling liberated upon completing their transition. They felt they no longer had to hide, deny, manipulate or control their 'wrong' objectified bodies. Several respondents very consciously planned to show their 'new' (post-surgery) naked bodies in places that they used to avoid, like swimming pools or saunas. Jeroen (47), for example, felt free to walk around on the beach bare-chested after his mastectomy. "And I did that, however cold it was. The only other person on the beach was wearing a very thick winter coat, but I was walking around bare-chested … Yes, I am proud of it, now I dare to show it to people!" Evelien (38) also 'celebrated' her final surgery by going to the swimming pool and changing in the women's changing room. Indeed, for many respondents their lived embodied experiences and sense of embodied subjectivity developed only after transitioning. Dorien, for example, was over 30 years of age when she started sport, with the welcome result that it "made me more physical on all kinds of different levels … I have become much more self-confident, much more conscious of everything."

Patrick's narrative illustrates how the negotiation of the safety of particular (leisure) spaces for trans people continues after transitioning (Lewis and Johnson 2011). And sometimes, after initial positive experiences, their trusting expectations may give way to feelings of exclusion. Dorien, for example, quit competitive sports directly after having experienced a painful public outing of her transgender identity, during a women's cycling competition where she had 'passed' unproblematically for several years. "[The speaker] yelled my biological gender through the microphone … If I were to consider competing again, you can be unmasked … so you can find yourself under extremely great public pressure". This example illustrates the continuing vulnerability of transgender people to the 'risk' of being outed. This was particularly the case for trans women who participated in women's competitive sport, even those who had fully undergone medical transition (cf. Tagg 2012). Marijke (43) and Ellen (35) expressed mixed experiences relating to their acceptance as trans women in competitive sport (table tennis and field hockey, respectively). In 2008, Marijke played at the highest competitive level and noted:

> I was one of the first openly transgender woman in competitive sports. Nowadays, things have changed. I think, there is more acceptance. But not always and everywhere. It seems you can be transgender in sport, except when you reach a high level.

This citation clearly notes a development towards a more inclusive environment for trans women on the one hand, whereas on the other hand this inclusion remains conditional. Especially at the higher competitive levels and when trans women win, the unfair advantage discourse tends to override the inclusion discourse.

Conclusion

The findings of our research partly affirm existing research that illustrates how transgender people, before, during and after transition, may feel excluded or forced to 'fit' into the binary gender structures and cultures of (competitive) sport spaces. But there were also counter narratives that showed how trans men and women may use sport to cope with their feelings or (re)build embodied gender identity. The narratives especially illustrated the extraordinary particularity of the body-self biographies and (changed) meanings of sporting practices and spaces. Sport spaces are often especially challenging during the 'liminal' transitioning process, involving the literal transgression of binary gender structures such as changing rooms and sex segregated sporting competitions. However, our findings challenge existing ideas that sports and physical activities are only disciplining – and sometimes shameful or even dangerous – practices for transgender people. We found that many trans men and women, as well as younger trans boys and girls, have positive experiences in different transition phases. Indeed, for some trans people, physical activities and sport were and are foremost enjoyable, empowering activities within supportive social environments, (re)creating body awareness, gender identification and a sense of belonging.

Notes

1 Exact figures are unknown, but recent findings among the Dutch population from 15–70 years, show that about 0.6 per cent of men and 0.2 per cent of women may have such experiences (Kuyper 2012).
2 Due to the strict binary gender structure and the gender policies aimed at unmasking unfair 'masculine' advantage in women's sport, only transgender women with complete gender reassignment surgery (including genital correction) and legal recognition of their new gender identity in their country of citizenship are allowed to participate. Hormone therapy must have been long enough to minimize advantage from the 'masculinizing' hormones their former male body produced – guidelines hold that to be more than four years – and they must live for a minimum of two years in their newly assigned gender.
3 Although transgender people in the Netherlands can legally change gender and receive official documents with their 'new' gender identity since 1985, until 2014, such a change required a 'complete' transition including hormonal and surgical treatment and sterilization to prevent transgender people from producing or conceiving children after transition. Since 2014, transgender people can also officially change gender, without such full surgical transition.
4 For example, the victory of Dutch trans woman Nathalie van Gogh at the national track cycling championships in 2009 led to public discussion. According to an online poll in a national newspaper, 70 per cent considered her victory to be unfair (Algemeen Dagblad, 11 October 2009).
5 The game of Quidditch is inspired by the books of Harry Potter. Inclusivity and diversity are very important for the game, as is most explicit in the 'four maximum rule', or the 'the gender rule', which allows each team to have a maximum of four players, who identify as the same gender in active play on the field at the same time. The gender a player identifies with may or may not be the same as that person's sex. USQ acknowledges that not all players identify as either male or female and welcomes players of all genders and identities (USQ Rulebook 8;www.usquidditch.org/about/rules).

References

Anderson, E. 2008. "Inclusive masculinities in a fraternal setting". *Men & Masculinities* 10(5): 604–620.

Anderson, E. 2014. *21st Century jocks: Sporting men and contemporary heterosexuality*. Basingstoke: Palgrave Macmillan.

Balzar, C. and J. S. Hutta 2012. *Transpect versus transphobia worldwide. A comparative review of the human-rights situation of gender-variant/trans people*. Berlin: TVT/TGEU.

Birrell, S. and Ch. Cole 1990. "Double fault: Renee Richards and the construction and naturalisation of difference". *Sociology of Sport Journal* 7: 1–21.

Bridel, W. and G. Rail 2007. "Sport, sexuality and the production of (resistant) bodies: de-/re-constructing the meanings of gay male marathon corporeality". *Sociology of Sport Journal* 24: 127–144.

Caudwell, J. 2014. "[Transgender] young men: gendered subjectivities and the physically active body". *Sport, Education and Society* 19(4): 398–414.

Cohen-Kettenis, P. T. 2013. *Agendering voor het nageslacht. Afscheidsrede 7 juni 2013*. Amsterdam: VUmc.

Connell, R. W. 1995. *Masculinities*. Berkeley: University of California Press.

Driessen, H. and W. Jansen. 2013. "The hard work of small talk in ethnographic fieldwork". *Journal of Anthropological Research* 69: 249–263.

Elling, A. and J. Janssens. 2009. "Sexuality as a structural principle in sport participation: negotiating sports spaces". *International Review for the Sociology of Sport* 44(1): 71–86.

Elling, A., P. De Knop and A. Knoppers 2003. "Gay/lesbian sport clubs and events: places of homo-social bonding and cultural resistance?" *International Review for the Sociology of Sport* 38(4): 441–456.

FRA 2013. *European Union lesbian, gay, bisexual and transgender survey*. Vienna: FRA-European Agency for fundamental rights.

Gagné, P., R. Tewksbury and D. McGaughey 1997. "Coming out and crossing over: Identity formation and proclamation in a transgender community". *Gender & Society* 11(4): 478–508.

Hargreaves, J. 1994. *Sporting females. Critical issues in the history and sociology of women's sports*. London: Routledge.

Johnson, K. 2007. "Changing sex, changing self: theorizing transitions in embodied subjectivity." *Men and Masculinities* 10(10): 54–70.

Kuyper, L. 2012. "Transgender in Nederland: prevalentie en attitudes." *Tijdschrift voor Sexuologie* 36(2): 129–135.

Lewis S. T. and C. W. Johnson 2011. "'But it's not that easy': negotiating (trans) gender expressions in leisure spaces". *Leisure/Loisir* 35(2): 115–132.

NOC*NSF 2015. *Transgenders en sport. Richtlijnen voor sportbonden, -verenigingen en sporters ten behoeve van de sportdeelname van transgenders*. Arnhem: NOC*NSF.

Roen, K. 2001. "'Either/or' and 'both/neither': Discursive tensions in transgender politics". *Signs* 27(2): 501–522.

Schleifer, D. 2006. "Make me feel mighty real: gay female to male transgenderists negotiating sex, gender and sexuality". *Sexualities* 9(1): 57–75.

Schrock, D., L. Reid and E. M. Boyd. 2005. "Transsexuals' embodiment of womanhood". *Gender & Society* 19(3): 317–335.

Spade, D. 2011. *Normal life: Administrative violence, critical trans politics, and the limits of law*. Brooklyn, NY: South End.

Sparkes, A. 1999. "Exploring body narratives". *Sport, Education and Society* 4(1): 17–30.

Sykes, H. 2006. "Transsexual and transgender policies in sport". *Women in Sport and Physical Activity Journal* 15(1): 3–13.

Tagg, B. 2012. "Transgender netballers: ethical issues and lived realities". *Sociology of Sport Journal* 29(2): 151–167.

Travers, A. 2006. "Queering sport: lesbian softball leagues and the transgender challenge". *International Review for the Sociology of Sport* 41(3–4): 431–446.

Travers, A. 2008. "The sport nexus and gender injustice". *Studies in Social Justice Journal* 2(1): 79–101.

Travers, A. and J. Deri. 2011. "Transgender inclusion and the changing face of lesbian softball leagues". *International Review for the Sociology of Sport* 46: 488–507.

UK Sport. 2009. *Transsexual people and sport. Guidance for governing bodies*. London. Department for Culture, Media and Sport

Wellard, I., ed. 2016. *Researching embodied sport. Exploring movement cultures*. London: Routledge.

Whittle, S., L. Turner, R. Combs and S. Rhodes. 2008. *Transgender study: Legal survey and focus on the transgender experience of health care*. Brussel: ILGA-Europe.

Wilson, M. 2002. "'I am the prince of pain, for I am a princess in the brain': Liminal transgender identities, narratives and the elimination of ambiguities". *Sexualities* 5(4): 425–448.

WPATH 2011. *Standards of care for the health of transsexual, transgender and gender nonconforming people. 7th version*. World Professional Association for Transgender Health.

Chapter 6

Athletes' perceptions of transgender eligibility policies applied in high-performance sport in Canada

Sarah Teetzel

Introduction

The International Olympic Committee (IOC)'s consensus statement on sexual harassment and abuse in sport called for the creation of 'a culture of dignity, respect and safety in sport' recognizing that sports organizations are 'gatekeepers to safety and should demonstrate strong leadership in identifying and eradicating these practices' (IOC, 2007). These sentiments are echoed in the IOC's reform strategy, *Olympic Agenda 2020*, which calls for a renewed effort to support athletes' wellbeing and welfare (IOC, 2014). As one step in a multipronged approach, the IOC has provided athletes with a greater presence in international sports governance through participation on influential IOC Commissions (IOC, 2016). Selected athletes now have a voice in shaping the policies that govern their participation in international sport. This increased recognition of the importance of athlete welfare, which seeks to reduce athlete exploitation, reduce harassment, and promote values-based sport, recognizes that athlete populations continue to face discrimination and abuse (Mountjoy *et al.*, 2016). The creation of athlete positions on influential committees is one of many steps to bring about positive change; however, it would be naïve to believe that any athlete representative can speak for the entire athlete population they are elected or appointed to represent. This is particularly the case when it comes to policies such as the so-called "Stockholm Consensus", which stipulates the conditions under which transgender athletes can participate in Olympic sports (IOC, 2003; IOC, 2015).

Athletes' perspectives on transgender athlete inclusion and exclusion policies, applied by international sports governing bodies, remain largely unknown. The development of fair and equitable eligibility policies in sport requires an awareness of transgender athletes' experiences in order to understand the barriers that remain in creating safe and inclusive sport spaces. The research literature has not yet established the impact of high-performance sport policies on transgender athletes' sport experiences and lives. Cisgender athletes' reactions to transgender sport policies, and their attitudes towards inclusive sport, are also relatively unknown, with the exception of the occasional, and often transphobic, quote from a high profile athlete published in media sources. For example, Ronda Rousey aggressively commented to reporters that she would not voluntarily fight Fallon Fox, a mixed martial arts fighter who had transitioned prior to beginning her professional career (Samano, 2013). We cannot assume that statements of this nature are representative of the views of the majority of athletes. Thus, this chapter presents the results of a small qualitative study designed to gain insight into transgender and cisgender athletes' perceptions of fairness in the regulation and inclusion of transgender athletes in high-performance sport.

Methods

Five transgender athletes and five cisgender high-performance athletes responded to posters (displayed at a national training centre and community resource centres) advertising a study on transgender athlete eligibility policies. Each participant took part in a semi-structured one-on-one interview where they were asked to share their perceptions of transgender eligibility policies applied in sport. Prior to the start of the recruitment process, approval was received from the University of Manitoba's Education/Nursing Research Ethics Board to conduct the study. Interested athletes reviewed and signed informed consent forms prior to their participation in interviews. Participants were asked to discuss their knowledge of and reactions to transgender policies in sport, as well as barriers and facilitators to their involvement in sport. In research of this nature, it is very important to consider athletes' lived experiences (Edwards and Jones, 2007) and participants were encouraged and prompted to share as much of their sport histories as they felt comfortable. Interviews lasted between 50 minutes and 2 hours and 15 minutes, and each interview was recorded, transcribed by a research assistant, and approved by the participant prior to being coded. Approved transcripts were coded using both priori and emergent coding techniques (Gratton and Jones, 2010).

Participants

Five cisgender female athletes volunteered to participate in this pilot study. All five had played at the provincial level, with three of the five participating on a Canadian national team. These athletes selected the pseudonyms Carlin, Leigh, Naomi, Rachel, and Sasha. Five athletes who identify as transgender (or two-spirited, non-binary, genderqueer, gender fluid, or gender non-conforming) also responded to the recruitment poster and volunteered to participate in an interview. All five participants had devoted time to training and competition prior to transitioning and now participate in sport at the recreational level. Three participants identify as men and had competed in women's sport in the past: Orlando competed in women's rowing at the university varsity level, Don competed in multiple sports at the provincial and university varsity levels, and Dylan was a multisport athlete now specializing in curling. Two participants once competed in men's sporting events and now identify as women: Gisele has earned a black belt in taekwondo, and Jen competes in curling at the provincial level with opportunities to play against national-level athletes. Jen and Don had both worked with sports organizations to draft transgender eligibility policies for specific leagues. The other eight participants had very little to no knowledge of the particulars of the Stockholm Consensus or the eligibility requirements for transgender athletes endorsed by the IOC.

Discussion

To help discern athletes' reactions to trans sport policies, participants shared their perspectives on sport policies regulating transgender eligibility with the understanding that their identities would remain anonymous. The focus of the discussion that follows emphasizes three themes that emerged from the viewpoints shared in the interviews: (1) uncertainty about what constitutes a performance advantage in sport, (2) a commitment to fairness, but genuine doubt as to what fairness entails, and (3) connections between participants' understanding of fairness and respect.

Uncertainty regarding where the science is at

Claims that transgender athletes compete with an unfair advantage often stem from ignorance about transitioning and gender normativity biases (Wahlert and Fiester, 2012). As a result of differing attitudes towards discrimination and inclusion, and different interpretations of the available research literature, the question of whether or not transgender athletes compete at a competitive advantage persists. Devries' (2008) comprehensive literature review of the scientific evidence addressing athletic advantages or disadvantages resulting from transitioning found no convincing or compelling evidence. However, as participants reflected in their interviews, it is not clear where the science is at in establishing competitive advantages, and conceptually what a competitive advantage entails. Sasha noted any advantage "comes down to a science, I think, more than ethical. Because do they have [pause] still a higher level of testosterone even though they have had this two year estrogen period or vice versa, right?" Sasha's questions demonstrate a curiosity to learn more, but a limited amount of time spent grappling with questions of trans athletes' participation in sport.

Other cisgender participants acknowledged a severe lack of awareness or understanding of transitioning. For example, Carlin acknowledged,

"I don't know exactly how it works, but I still think it [testosterone] will be higher than normal levels found in these people." Regarding the requirements of competing in sport, Naomi asked:

> Like you obviously need some [requirements], you know, you can't just have a man just um taking a few pills and saying he is a woman, you know and competing with women, but at the same time, transgenderism, or, I don't know how you say that, has become more popular, it's um not something that, you know, you can't just say like 'oh you were born a man you have to compete with men' or you know or anything like that.

Rachel had not considered competing against transgender athletes prior to her interview, but attempted to make sense of her initial thoughts about appropriate criteria for inclusion:

> I mean it's, it's like a whole other world. I can't even imagine like being in that position and I'm trying to think of myself, if I was in the position where I had the desire and passion to play that much.... I think there has to be some, a very, like a strict guideline and it can't be wishy washy and if they have, you know, three things, like here are the things we need from you and then you make your decision from there. I mean it's like a whole other world, I can't even imagine in my head, how do you make those decisions?

In a similar vein, Sasha noted that transgender athletes' participation does not impact her personally, but she thinks, "Some athletes would be intimidated by it or, use it as sort of an excuse to say maybe why they lost or why they didn't perform as well, there's tons of ethical reasons behind that" then elaborating, "Personally I don't find that a lot of the external stuff really matters to me so I don't, I don't think it would bother me, but I could see there being ethical reasons behind others' [opposition]." The five cisgender athletes in the study, however, all eventually reasoned their way through to positions based in inclusion. For example, Carlin reflected:

> Yes, it is an unfair advantage that she has, but it's the same as somebody who could be very smart in a field of study and there is somebody else who doesn't study or retain information as well, that person is obviously going to excel. Do we have to hold that person back because that is just her specialty in life?

Responding no to the rhetorical question posed, Carlin articulated that without clearly established scientific advantages, limiting trans athletes from competing is unacceptable.

Trans participants also raised questions about whether athletes compete at an advantage or disadvantage after transitioning, and how performance advantages are conceptualized and measured. Gisele raised the issue of determining 'normal' levels of testosterone in bodies, and how athletes' bodies fit within norms established for the general public. She noted that current regulations that require hormones implies scientists know,

> ...where the outliers are. If you are, if you are dealing with elite athletes, you're dealing with, with people who are you know within the fractions of, of a, of the top percent of athletes in a, in a pool. Will those people be representative of the population as a whole? And per chance does, you know, a woman skier, a female athlete of any kind, if her testosterone levels are on the high side of normal, or even what would be considered normal for the population as a whole, should she be excluded? Probably not! It should be up to the anti doping people to be able to prove that the testosterone flowing in that woman's blood was produced by her it wasn't synthesized testosterone that she was taking to enhance her performance.

In a similar vein, Jen speculated that concerns about the science of advantages are impacted by transgender athletes' ability to pass and not have their gender identity questioned by their competitors. As she explained:

> You know I think a lot of it has to do with passability. Um, so and this is perhaps wrong, but the better a person looks, the better that they get treated. And that's really hard for us transwomen is looking, um, acceptable. It takes a lot of work. It takes, um it takes, it's hard. I mean your body structure is larger, your bone structure. I had the facial feminization surgery so you know there's some advantages to that but still you know on a body realm, um you still have to use hip padding and things like that to try to have a more female shape and I think that's ultimately, a more female shape as well as a female looking face, that just is like the ticket to no problems.

Finally, Don pointed out that while more research is necessary to establish specific competitive advantages, establishing this answer is not a major focus for the transgender community. He noted, "I understand that like there's not a lot of, like we don't have a lot studies on the effects on someone's performance." Elaborating on his view, Don added:

> I guess one of the reasons that I struggle so much with this, I don't know if this makes any sense but like we're having enough trouble surviving as a trans population that like fighting about Olympic inclusion is one of those things where it's, like, I think it's really good that there

are people advocating for this, don't get me wrong. I mean we're about to go to the Olympics in Brazil which is like the world like, [sigh] the world capital of transgender murders and I'd really like to see the Olympic Commission say something about that, as we're like filling their economy with funds.

While the five cisgender participants in this study had the privilege of not needing to think about eligibility and inclusion policies in sport prior to their interviews, the athletes identifying as trans had clearly spent more time thinking about trans athlete inclusion, safety, and respect in sport. None of the participants voiced outright opposition to or displeasure at the current policies, once the policies were explained to them, and all acknowledged the issue was important to address and terribly complex.

A commitment to some sort of fairness

An overarching theme expressed in the interviews with the ten athletes who participated in this study was a desire and commitment to maintaining a fair playing field in sport, but uncertainty over what a fair playing field actually involves and requires. None of the participants believed a trans athlete would transition for the potential rewards of success in sport. Various conceptions of fairness were put forward by participants. Describing fairness as "a more foggier concept than one would have thoughts", Naomi expressed her conception of fairness in terms of equality of opportunity:

> [Is] making it fair, essentially for everyone, is that even possible? Really? … For example, I'm thinking of figure skating, you have the rich people who can afford like the pro coaches, like for hours a day, you have the ones who are like figure skating on a pond, you know? Like they could have potentially, had they been given the same amount of money growing up, gotten to like the same level, but the person with the training as opposed to the person figure skating on a pond are not going to reach the same level. Hmmm, I don't know if there really is fairness in sport!

For Rachel, fairness involved equality and equal access. Sasha explained that her thoughts on fairness focus on anti-doping and ensuring athletes compete cleanly. In addition to a commitment to anti-doping, Sasha equates fairness with hard work:

> I think it more comes down to a work ethic and being willing to work and compete and wanting to train and what not. So I mean if you're willing to train on a year round and your body is used to it then that's,

that's an advantage in itself. I don't think that there's sort of a fairness of having to take this time off [to meet the eligibility requirements]. I think the drug part is probably the biggest part of it that, that determines fairness in sport.

Leigh took her time composing her thoughts on what fair sporting environment looks like, and eventually landed on a conception of fairness rooted in inclusivity, stating: "I don't know, what's fair anymore? [laughs] It's like fair to me might not be fair to you.... I don't, it's hard to verbalize! And I'm trying to find the words. It's a touchy subject [long pause]." After additional thought, Leigh added that fairness in sport is "a standard that you hold everyone to. So if you're going to set guidelines, then you hold everyone accountable. You don't just pick and choose who you want to attack! You have to say, and it can't be biased." Like Leigh, Carlin highlighted the contradictions in her thinking about fairness, wavering back and forth between wanting to include transgender athletes without case-by-case examinations and wanting to ensure everyone has a chance to compete on a level playing field. These views of fairness demonstrate the complexity of the ideal of fairness. While fairness was raised by every participant, explaining what fairness means was a challenge for each participant.

Connecting inclusion and respect

The tension between trans inclusion and the idea of a fair playing field are complicated further when discussion moves from participation to winning. Several participants in this study shared the view of Bruce Kidd, a Canadian Olympian, researcher, and activist, who advocates for athletes to be able to compete in the sex category of their choice without facing testing or mandatory treatments. Kidd's (2011) calls for self-identification to be the only criterion for participation in the men's and women's categories at all levels of sport stems from the view that unequal playing fields are created by myriad factors, including access to coaching, nutrition, and equipment, and are not restricted to an athlete's sex at birth or testosterone level. Historical analyses of eligibility rules in sport demonstrate that 'there is nothing in the nature of sport itself that determines who can and cannot play. In the purest form of sport only self-exclusion should apply' (Vamplew, 2007, p. 851).

As noted by several participants in this study, the idea of gender self-declaration applies not only to trans athletes but also to intersex athletes, and it would be highly complex and difficult to apply as a policy. Many participants echoed support for women athletes who challenge sport's gender binary, including Caster Semenya and Dutee Chand, and voiced support for these athletes to be immediately permitted to run in women's races. Yet none of the participants reflected aloud about racialized notions of the hyperphysicality of brown and black bodies. Instead, discussions continued to focus on the idea of fairness and equality of opportunity. One trans athlete, Sophie, spoke at length about how a policy of self-declaration is desirable on paper, but would be hard to enact. Noting a trans athlete who wins at the elite level can expect to have the legitimacy of their victory questioned, Sophie drew on personal experiences to characterize some competitors' automatic responses that success stems from unfair advantage. However, she rejected that view, explaining, "That's sour grapes, that's pure sour grapes." Jen, who had recently participated in developing a transgender eligibility policy for a team sport, did not endorse gender self-declaration policies despite appreciating the fundamental idea motivating them:

> I do also think that there's um there has to be something because otherwise it's just, how do I say this without, there has to be some lev-eling of the playing field to start with it. And I keep coming back to weightlifting. You know if that was the particular sport and there was somebody not on hormones, not anything, you know that would, just wouldn't be a fair sport. So, umm, so I don't know. Yeah I guess you know it's just the surgery and the hormone requirements that seems to be the best that we can think of at this time.

Orlando, a trans man who had a successful career in varsity women's rowing prior to transitioning, highlighted the tensions in applying a gender self-declaration only policy:

> My trans advocacy says that that is awesome, that is incredible. And I think in many ways as a society, I think that is an amazing model and push forward.... My arcane athletic side, and especially when you're looking at your entire life is dictated by becoming the best, like that is the commitment, that there is so much focus, passion, and pain. I think it would, I think it would be hard for me as say that twenty year old female bodied athlete to look over and be like 'Okay there is, you know somebody who appears to be a cis dude, who is identifying as a woman and we're about to go at it' and so, you know, that's one thing that I think I would really struggle, where I'm like okay, where is this, what is this going to do for me ultimately, overall in my ability to say get to the podium? So even though, like it really conflicts, I'm, I'm, I'm conflicted inside, so much emotion!

Orlando raised the thought experiment of whether when competing as a female athlete he would've been comfortable racing in a heat against cis-gender women, women with hyperandrogenism, and trans women, noting the different dynamics each athlete's presence raises. Reflecting on his reaction, Orlando continued,

> ...it's because as, as trans man I know well how powerful testosterone is, and I think I would be really challenged because you know, while I respect that person's gender, I also recognize that [sigh] that's big, that's a big advantage.

He posits a potential solution as a "revolutionary revisioning" of sport that does not place so much emphasis on categorization but instead requires specific sport skills that are not gendered, and where categories beyond women's and men's are contested. In short, what Orlando proposes is a move from fairness to respect.

Orlando's connection of fairness with respect provides a framework for further analysis. The concept of respect includes an extremely broad category of attitudes, emotions, and behaviours, ranging from self-respect to respect for persons, to respect for authority and the environment (Cureton, 2013). Because ideas about respect are intricately tied to discussions of 'justice and equality, injustice and oppression, autonomy and agency, moral and political rights and duties, moral motivation and moral development, cultural diversity and toleration, punishment and political violence' (Dillon, 2014, p. 2), the concept requires unpacking in the context of transgender sport policies and practices. Respecting a person is understood to require recognising another person as a moral agent (Carter, 2013). However, it's not clear that this is occurring in sport as respecting difference is different from accommodating differences.

As Peter Balint (2013) notes, "Sometimes respect for difference will lead to its accommodation, sometimes it will not, and sometimes accommodation can occur with no accompanying respect" (p. 255). Our current sport system can be accused of not yet making the jump from merely respecting difference to taking active steps to accommodate difference. Stephen Darwall's (1977) distinction between appraisal respect and recognition respect helps illustrate this point. Appraisal respect acknowledges another person's merits, ideas, actions, or characteristics, is attitudinal in nature, and can occur in a range of degrees or as a result of comparisons (Benditt, 2008). Recognition respect, on the other hand, is action oriented and directly linked to our actions towards others as it "reflects an attitude or belief about how people should be treated generally, and as such transcends the characteristics of the individual target of respect" (Grover, 2004, p. 34). Consequently, recognition respect refers to one's intentional actions stemming from their intentional decisions and thereby actively demonstrates respect through accommodation. Merely respecting difference without taking corresponding actions to accommodate can lead to accusations of not 'walking the talk'. A lack of recognition respect in sport seems to be inherent in sports organizers' decisions to schedule international competitions during religious holidays, in allowing International Federations to ban athletes from wearing the hijab in competition, and in trying to enforce regulations regarding who can and cannot compete in the women's and men's divisions of sport.

Conclusion

The views shared by participants in this study provide insight into the barriers to inclusive sport that eligibility rules create for transgender individuals, but are not intended to represent all athletes' perspectives or ways of thinking. Many researchers have pointed out the continued unfairness of discriminating against transgender athletes (e.g. Bostick and Joyner, 2012; Heggie, 2010), and today high-performance sport remains a sex-segregated space that can condone gender injustice (Tännsjö, 2000; Travers, 2008). As explained by Cunningham (2012), 'sexual prejudice and heterosexism have been and still are pervasive in many areas of sport. Trans athletes, coaches and administrators … represent just some of the persons or groups facing negative treatment and limited opportunities in sport' (p. 70). The research literature does not yet address fully how comfortable trans and high-performance athletes feel expressing their views on rule and policy changes related to transgender inclusion.

Athletes concerned about performance advantages associated with testosterone levels may feel silenced out of fear of appearing intolerant or politically incorrect. On the other hand, athletes who vocally oppose sport governing bodies' decisions can face criticism, chilly climates, and repercussions that impact future participation and sponsorship opportunities (Ljungqvist and Genel, 2005; Martínez-Patiño, 2005). In support of the sex verification procedures utilized in sport to measure women's testosterone levels, American Olympian Summer Pierson (2011) has argued against an "intrinsic or explicit right to compete" instead stating, "it is a privilege to compete, and in order to enjoy such a privilege, the sacrifice of certain rights is required" (p. 323). The extent that other high-performance athletes share her view is unclear.

Adding a rule or eligibility requirement in a policy or rulebook does not make the rule fair, even if the sports organization can legally enforce the addition (Schneider, 1992) as doing so can fail to accommodate differences. While there has been modest critical evaluation of transgender eligibility sport policies by researchers (e.g. Cavanagh and Sykes, 2006; Coggon *et al.*, 2008; Teetzel, 2014) few studies have included athletes' perspectives on the rule changes, or the resulting impacts on their lives that the changes create. While this pilot study begins to contribute to this gap, it needs to be expanded to include more voices and perspectives to gain new knowledge about how barriers to participation are influenced by gender norms, racial and gender stereotypes, and intentional or internalized transphobic attitudes. The resulting information can then be used to design more inclusive sport policies and educational resources for teachers, coaches, athletes, and other stakeholders in sport. Thus, many more voices are needed in this dialogue, including both supporting and dissenting voices, in order to work towards solutions that not only respect but accommodate differences among athletes.

References

Balint, P. 2013. "Against respecting each others' differences". *Journal of Applied Philosophy* 30(3): 254–267.

Benditt, T. M. 2008. "Why respect matters". *The Journal of Value Inquiry* 42(4): 487–496.

Buzuvis, E. 2012. "Including transgender athletes in sex-segregated sport". In *Sexual Orientation and Gender Identity in Sport: Essays from Activists, Coaches, and Scholars*, ed. G. B. Cunningham, 23–34. College Station, TX: Center for Sport Management Research and Education.

Carter, I. 2013. "Are toleration and respect compatible?" *Journal of Applied Philosophy* 30(3): 195–208.

Cavanagh, S. and H. Sykes. 2006. "Transsexual bodies at the Olympics: the International Olympic Committee's policy on transsexual athletes at the 2004 Athens summer games". *Body & Society* 12(3): 75–102.

Coggon, J., Hammond, N., and S. Holm. 2008. "Transsexuals in sport – fairness and freedom, regulation and law". *Sport, Ethics and Philosophy* 2(1): 4–17.

Cunningham, G. B. 2012. "Bridging the gap: researchers and activists pursuing LGBT equality in sport". In *Sexual Orientation and Gender Identity in Sport: Essays from Activists, Coaches, and Scholars*, ed. G. B. Cunningham, 69–77. College Station, TX: Center for Sport Management Research and Education.

Cureton, A. 2013. "From self-respect to respect for others". *Pacific Philosophical Quarterly* 94(2): 166–187.

Darwall, S. 1977. "Two kinds of respect". *Ethics* 88(1): 36–49.

Devries, M. C. 2008. *Do Transitioned Athletes Compete at an Advantage or Disadvantage as Compared with Physically Born Men and Women: A Review of the Scientific Literature*. Ottawa: Promising Practices.

Dillon, R. S. 2014. "Respect". *Stanford Encyclopedia of Philosophy*. Available: http://plato.stanford.edu/entries/respect/

Edwards, L. and C. Jones. 2007. "A soft gynocentric critique of the practice of modern sport". *Sport, Ethics and Philosophy* 1(3): 346–366.

Gratton, C. and I. Jones. 2010. *Research Methods for Sports Studies*. Oxon: Routledge.

Grover, S. L. 2014. "Unraveling respect in organization studies". *Human Relations* 67(1): 27–51.

Heggie, V. 2010. "Testing sex and gender in sports: reinventing, reimagining and reconstructing histories". *Endeavour* 34(4): 157–163.

IOC. 2003. *Statement of the Stockholm Consensus on Sex Reassignment in Sports*. Available www.olympic.org/news/ioc-approves-consensus-with-regard-to-athletes-who-have-changed-sex

IOC. 2007. *IOC Consensus Statement: Sexual Harassment and Abuse in Sport.* Available   www.olympic.org/news/ioc-adopts-consensus-statement-on-sexual-harassment-and-abuse-in-sport

IOC. 2014. *Olympic Agenda 2020.* Available www.olympic.org/olympic-agenda-2020

IOC. 2015. *IOC Consensus Meeting on Sex Reassignment and Hyperandrogenism November 2015.* Available https://stillmed.olympic.org/media/Document%20 Library/OlympicOrg/IOC/Who-We-Are/Commissions/Medical-and-Scientific-Commission/EN-IOC-Consensus-Meeting-on-Sex-Reassignment-and-Hyper androgenism.pdf#_ga=1.131628173.323004607.1418324623

IOC. 2016. *IOC Implements Measures to Safeguard Athletes from Harassment and Abuse in Sport.* Available: www.olympic.org/news/ioc-implements-measures-to-safeguard-athletes-from-harassment-and-abuse-in-sport

Kidd, B. 2011. "For gender self-declaration". Paper presented at *Play the Game*, October 5, Cologne, Germany. Available: www.playthegame.org/conferences/ play-the-game-2011/presentations.html

Ljungqvist, A. and M. Genel. 2005. "Transsexual athletes: when is competition fair?" *Lancet* 366: S42–S43.

Martínez Patiño, M. J. 2005. "Personal account: a woman tried and tested", *Lancet* 366: S38.

Mountjoy, M., Brackenridge, C., Arrington, M., Blauwet, C., Carska-Sheppard, A., Fasting, K., Leahy, T., Marks, S., Martin, K., Starr, K., Tiivas, A., and R. Budgeett. 2016. "The IOC consensus statement: harassment and abuse (non-accidental violence) in sport". *British Journal of Sports Medicine.* doi:10.1136/ bjsports-2016-096121

Pierson, S. T. 2011. "The culture of the elite athlete: an enhanced perspective on the case of Caster Semenya, and gender verification testing". *Journal of Genetic Counseling* 20(3): 323–324.

Samano, S. 2013. "Ronda Rousey: 'I don't think it's fair' transgender fighter Fallon Fox faces women". *USA Today Sports*, April 11. Available: www.usatoday.com/ story/gameon/2013/04/11/ufc-ronda-rousey-transgender-fighter-fallon-fox/2072937/

Schneider, A. J. 1992. "Harm, athletes' rights and doping control". In *Proceedings: First International Symposium for Olympic Research*, eds. R. K. Barney and K. V. Meier, 164–175. London, ON: The Centre for Olympic Studies. http://library. la84.org/SportsLibrary/ISOR/ISOR1992q.pdf

Tännsjö, T. 2000. "Against sexual discrimination in sports". In *Values in Sport: Elitism, Nationalism, Gender Equality and the Scientific Manufacture of Winners*, eds. T. Tännsjö and C. Tamburrini, 101–115. London: E&FN Spon.

Teetzel, S. 2014. "The onus of inclusion: sport policies and the enforcement of the women's category in sport". *Journal of the Philosophy of Sport* 41(1): 113–127.

Travers, A. 2008. "The sport nexus and gender injustice". *Studies in Social Justice* 2(1): 79–101.

Vamplew, W. 2007. "Playing with the rules: influences on the development of regulation in sport". *International Journal of the History of Sport* 24(7): 843–871.

Wahlert, L. and A. Fiester. 2012. "Gender transports: privileging the 'natural' in gender testing debates for intersex and transgender athletes". *The American Journal of Bioethics* 12(7): 19–21.

Chapter 7

Sport and physical exercise among Spanish trans persons

Víctor Manuel Pérez Samaniego,
Sofía Pereira-García, Elena López-Cañada,
Jorge Fuentes-Miguel and José Devís-Devís

Introduction

The few surveys exploring the relationship between sport and physical exercise (SPE) among trans people find numerous barriers, and an alarming number of situations of harassment and violence. For example, in Scotland Smith *et al.* (2012) pointed out that 79 per cent of 115 trans participants declared that homophobia and transphobia were barriers for their sport participation. Symons *et al.* (2010) found that 25 per cent of surveyed trans participants in Victoria (Australia) were verbally hounded. Furthermore, 14.3 per cent of a sample of trans students in the UK did not participate in SPE due to the homophobia, biphobia and transphobia, and 27.8 per cent of trans students who participated in the National Union of Students LGBT Campaign were worried about verbal or physical abuse (NUS, 2012). Similarly, a recent paper reported that 18.9 per cent of trans participants suffered harassment in sport facilities and spaces in Spain (Devís-Devíset al., 2016).

Although studies above mentioned reinforce the idea that SPE are hostile environments for trans people and they hardly participate in them, however, a search of evidence for this sort of statement is still needed. In so doing, two preliminary concerns are worth considering. First, although in most survey studies SPE appears as static and single realities, in fact, they involve many different modalities, which may have diverse implications in their embodied experience of practice (Agans and Geldhof, 2012). In particular, characteristics and features of different types of SPE practiced by trans persons may entail differences according to their self-defined gender identities. Second, it is essential to know how trans persons' personal and social practices, such as SPE, are actually framed within different cultural contexts. Accordingly, studies comprising SPE practice at a national scale may contribute to assess transcultural and transnational differences and similarities in trans persons' patterns of practice.

Against this backdrop, the purpose of this chapter is twofold: (1) to describe the participation of Spanish trans persons in SPE; and (2) to relate participation with self-defined gender and type of SPE practiced by trans persons in Spain.

Method

This chapter is based on a research project developed between 2012 and 2015 aiming to study trans persons practice of SPE in Spain. For that, a two-phase study combining quantitative and qualitative methods was designed. The quantitative phase was based on a survey study designed to obtain information about different psychosocial issues related to trans people's experiences in different moments and contexts of their daily life. In this chapter, we use only data from the quantitative phase related to SPE practice after gender disclosure, that is, the moment in which trans persons made public and started to live according their gender identity.

Participants were recruited from LGBT collectives and through snowball sampling, a strategy suitable for finding participants from hidden and marginal populations (Faugier and Sargeant, 1997). In total, 212 trans people from different Spanish regions participated voluntarily in this study. This sample is thus one of the largest in international studies on SPE practiced by trans persons.

The average age of participants was 30.63 (SD = 10.75). Measures of socio-demographic data also included self-definition gender and age of gender disclosure. 44.1 per cent (n = 93) of the participants defined themselves as 'girls' or 'trans women' (TW), 51.2 per cent (n = 108) self-defined themselves as 'boys' or 'trans men' (TM) and 4.7 per cent (n = 10) opted for different gender categories we globally labelled as 'other' (O). Although small in number, data about this group is also included, as they offer a different perspective on traditional gender dichotomy in studies on SPE. The average age for gender disclosure was 22 (SD = 9.7). Those who had not transitioned or did not answer the question were coded as missing.

Surveys were administrated face-to-face in small groups, following a protocol designed by the research team. Participants were informed that questions related to SPE referred to any kind of sports and exercise practiced after gender disclosure. The questionnaires were filtered in order to detect possible errors by individually analysing invalid or inconsistent values and the aggregate behaviour of some variables. Data contained in questionnaires underwent a series of treatments in order to be ready for full utilization as results. We present a preliminary description of the results obtained using frequencies and percentages of SPE participation as a whole and by self-defined gender in this chapter.

As part of the wider project, all materials and procedures were approved by the Ethics Committee of the Universitat de València (Spain). The survey respected the self-determination of trans people's gender identities and no personal data was requested. Informed consent forms authorizing the

research team to publish the data of this study were signed by adult participants or by parents or guardians of participants under 18. The surveys
and informed consent forms were kept separately and the data was entered
in a database for its subsequent statistical analysis.

Results

Global participation of transgender persons in SPE shows that almost three
out of four trans persons (74.9 per cent) participate in some form of SPE.
Any of these forms is practiced at least once a week for 62 per cent of the
sample, being the most frequent practice of three or more times a week
since 45 per cent of participants fall under this category. Regarding self-
defined gender identities, Figure 7.1 shows that participation in SPE of TM
(77.7 per cent) is higher than TW (71.1 per cent) and similar to O (77.8
per cent). Practice on a weekly basis is near or above 60 per cent in the
three groups.

Distribution of participants by percentages in the main types of SPE
practiced by trans people is presented in Figure 7.2. It shows that individual

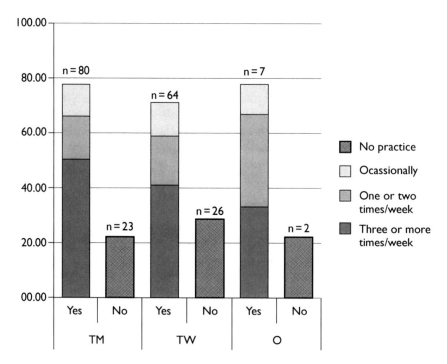

Figure 7.1 Participation in SPE by gender.

Note
There are ten participants with missing data.

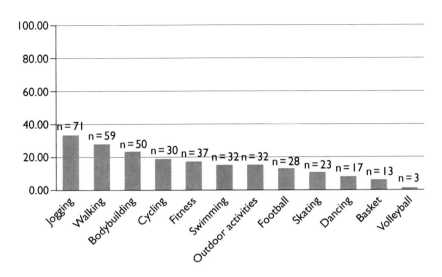

Figure 7.2 Participation in main types of SPE.

SPEs are predominant, while percentages of participation in collective SPEs are considerably lower. Among these, football (soccer) is the most practiced team sport (13.20 per cent).

Figure 7.3 shows the participation of trans persons in individual SPE by self-defined gender. Jogging and walking are the preferred activities in all groups. The participation of TM is higher than in TW in jogging (TW = 22.6 per cent; TM = 40.7 per cent) and the participation in walking is higher in TW than in TM (TW = 32.3 per cent; TM = 22.2 per cent). Bodybuilding shows the biggest difference of participation between genders

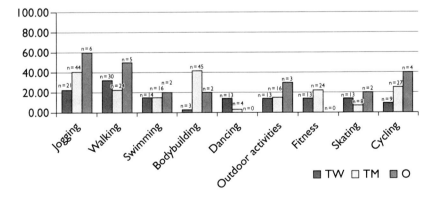

Figure 7.3 Participation in individual SPE.

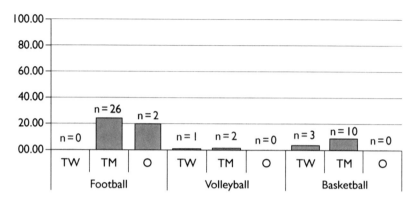

Figure 7.4 Participation in collective SPE.

in favour of TM compared to TW (TM = 41.7 per cent; TW = 3.2 per cent), followed by dance, which shows predominance of TW in comparison to TM (TW = 14 per cent; TM = 3.7 per cent). In the group of O, jogging (60 per cent), walking (50 per cent), cycling (40 per cent) and outdoor activities (30 per cent) are the more practised individual SPEs.

In collective SPEs, participation of TM and O is remarkably higher than TW's (see Figure 7.4). In fact, no TW practice football, which is by large the most practised collective SPE among TM (24.1 per cent) and O (20 per cent). In basketball and, especially, volleyball, differences are not so striking, though always favourable for TM. TW participation in collective sports is always under 5 per cent.

Discussion

Results presented in this chapter provide a first attempt at describing the SPE participation of trans people in Spain. In particular, it provides data regarding the overall participation and types of SPE by the whole sample and according to the self-defined gender identities of participants. The discussion of these results is organized around two axes.

First, in order to determine the possible distinctiveness of trans persons' involvement in SPE, results on overall participation need to be contrasted with indicators from the general Spanish population. Compared with data from the *Survey on Sporting Habits in Spain* (2016), analysis of the rates of practice shows that the number of trans persons practicing SPE either regularly or occasionally (74.9 per cent) is considerable higher than the overall population of persons 15 years old and over in Spain (53.5 per cent). However, considering the average of age of participants in this study (30.6), rates of participation are rather similar to age group between 25 to 34 years in the general Spanish population (72.6 per cent). In addition,

SPE practiced on a weekly basis by transgender persons (62 per cent) is higher compared to the group of age (between 25–54) in the general Spanish population (53.2 per cent). Consequently, with cautions about possible overestimation of trans persons' participation in SPE (see limitations), results indicate that involvement of trans persons in SPE is similar or slightly higher than that of the general population in Spain.

A second theme for discussion is with regard to emergent patterns of practice regarding self-defined gender identities. Similar to the general population in Spain, although with less difference, results show that gender becomes a determining variable for the involvement of trans persons in SPE. TM (77.7 per cent) and O (77.8 per cent) are more involved in SPE than TW (71.1 per cent), while the Survey on Sporting Habits in Spain (2016) shows 59.8 per cent of men's participation and 47.5 per cent of women's participation. TM predominance in SPE is also remarkable when considering the age of participants in relation to frequencies of practice. Figures of TM practicing SPE on a weekly basis (66 per cent) are higher than the rest of Spanish men within the equivalent age group of 25–54 (44.6 per cent). Similarly, at 59 per cent, the percentage of TW practicing SPE on a weekly basis is also higher than the rest of women (32.6 per cent) within that age range.

Self-defined gender identities also influence the type of activities chosen by trans persons. Remarkably, the most common forms of SPE participation among trans persons are individual and unregulated practices such as jogging, walking and cycling. By unregulated practices we refer to SPE, which are not formally or informally controlled by sporting institutions or regulations to any extent, including access to facilities.

This not surprising considering some barriers, which hinder the access of trans persons to regulated or organized forms of SPE. For instance, having an Identity Card (ID) is a necessary requisite to join sport teams, as well as to access most sport facilities and fitness clubs in Spain. As modifying the gender category on the ID is a long process that can take many years and that is not available to everyone, a large number of trans people's IDs do not accurately reflect their gender identities. This poses a serious problem as IDs actually exert the legal power to determine who is a man and who is a woman (Schilt and Westbrook, 2009).

The use of locker rooms is another example of how informal barriers influence trans people's participation in SPE. As Smith *et al.* (2012) and Hill (2013) have claimed, locker rooms are seriously problematic spaces for some trans people, as they become forced to expose their bodies to a social gaze most try to avoid. Trans persons who are unable to pass as heteronormatively gendered persons tend to experience more gender policing and challenges about their right to access sex segregated spaces (Caudwell, 2014; Hill, 2013). It makes sense therefore, that besides other common considerations (e.g. low cost, easy access, flexible use) that the particular inclination of trans persons towards unregulated SPE practices may be a strategy to overcome legal and informal barriers hindering their participation in more regulated forms of SPE.

However, whenever trans persons get involved in more regulated forms of SPE, a gender pattern characterized by TM predominance emerges. Trans persons' participation in collective sports is much lower than in the general Spanish population. Only 28 trans persons (13 per cent) declared to have practiced some collective sport, whereas the Survey on Sporting Habits in Spain (2016) shows 41.9 per cent of participation in at least one collective sport. In the practice or collective sports, TM predominance becomes evident in the case of football, which is practiced by 24.1 per cent of TM and 20 per cent of O, whereas not a single TW indicates participation football. In individual SPE, bodybuilding stands out as a practice preferred by TM, in contrast to dance and skating, in which TW are clearly predominant. These patterns indicate that trans persons involvement in SPE somehow reproduces stereotypes of gender binarism, insofar as TM are more inclined towards socially considered masculine and masculinizing practices, precisely those rejected by TW, and vice versa. Accordingly, it seems that, at least for a part of Spanish trans people, SPE participation may seem to play a gender conforming role, insofar as their choice of activities strategically accommodate to gender normativism (Travers, 2006). However, other alternative explanations are also possible. For instance, TW participating in collective sports might be accused, however falsely, of having an inherent *masculine* advantage. Besides, considering the average age of gender transition of the sample (22), adult trans persons may finally practice SPE that they could not do when younger.

Conclusions and limitations

The findings of this study can be summarized as follows. First, in terms of overall participation trans persons are similarly or, even, more involved in SPE than the rest of Spanish population. Second, trans persons are more involved in individual and unregulated types of SPE practice than in collective and regulated sports. Third, TM and O are more involved in SPE than TW. TM and TW patterns of participation in regulated and organized practices tend to reproduce binaryconforming rather than binary transforming (Travers, 2006) gender patterns in SPE, although reasons for this are potentially complex, calling for further study.

Some potential weaknesses need to be considered in this study to accurately interpret these findings. First, it was not possible to establish a representative sample due to the inexistence of a register or reliable estimation of the number of trans people who reside in Spain. However, this limitation is a common factor in most studies concerning trans people (FRA, 2014; Grant *et al.*, 2011; Grossman and D'Augelli, 2007). Second, the way we have delimited the time range of SPE participation in our study (SPE practiced after gender disclosure) must be considered more comprehensive than the one used in the *Survey of Sporting Habits in Spain* (2016) (participation in sporting activities during last year). This has probably caused an overestimation of participation in comparison to that study. Third, variables influencing participation in SPE such as age, educational level or time period in which SPE are more frequently practiced (e.g. weekends, holidays) have not been considered in this study. Inclusion of such variables, as well as analysing how gender identities intersect with other identities such as, race, social class and religion (Kauer and Krane, 2010), would be a prospective for future survey studies on trans participation in SPE.

Implications

Despite these limitations, this study offers useful insights about the patterns of SPE among Spanish trans people. On one hand, the similarity of participation between trans people and the rest of the Spanish population tells us that, at least in unregulated and unorganized modalities, trans people are equally as involved as the general population in such an important social practice as SPE. Beyond personal benefits related to SPE, this may help to overcome certain negative stereotypes, prejudices and negative attitudes towards trans people participating in social life. However, when analysing results in detail, it becomes evident that trans people are disproportionately excluded from/excluding themselves from regulated/team-based forms SPE. Trans persons, especially TW, rarely participate in any team sports or get involved in activities requiring access to sports facilities. In this regard, they remain excluded from the SPE system.

This exclusion should be interpreted as a call for policy makers, sporting professionals and educational agents to work on expanding the inclusion of trans persons in team-based and regulated forms of SPE. As Krane (2016) remarks, having more inclusive SPE policies and climates for trans persons will provide many advantages. First, it is obvious that it would provide more and better opportunities for all people to participate in SPE. Given the strong emphasis on educational and health implications related to SPE, it seems logical that institutions and policymakers should provide fair opportunities for everybody. Second, challenging assumptions about gender identities will contribute to promoting *inclusive excellence*, that is, excellence that is "achieved by embracing multicultural and diverse individuals" (Kauer and Krane, 2010: 414). As intrinsically embodied practices, SPE can do a lot to improve acceptance and social recognition of persons and groups with controversial body-selves. This study shows that trans persons are already involved in SPE in Spain, although many of them discreetly. Keeping this in mind, being inclusive and supporting the participation of trans persons would make SPE something even worthier to be promoted and practiced.

References

Agans, J. P. and G. J. Geldhof. "Trajectories of participation in athletics and positive youth development: the influence of sport type". *Applied Developmental Science* 16.3 (2012): 151–165.

Caudwell, J. "[Transgender] young men: gendered subjectivities and the physically active body". *Sport, Education and Society* 19.4 (2014): 398–414.

Devís-Devís, J., Pereira-García, S., Valencia-Peris, A., Fuentes-Miguel, J., López-Cañada, E. and Pérez-Samaniego, V., "Harassment patterns and risk profile in Spanish trans persons". *Journal of Homosexuality* (2016): accessed 30 May 2016, doi:10.1080/00918369.2016.1179027.

Faugier, J. and M. Sargeant. "Sampling hard to reach populations". *Journal of Advanced Nursing* 26.4 (1997): 790–797.

FRA (European Union Agency for the Fundamental Rights). *European Union LGTB Survey*, 2014. Accessed 30 May 2016. http://fra.europa.eu/sites/default/files/fra-eu-lgbt-survey-mainresults_tk3113640enc_1.pdf

Grant, J. M. *et al.* "Injustice at every turn: a report of the National Transgender Discrimination Survey. 2011". Washington, DC: National Center for Transgender Equality and National Gay and Lesbian Task Force (2015). Accessed 30 May 2016. http://goo.gl/dcBEi0

Grossman, A. H. and A. R. D'Augelli. "Transgender youth and life-threatening behaviors". *Suicide and Life-Threatening Behavior* 37.5 (2007): 527–537.

Hargreaves, J. and E. Anderson. *Routledge Handbook Of Sport, Gender and Sexuality*. London; New York: Routledge, 2014.

Hill, J. "Queer bodies: sexualities, genders and fatness in physical education". *Sport, Education and Society* 18.3 (2013): 428–432.

Kauer, K. and V. Krane. "Diverse sexual and gender identities in sport". *Routledge Handbook of Applied Sport Psychology* (2010): 414–422.

Krane, V. "Inclusion to Exclusion. Sport for LGBT athletes". *Routledge International Handbook of Sport Psychology*, 238–247. London; New York: Routledge, 2016.

Muñiz, C., Rodríguez, P. and M. J. Suárez. "Sports and cultural habits by gender: an application using count data models". *Economic Modelling* 36 (2014): 288–297.

NUS "Out in sport. LGBT students' experiences of sport" 2012. Accessed 30 May 2016. www.nus.org.uk/Global/Final%20Out%20in%20Sport_NEW_web.pdf

Schilt, Kr. and L. Westbrook. "Doing gender, doing heteronormativity 'gender normals', transgender people, and the social maintenance of heterosexuality". *Gender & Society* 23.4 (2009): 440–464.

Smith, M., Cuthbertson, S. and N. Gale. *Out for Sport*. 2012. Accessed 30 May 2016. www.equality-network.org/wp-content/uploads/2013/03/Out-for-Sport-Report.pdf

Survey of Sporting Habits in Spain 2015. 2016. Accessed 30 May 2016. www.csd.gob.es/csd/estaticos/dep-soc/sintesis_ehd_2015_ingles.pdf

Sykes, H. "Transsexual and transgender policies in sport". *Women in Sport & Physical Activity Journal* 15.1 (2006): 3.

Symons, C. *et al.* "Come out to play: the sports experiences of lesbian, gay, bisexual and transgender (LGBT) people in Victoria" (2010). Accessed 30 May 2016. www.glhv.org.au/files/ComeOutToPlay.pdf]

Travers, A. "Queering sport lesbian softball leagues and the transgender challenge". *International Review for the Sociology of Sport* 41.3–4 (2006): 431–446.

Chapter 8

Honesty and discipline

Identity management of transgender netballers

Brendon Tagg

This chapter discusses the experiences of three New Zealand female trans-gender netball players, specifically examining aspects of their identity management. The sport of analysis, netball, was invented as a late Victorian-era form of women's basketball. Throughout the twentieth century it came to be seen as both a good girls' game (i.e., a game women enjoy playing, see Andrew 1997, 1) and a good girl's game (a game that reflected and reinforced conservative gender norms, see Nauright 1999, 47). Yet increasingly men also play the game. Most early members of the New Zealand Men's Netball Association (NZMNA), formed in the 1980s, were Māori and Pacific Island gay men and transgender women in New Zealand's North Island (Tagg 2008a, 461). Transgender players helped form this association after having been officially excluded from Netball New Zealand (NNZ) (Tagg 2008a, 459). By the early 1990s, however, overtly queer players were also forced out of the NZMNA as it coveted a more hetero-normative image. This subsequently forced the remaining queer players into increasingly homo-normative performances (i.e., acting in line hetero-normative standards of behavior). Part of the impetus for this appears to have been the inclusion of teams from New Zealand's relatively conservative and White-majority South Island, and subsequent efforts to build a larger, more mainstream, organization. This chapter discusses the experiences of three transgender players who were NZMNA members at the time.

The participants, all of whom were of Māori or Pacific Island descent, described educating early South Island NZMNA members, especially heterosexual White men, about relevant cultural and gender issues. But they also describe feeling betrayed by some Māori and Pacific Island gay men, mainly also from the South Island, who the participants felt should have expressed greater queer solidarity. The participants speculated that gay men playing netball often felt more threatened by transgender women than heterosexual men did, because transgender netballers drew attention to the queer subculture of men's netball and therefore undermined the men's ability to easily *pass* (Goffman 1963) as heterosexual. Interestingly, though, the participants also pushed back in the opposite direction: partially blaming gender-transforming transgender people (i.e., those who *disrupt* the two-sex model rather than transition across it (Travers 2006) for starting the struggle that the South Island administrators ultimately won. It involved "radical transgender netballers 'who would turn up with false tits, eyelashes, and makeup ... just to be defiant'" (Tagg 2008a, 468). Not everyone accepted or was able to perform acts of homo-normativity and indeed the intersection of culture and sexuality appears critical here. As being queer has become increasingly mainstream in Western cultures, this has happened in ways that the "relative privilege of White, middle-class lesbians and gay men appears to have been entrenched" (Brown 2012, 1065).

It is perhaps helpful to clarify the relationship between netball's early development as a sport and the geographical and demographic features of the New Zealand men's netball scene. Netball was invented in the late nineteenth century as a modified "ladies" version of basketball and was designed to reflect and reinforce patriarchal ideas of femininity. By the 1920s in New Zealand it 'was given validity as the most suitable team sport for women by the 1920s and has been promoted as the sport that New Zealand "girls" should play' (Nauright 1999, 47). Historically within Anglicized cultures it has been considered inappropriate for men to play, while Pacific cultures often have more fluid gender categories. In the early 1980s, pre-NZMNA players were comprised mainly of people of Māori or Pacific Island descent, and were often also gay or transgender (including third gender categories such Samoan *fa'afafine*). The early NZMNA coalesced from teams in the two largest North Island cities (Auckland and Wellington) and small towns in the North Island's Bay of Plenty region. Most early South Island players were heterosexual White men, with a few influential gay Pacific Island men. Canterbury was the first South Island-based team to participate at the national championships, in 1989, followed by Otago in 1991 (Tagg 2008b, 425).

Theoretical framework

This chapter is based around Goffman's (1963) *Stigma: Notes on the Management of Spoiled Identity*, and specifically Orne's (2013) reconfiguration based on analyzing "coming out" narratives. This important context for identity management shares common features with the present focus on transgender netball players' narratives surrounding (successive waves of) heterosexual men "coming in" to this historically queer-centric space. The North Island-dominated men's netball scene of the late 1980s was predominantly a Māori and Pacific Island-based queer and queer-friendly space, although this began to change from the early 1990s. As increasing numbers of mainly White heterosexual men entered the NZMNA, both they, and the existing members, performed various identity management techniques. The earliest South Island men's netball players to participate at national championships found themselves in a context in which they were in the minority in terms of both their heterosexuality and their White ethnicity.

Orne emphasizes how "coming out" has historically been analyzed from a now-discredited linear model, "as though once someone has done the work of coming out they will never have to do it again" – and how queer people often fit their narratives to this model (2013, 239). Rather than emphasizing a singular moment, it is more helpful to consider the strategic management of other's knowledge of one's identity; "outness" should be understood "not as a quality of a person but as an interactional accomplishment ... existing along a continuum between acceptance and hostility" (2013, 240). This is relevant to the present case, where at each annual national championship *uninitiated* men – see below – from New Zealand's relatively conservative South Island enter the New Zealand's men's netball scene.

Orne proposes a category between acceptance and hostility – "a space where others are ambiguously hostile, uncertain, 'tolerant,' socially awkward, or invasively questioning of them upon learning of their sexuality" (2013, 230) – in which stigmatized individuals may choose three potential strategies. The first is to "take the bullet" and respond to potentially invasive questions in the "hope to educate the uninitiated and change their image of queer people" (2013, 242). Here, one both develops one's own "double consciousness" and promotes "ally-consciousness" among non-queer people (i.e., what Goffman named "the wise"). Double consciousness is a term introduced by W. E. B. Du Bois in his 1903 publication, *The Souls of Black Folk*. While Dubois focuses on the dual – and incommensurable – identities of "Negro" and "American," Orne applies the term to the experience of stigmatized individuals in general. The second strategy is to "deflect the bullet," or modify one's identity label so to assist understanding or acceptance. This involves presenting a different, better-understood but still-stigmatized identity depending on the audience; for example, bisexual (rather than pansexual) or gay (rather than bisexual) (2013, 244–245). The third strategy is to "dodge the bullet" by cutting off further contact. One might simply lack the energy or time to deal with people or environments that regularly put one "in the line of fire." Importantly, Orne (2013, 246) observes that even queer-identified spaces are not always "safe" – bisexual men, for example, are subject to a litany of what Anderson and McCormack (2016) call bisexual burdens, above and beyond what gay and lesbians people experience.

Orne (2013) outlines four ways his argument diverges from Goffman's. First, he disputes the idea that stigma management is primarily about evading or minimizing hostility. Indeed, individuals often intentionally "take the bullet" for the purposes of educating others; this is quite different to the more politically oriented flaunting or celebration of identity (Orne 2013, 247). While "flaunting" is a loaded term it has also been reclaimed as a strategy for social resistance in similar ways to the Slutwalk movement. Second, the plethora of gender/sexuality identity labels allows the stigmatized to deflect the line of fire without necessarily passing as normal. One can, for example, adopt alternative – better-understood or better-accepted – labels if the need arises, and not necessarily just for the benefit of the recipient (Orne 2013, 248). Third, by noting disputes within the queer community, Orne specifically critiques the assumption that "everyone with the same stigma is going to be a so-called sympathetic other" (2013, 248). Fourth, Orne questions the shared frame of reference between stigmatized and "normals" by invoking the concept of double consciousness; the stigmatized "can simultaneously be aware of the stigmatizing views against them while also remaining 'stigma resistant'" (2013, 231).

Methods

This chapter forms part of a mixed-methods ethnographic study of competing discourses within New Zealand men's netball (Tagg 2008b). The larger study began with participant observation with the Otago provincial team, based in New Zealand's lower South Island and also involved textual analysis and 23 in-depth semi-structured interviews with Otago team players, former NZMNA senior administrators and these transgender participants.

After interviewing Otago players, snowball sampling helped me locate the administrators and transgender players. Some of the limitations of snowball sampling were partly mitigated by the small size of the New Zealand men's netball community; some participants criticized the very people who had recommended them while others intentionally gave details of those with alternative perspectives. During the interviews, I attempted to operate as both insider and outsider; as a fellow player who understood the game but also as researcher from a more conservative part of the country, for whom they sometimes needed to explain the obvious. The intrinsic power imbalance within the interview format was strong enough that the first two participants wished to be interviewed together but weak enough that they felt comfortable suggesting this arrangement. Finally, pseudonyms are used throughout both this chapter and the larger study.

This chapter's structure reflects the structure of the interview process: the first two sections discuss the nature of the early association and the changes associated with the incoming South Islanders; the last two emphasize the distinction between heterosexuality and hetero-normativity and the experiences playing with heterosexual men. Following Travers (2006), I distinguish between gender transforming transgender men's netballers (people assigned a male sex at birth but who subvert gender binaries within men's netball) and gender conforming transgender men's netballers (people assigned a male sex at birth, that identify as female but play men's netball). This reflects the participants' desire to be seen *as* female – and as transgender only as a subgroup of female or out of necessity (see Tagg 2012, 157). Unfortunately, no early gender transforming transgender players were located; after being excluded from the NZMNA many transgender players lost contact with each other and this potential archive may have been lost.

The early association

A short introduction to the participants may also be useful. A fuller description of Amy and Brenda's background is presented in Tagg (2012, 156) and that article provides a general background for this chapter. Amy grew up in a regional North Island city before moving to and fro with Auckland, where she currently lives. She started playing men's netball at the local level in the late 1980s. Brenda grew up in a small North Island town before moving to Auckland, where she started playing men's netball in the late 1970s. Later she become heavily involved with the Night Owls, a well-known Auckland-based team mainly composed of transgender prostitutes.

Despite its name, the early NZMNA was in many ways a gender-neutral and queer-centric place of acceptance, largely operating outside the two-sex system and the public eye. Although most players were gay men, transgender women were welcomed and formed their own teams (Tagg 2008a, 461, 466–467). Carla described pre-NZMNA men's netball in the early 1980s as friendly Sunday morning games involving "all the Island queens … because it was the day in Samoa you weren't supposed to drink because it was religious." Brenda added that in the early 1980s, transgender women were running the Auckland association and that "the men were all gay men." A transgender-based team called the Night Owls was especially well known in Auckland; according to Amy, they even welcomed certain heterosexual men whom they deemed to be "well-educated around the sisterhood."

There were also family associations across the North Island; Amy said that Māori and Pacific Island-based extended families "created good associations." Although there was occasionally "that guy with the homophobia," in general they felt they could shift such players' perceptions as new members realized they enjoyed "playing it with all these gay guys because they could really play." This matches evidence presented elsewhere suggesting that the early NZMNA was a queer-friendly space with, in the words of one former player, "hardly any straight men" (Tagg 2008a, 462).

The participants suggested that transgender women originally started playing in the early competitions that preceded the NZMNA because they lacked legal recognition as women. Carla apparently accepted this and cited certain advantages in terms of agility, flair and general strengths – reflecting both her female identity *and* support for the two-sex model. However, Amy described transgender women's "covert operations" within NNZ, and even Carla mentioned one Tongan transgender woman who played into her early sixties, even though "she's still got Willie the Whaler!" Conversely, Brenda was prepared to "dress as a man" (see Tagg 2008a) within the NZMNA but only as long as she could wear "some kinky shorts and some white tops." She also suggested that one early player so convincingly passed as cisgender that she worked as a female model; before representing New Zealand, the Australian players apparently successfully demanded a medical examination "to make sure she had balls." These statements draw attention to the gender fluidity within certain Pacific communities.

The player referenced at the end of the paragraph was allowed to play men's netball because at the time opportunities for gender reassignment surgery in New Zealand present extremely limited; according to Roy (2016) the government funds just three male-to-female surgeries and one female-to-male funded every two years and there is no qualified surgeon in the country to perform the operations. While for example *fa'afafine* are less likely to seek this surgery than White transgender people, Māori and Pacific Island people in New Zealand are in general less able to pay for either the out-of-pocket cost should they reach the top of the waiting list or the prohibitive costs associated with seeking surgery aboard.

The participants described two key changes to men's netball in New Zealand over time. The first was from a generally gay and transgender-centric environment to a highly charged one, in which queer masculinities were increasingly strictly policed in the early 1990s. The second transition, later in the 1990s, was toward men's netball as a somewhat mainstream athletic space. This cumulated in a dramatic 2004 Annual General Meeting (AGM) in which the NZMNA was replaced with the New Zealand Men's and Mixed Netball Association (NZMMNA), which accommodates mixed-gender teams and projects a more hetero-centric image (Tagg 2008a, 471). This reflects a sort of gentrification, where minority group members are forced out by the influx of members with greater capital. The participants suggested NZMNA administrators marginalized transgender and overtly "camp" gay players to harness the symbolic power associated with hegemonic masculinities. They apparently intended to increase the player base and to build bridges with NNZ, who – in the words of one cisgender female men's netball administrator – "didn't want men parading on their courts in skirts" (Tagg 2008a, 463). Indeed, there was even resistance to cisgender men playing netball because women's netball administrators were concerned that the men would take over (Tagg 2008a, 459). Interestingly, the NZMNA began excluding transgender players in the early 1990s

– i.e., even after the 1986 Homosexual Law Reform Bill, which decriminalized male same-sex relationships (Brickell 2000, 169).

Entry of South Island teams

Brenda described Canterbury as the first "white man, straight man" team. Based in Christchurch, the South Island's largest city, they have dominated New Zealand men's netball since the mid-1990s, both athletically and organizationally. Amy described a conflict of interest "because we had so many players that are current champions – i.e., the Canterbury men's – yet they're all executive officers as well." But at their first national championships, Canterbury apparently, "didn't know how to take it ... they had never seen a queen – a proper queen – before, but they came to Auckland and they played *us!*" She suggested that with only "a couple of gay boys ... [on their team, it was] quite freaky for the South Island men." Brenda described their shock at her teammates "wandering around going 'hiiii!'" in an overtly camp tone, dressed in high heels and long nails. She said they, "couldn't believe how queens can play netball." The Canterbury players' girlfriends and wives – who also "didn't know what a queen was" – apparently enquired why women were playing men's netball. According to Carla they "used to get a bit of a shock ... because they'd be trying to figure out 'is that a guy or a girl?'" Feeling empowered within a queer-centric space there was little need for strategic identity management, although their playful antics could be interpreted as "taking the bullet."

The South Islanders' anxiety was most acute at end-of-tournament social events. While Brenda understood the cultural differences, she insisted "Everybody loved it; you know they made *them* feel welcome." Sometimes, however, at the social function "everyone got a bit too much ... all the gay guys in those days, they were – well, excuse the word – they were *sluts.*" While she apparently prevented her transgender teammates from propositioning heterosexual players, she also joked that if "they came to us that was a different story; we were allowed to do that!" Carla, however, described her teenage years as going "out on the piss [binge drinking] on the street, pick up a man, going to work, netball Sundays." Given that this statement hints at employment in the sex trade perhaps the conservative South Islanders interpreted their antics in a different way than intended; efforts to restrain the transgender players' desires might therefore constitute "deflecting the bullet."

Transgender players also seemed shocked to meet netballers who were heterosexual men. The following story suggests they challenged Carla's assumption about the sexuality of netball-playing men:

> "oh, here's a nice gay boy" – you know what I mean – "here's a nice gay boy girl!" And then you know, you'd get on the piss and ... if your

[the player's] woman [girlfriend or wife] walked in [Carla and her friends would say] "oh my *god*!" Just to ourselves, not to you, you know, but that's how it was.

The South Islanders precipitated a more hetero-centric national association. Carla said only after Canterbury joined in 1989 was men's netball "toned down ... to entice straight men to play," with rules specifying "no eyeliner, no foundation." Unlike the "flair," "agility" and "fastness" of early men's netball, the game also became "more structured to be 'uh!'" (i.e., a hegemonic masculine grunt; for an illustration, see Tagg 2008b, 417). While many transgender players gave up "because of the political bullshit of straights, 'uh,' of it" she admired one Canterbury player; because "it was the queens that taught him to play netball ... he has that flair." Therefore, as men's netball became more hetero-centric, transgender players increasingly opted to "dodge the bullet." Despite Canterbury's long-running success at the national championships, Carla described them as "fucking shit" because "there was no massive passes or no flying out of the court and flicking it back in like you were at the circus; there was no acrobatics in it." Amy separated the two concerns; while disagreeing with the Canterbury-led policies, "Canterbury played a very *good* game." Carla was clearly upset about netball becoming mainstream and heterosexist.

Heterosexual versus hetero-normative

While lamenting the increasing hetero-centricity of the league, the participants were most angry with certain gay men in the NZMNA. Certainly the push to exclude transgender women from the NZMNA was a direct result of the Anglicized sensibilities of the incoming South Island-based players – the majority of which were heterosexual White men (Tagg 2008a, 464). However, these teams also included a small number of Māori and Pacific Island men, some of whom were both gay and came to be increasingly influential within the association. Indeed, Brenda said she was especially hurt by "the gay guys ... that had the real issue with the transgenders" because it came from "your own circle." This reflects Orne's (2013, 246) point about how queer spaces are not necessarily 'safe' for transgender people.

Brenda noted that while gay men "could go butch or go and pass [deliberately using Goffman's term] if you like," many transgender players could not "blend in." Instead, they responded by "flaunting." Amy described transgender players who refused to "be something less than what they are [and] ... would turn up with false tits, eyelashes, and makeup and still run around in a men's netball tournament, just to be defiant" (see also Tagg 2008a, 468). In Amy's words, transgender people must "have thick skin like an alligator" and make it clear that "whether you like me being a queen or not, I don't really give a fuck." Not only was she herself "not frightened to die," she found that if she was "just true to yourself then people will ... tend to accept you because you're not creating an illusion for people to think 'is, am, I, er, um.'" This emphasis on authenticity, could explain the resistance to gender transforming transgender people. Here, Goffman's (1963) analysis is useful.

The participants were critical of the NZMNA for seemingly abandoning them out of shame. Carla found it ridiculous that the NZMNA "worried about what people think of them rather than just focusing on what the men's netball was all about in the first place" and suggested that this reflected the men's insecurities. Gay men may have sought to pass as hetero-normative (by repressing gay subculture mannerisms) so as to not alienate both heterosexual men and the relatively conservative NNZ officials (Tagg 2008a, 466). Amy specifically criticized an NZMNA president/ Canterbury coach that had "the cheek to say that us going to the social in drag is unprofessional" who "abused the umpires ... in the middle of the [national championships] grand final" (I also was watching this match). Many of the players who resisted such pressures were in fact transgender people of Māori and Pacific Island descent and who were less inclined to practices of homo-normativity. It is important to reiterate that not all queer people have equal desire to participate in the privatization, domestication and depoliticization of gay life.

Brenda, in particular, distinguished herself from gender transforming transgender players by emphasizing professionalism. She suggested players should follow the rules and even "go on court with no makeup" and appreciated being praised by elite women's coaches for "the discipline and how we held ourselves up in public." While the strict *dress as a man* rules posed problems just when "most of us were developing our tits" she both strongly disliked gender transforming transgender players' "false impressions" and criticized younger "man-acting" (cf. "straight-acting") transgender players, saying: "as long as you're playing in that association and playing in shorts looking like that don't call me 'sis.'" Her solidarity was with "up-and-coming" transgender players who "don't want anything to do with it [the national association] because they get shot down all the time." Interestingly, her queer solidarity did not extend to gender transforming transgender men netballers; a second example of queer spaces not necessarily being "safe." It is also, perhaps, an example of "dodging the bullet."

An interesting tension, however, surrounded the occasional need to respond to harassment with violence. Carla described an altercation with an early South Island player who apparently later came 'out' as gay:

> He walked past and said "you fucking faggot" and I said "you'd better not be talking to me," so we went outside and punch in the mouth!

"Don't you come into netball and say that I'm a fucking poofter – who do you think you are? You haven't been around, you're a child; you've just started."

Carla suggested that a more rational response would be to say she's, "not a threat to you because you're not insecure." While clearly an instance of hostility, Carla's reaction was also framed to target South Island players who "hated coming up against us because … we didn't give a fuck if they liked us being queens or not." She saw being asked to tone it down as giving up part of her identity because transgender players "loved having that center of attention … [even as] a freak show for the straights; of 'fucking poofters down the road playing netball.'" In the face of such hostility, flaunting was an act of resistance that overrode any desire to "take," "deflect" or "dodge the bullet." There are tensions here between Carla's flaunting (including the rough language) and Brenda's adherence to emphasized femininity (Connell and Messerschmidt 2005) as a tool of identity management.

The aggressive strategies increasingly backfired as the proportion of South Islanders in the NZMNA grew, emphasizing the non-linear nature of "coming out." When describing an emerging Wakatipu team (from the conservative rural Central Otago region) gradually adjusting to training with an openly gay Otago player, Carla retorted: "Get fucked, I was playing netball when you were still in nappies!" This aggressiveness, although understandable, was clearly not being applied strategically; it took courage for these heterosexual men to play men's netball. Possibly in response to my surprised reaction, she immediately conceded that men's netball was "not about that" but "being able to be yourself" because, again, many South Island players "didn't see the queens as a threat." Here, Carla changed her strategy from responding to apparent Goffman-style aggression to recognizing it as a more ambiguous case and modifying her response all the way back to in fact "taking the bullet."

Another useful conceptual frame is that of public vs. private space. While homosexuality in New Zealand is typically tolerated within the private realm "heterosexuality's omnipresence 'in public' is not recognised, leading to [false, hetero-normative] claims that heterosexuality is not publicly 'flaunted'" (Brickell 2000, 165). From a heterosexist perspective, pride parades – rooted in the larger carnivalesque tradition of public display of sexualized bodies – intrude into "the 'public' space of the city street and, in turn, the 'private' space of the minds of heterosexuals" (Brickell 2000, 164) even though public spaces organized explicitly and implicitly around hetero patriarchal family structures. Similarly, heterosexist concerns about men's netball reflect the transition from the early 1980s private gatherings of largely queer people to a public-space event involving heterosexual men. Indeed, according to one cisgender female men's netball administrator, a triggering factor for the heterosexualization of the

NZMNA resulted from early attempts to promote the sport more widely, which led to certain players being "called faggots and there was all these [newspaper] write-ups that was all bad" (Tagg 2008a, 463). This perhaps explains Amy's view that "if you're going to carry on behaving like what you seen in the news ... then expect ramifications" (Tagg 2012, 164).

Playing with heterosexual men

Carla has played netball *with* South Islanders as well as in teams that played against them. Overall, she said, "nine times out of ten, the straight guys are fun" and her only major complaint was how "all they were talking about was pussy [sexual conquest]." Both transgender and hetero-normative players just want "to laugh and be silly and play drinking games and fine, go to sleep under the bush and in a silly area." A minor distinction was that transgender players typically drank heavily the night *before* the games – apparently because "You will play better because you're relaxed ... [compared to being] so worked up and so tense ... you get intimated by these other teams." It also, perhaps, reflects their realities of working on Saturday nights and playing on Sunday mornings. She described binge drinking before an important match in which scored on every attempt, "But when I sobered up I couldn't hit the fucking thing." This state of inebriation may represent the conditions under which she normally played. It also, it seems, reflects pre-gentrified men's netball.

While Amy and Carla suggested hetero-normative men netballers no longer felt threatened by transgender players, Brenda disagreed. Amy suggested that current players "were a lot more patient with numbers as we called them" and that the Australian team in particular "don't give a shit if you're gay, if you're queer, if you're what! They want to get on there and they want to annihilate!" Carla said that while many heterosexual men "wouldn't be seen *dead* on a netball court," she "kept persisting" and, optimistically, now "it's accepted by society." She felt transgender-centric teams "made it easier and more comfortable for other transgenders to play in those days." Brenda, however, suggested that this simply reflected transgender players' invisibility and the few remaining transgender players' careful identity management. When Amy suggested that now "it should be a little bit easier for them" Brenda disagreed sharply saying "No. It's not.... Because it's indirect; it's very discreet; it's behind closed doors." While in the early days "we'd have it out on the court" they are now "really quite nasty about it ... let's keep it as discreet as possible." She resented both the restrictive policies and being told to keep quiet. This shows how transgender netballers may interpret the same political context quite differently, and choose different identity management strategies. Not only should we be cautious about the idea of queer solidarity, but perhaps of transgender solidarity as well.

Discussion

The narratives of these three transgender players highlight the usefulness of the gender-conforming/gender-transforming distinction (Travers 2006) and the limitations of focusing just on queer versus straight identities, and in particular queer solidarity. The participants described alliances with some heterosexual South Islanders that depended on the latter recognizing that transgender players need not threaten their identity. While the participants identified as female and wished to be considered feminine, this did not prevent them from breaking with emphasized femininity and actually using direct violence as a response to harassment. While the transgender people I interviewed lamented the NZMNA's hetero-normativity, they were also dismissive of gender transforming transgender people. Perhaps the emphasis on authenticity made it difficult to put aside identity politics and understand others' point of view. Their concern that gender-transforming transgender people give off "false impressions" in the same way as "straight-acting" gay men reflect their own investment in the two sex system.

Orne's (2013) refinements of Goffman's (1963) analysis of identity management seem useful for conceptualizing situations in which transgender people face neither clear hostility nor are clearly accepted. Identifiable are potential examples of participants "taking," "deflecting" and "dodging" the bullet and even one example of a participant reinterpreting Goffman-style hostility to be an opportunity to "take the bullet." The recognition that coming out is not a singular moment is extremely helpful for understanding the transition from an unambiguously accepting space in the early 1980s into a space with both significant open hostility and ambiguous interactions. Finally, Brickell's (2000) distinction between public space and private space provides clarity, since the effort to expand the NZMNA from small private gatherings into a mainstream sporting association precipitated the changing character.

The concept of queer solidarity appears especially problematic. The participants suggest that, in important ways, many openly gay men were *more* hostile to transgender women than were heterosexual men netballers. Even transgender solidarity seems problematic; both gender transforming transgender people and "male acting" transgender women undermine the two-sex system, which seems to be a key foundation of gender conforming *trans*-gender women's identity management. Therefore, in a single moment, one can be both "stigmatized" and "normal" (in the sense of being a stigmatizer). One may, for example, possess "double consciousness" when deciding how to respond to an ambiguous situation involving a gay or heterosexual man, and yet be entirely blind about, for example, gender transforming transgender people, "male-acting" transgender women, oreven heterosexual men. This is especially problematic in the case of deciding appropriate transgender netball attire, considering the clear range of what women, including transgender women, feel comfortable wearing; many cisgender women, in fact, play sport in trousers and all three participants criticized aspects of the NZMNAs regulations about appropriate dress.

References

Anderson, Eric and Mark McCormack. *The changing dynamics of bisexual men's lives: Social research perspectives.* New York: Springer, 2016.

Andrew, Geoffrey. "'A girl's game, and a good one too': A critical analysis of New Zealand netball." Master's thesis, University of Canterbury, 1997.

Brickell, Chris. "Heroes and invaders: Gay and lesbian pride parades and the public/private distinction in New Zealand media accounts." *Gender, Place and Culture: A Journal of Feminist Geography* 7, no. 2 (2000): 163–178.

Brown, Gavin. "Homonormativity: A metropolitan concept that denigrates 'ordinary' gay lives." *Journal of Homosexuality* 59, no. 7 (2012): 1065–1072.

Connell, Robert W. and James W. Messerschmidt. "Hegemonic masculinity rethinking the concept." *Gender & Society* 19, no. 6 (2005): 829–859.

Goffman, Erving. *Stigma: Notes on the management of spoiled identity.* New York: Simon and Schuster, 1963.

Nauright, John. "Netball, media representation of women and crisis of male hegemony in New Zealand." *ASSH Studies in Sports History,* no. 11 (1999): 47–65.

Orne, Jason. "Queers in the line of fire: Goffman's stigma revisited." *The Sociological Quarterly* 54, no. 2 (2013): 229–253.

Roy, Eleanor Ainge. "Transgender New Zealanders face 30-year wait for surgery after only specialist retires." *Guardian,* April 22, 2016.

Tagg, Brendon. "'Dress as a man': New Zealand men's netball as contested terrain." *Ethnography* 9, no. 4 (2008a): 457–475.

Tagg, Brendon. "'Imagine, a man playing netball': Masculinities and sport in New Zealand." *International Review for the Sociology of Sport* 43, no. 4 (2008b): 409–430.

Tagg, Brendon. "Transgender netballers: Ethical issues and lived realities." *Sociology of Sport Journal* 29, no. 2 (2012): 151–167.

Travers, Ann. "Queering sport lesbian softball leagues and the transgender challenge." *International Review for the Sociology of Sport* 41, no. 3–4 (2006): 431–446.

Chapter 9

The experiences of female-to-male transgender athletes

Mark F. Ogilvie

Introduction

Men's sports have traditionally been characterized by high levels of homophobia, perpetuating aggressive and misogynistic archetypes of male athletes, particularly throughout the 1990s. The domain of male sports, which was once a hostile environment for gay and bisexual men, has shifted toward a more inclusive environment (Anderson, 2011a). In more recent years, researchers have found that male athletes, as well as fans of male sport, have improved attitudes toward gay men in sport (Anderson & McGuire, 2010; Cashmore & Cleland, 2012; Magrath, 2012). Additionally, openly gay athletes have reported less homophobia on their teams, a decrease in homophobic language from teammates (McCormack, 2011; Hargreaves & Anderson, 2014), and better experiences in general (Anderson, 2011b).

The acceptance of mainstream transgender athletes, such as Chris Mosier and Caitlyn Jenner, has increased cultural awareness and sparked a cultural dialogue about transgender athletes and their role in sport. However, as of now, there is a lack of literature on transgender athletes' experiences. Successful transgender athletes started the conversation. Now, policymakers have the opportunity to create sporting policies that promote the inclusion and acceptance of transgender athletes in the context of athletics, which holds the possibility of transcending throughout the rest of society by extension through their example, leadership, and influence (Buzuvis, 2011). Research that supports this endeavor by documenting the experiences of transgender athletes is thus important.

In this chapter, I will discuss the experiences of five transgender athletes from various regions of the US, with data collected via interviews I conducted in May, 2016. All participants are Female-to-Male (FtM) transgender athletes and the interviews are focused on their experiences with sport from childhood, through their transition, and into their current day-to-day lives. The aim of this research was to learn about their everyday experiences and to showcase the voices of competitive athletes who are not celebrities or in the media spotlight.

The story of Alex

Early school years can be challenging and confusing for children who diverge from dominant heteronormative and binary gender schemes. This was certainly true for Alex while attending an all girl's private school in the Midwest during the 1980s. This was an era in the USA characterized by extreme, and politically mobilized, homohysteria (McCormack & Anderson, 2014). This homophobic context reinforced what we would today refer to as transphobic attitudes, with the result that Alex had no language about transgender identities, let alone role models, to aid him in his transition into the man he is today.

Socially ostracized, Alex found himself surrounded by what he perceived as graceful, socially adept young women – his peers. At an impressionable age, Alex felt isolated and bullied at times; having sexist profanities written on his locker and having classmates openly question his sexuality. Alex's life was not a primetime TV show with helpful teachers to get him though confusing times and there was no Gay Straight Alliance to support him and celebrate his differences. There was only one safe place for Alex – sport.

Alex grew up playing a wide range of sports: basketball, fencing, cycling, rugby, tennis, and field hockey. In high school, Alex was a two-sport varsity athlete on the female basketball team and the female field hockey team. Alex proved himself to be a talented goal keeper in field hockey, which has led to a long career of playing the sport he loves and gaining love and support from teammates who are now life-long friends of his; however, Alex's journey to success in field hockey was not always an easy path to follow.

Alex, now 43 years old, discussed his experiences of the earlier days in his sporting career as a time of uncertainty. Towards the end of high school, many universities had attempted to recruit him as a player. At the time, he had considered trying out for the US women's national team. Confident in his skills on the field, he said he had a good chance of making the team; however, one thing stood in his way at the time:

> It was made very clear to me that openly gay [lesbian/queer] athletes were not welcome on the national team. There were plenty of gay athletes on the team, we just weren't allowed to be out and open. That bridge had already been crossed in my life and I wasn't comfortable pretending otherwise. I had not begun transitioning at all, but I was definitely on the very masculine side of the spectrum to begin with and it felt like a very unnatural fit for me when I would go to the women's national team events. I got a really strong feeling of 'the cold shoulder' in an indirect way through comments which made it clear that it wasn't going to be a good fit for me.

At this point in Alex's life, he decided to attend college and to take a break from higher levels of organized sport, but his love for field hockey never faded. Alex continued to play in club events and on co-ed teams throughout college and after graduating.

In Alex's late twenties, he followed his heart and embraced his true gender identity, first consulting his doctor, then beginning his transition and taking testosterone. During this time, he continued to play field hockey at a recreational and club level of competition. When discussing his experiences of field hockey during the beginning of his transition, Alex commented that:

> Hockey has always been a place where I don't have to think real hard, its time out of space where I don't have to worry about outside factors. So, the actual competition hasn't really changed. On the other hand, what changed was my experience of it. Starting to take testosterone, I felt a lot of changes internally. I was willing to take a lot more physical risks and push my body harder. I put on a lot of muscle mass and my quick twitch reflexes have changed. My entire relationship with my body had changed as the testosterone took hold in my system. It wasn't an uncomfortable change, but I definitely noticed that I was playing harder, taking more risks, and became more protective of my teammates in some interesting ways as well. I definitely think that some of those characteristics that are traditionally seen as male characteristics had come out in the way I started to play hockey.

Alex also commented on the irony of being the goal keeper in field hockey during his transition: In co-ed leagues, there is a quota on the men to women ratio of field players, but the gender of the goal keeper is not a part of that ratio, meaning the goal keeper's gender is non-essential. Describing himself as 'a goal keeper for cheap hire,' he finds the non-gender binary position in co-ed field hockey both comical and fitting to his circumstances, and is happy to embrace the one position on the field in which talent trumps gender.

An already talented goal keeper, Alex has become a successful player, umpire, and coach in the world of field hockey. He has played for the US Men's Masters Team, and continues to play field hockey competitively and recreationally, contesting gender binary barriers in field hockey. He is an openly transgender athlete with immense talent and a passion to make the world of sport a better place for the generation of athletes who hope to follow in his footsteps. As a final statement in a powerful interview, Alex poured his heart out:

> I think it's been an ongoing theme in my life - sports can be a port in the storm for people. For me, it very much was a safe place when

things got stressful and difficult in my life, I always had sports. For the transgender community, that port should always be available to anyone who wants it. I think that as we grow and learn and understand, there is going to be more and more non binary athletes that want to participate in sport, and I really hope to be in a world in such a way that we encourage that participation instead of discourage it. I was discouraged, but I would like to empower. I'd like to see young non binary athletes be able to play and be involved instead of give up on sports because they feel like they don't have a home there.

Stories like Alex's highlight some of the positive effects sports can have on youth in Western societies, even in periods of time where society and sport have been seen as oppressive to sexual minorities. At a recreational level, sports participation can promote physical and mental health. Many young students join sports to make friends, have fun, and to be part of a team. Socially, sports can give students the opportunity to make connections with one another and strive for a common goal while building confidence and cultivating leadership skills, leading to social inclusion (Bailey, 2005). Although it is not always the case, some research suggests that sport can also be a gateway to academic achievement, better grades, and a higher likelihood of attending college (Rosewater, 2009).

However, organized sport remains trapped in a male/female dichotomy (Foddy & Savulescu, 2011). This structure of sport has consequently excluded athletes that maintain other gender identities. Transgender youth, having an internal sense of self that does not match their sex assigned at birth, are often forced to comply with the dichotomy of organized sport in order to reap the physical, mental, social, and academic benefits of their cis-gender peers. As adults, transgender athletes have been granted access to competing in NCAA and Olympic level sport, as long as they prescribe to the historically horrific tests of sex-verification, which currently revolve around hormone testing.

Meet the roster

In addition to Alex, four other FtM athletes were participants for this research:

Sam, a CrossFit competitor, has a strong support system with his Cross-Fit Box in Southern California. His current participation is recreational. He also competes in informal, local men's CrossFit competitions. He hopes to one day be able to compete in official competitions; however, the Cross-Fit rules, as of now, do not accommodate for transgender athletes.

Blake and Casey, American football players from the American South, continue to compete in women's leagues and in LGBTQ leagues. They have yet to make the transition into playing in men's leagues. As of now, they do not feel as if they have to change leagues. They have not been pressured to change leagues by teammates, coaches or opponents, and they are in no rush to leave a league filled with their closest friends. Everyone they have encountered in their current leagues have been supportive of their transitions; however, they feel a lack of organizational support, and are apprehensive about the possibility of being forced out of their current leagues.

Dylan, a multi-sport athlete with a particular talent for softball, spent his life in women's recreational sports programs on the east coast. Transitioning in his late fourties, he now competes in recreational co-ed softball leagues. Having great experiences since his transition, he often thinks about growing up in the 1960s and the amount of discrimination he faced as a young queer woman in sport.

Increased inclusivity

Since sport became socially valued in the late 1800s, homophobia has policed players' behaviors and has encouraged non-heterosexual players and other sexual minorities to 'pass as straight' in order to fit the role of an athlete (Anderson, 2014). In recent years, Western countries have rapidly recognized sexual diversity, which has led to a greater tolerance of lesbian, gay and bisexual players. This newfound tolerance has translated into the sport domain, lessening homophobia and biphobia in sport (Anderson & McCormack, 2016; Anderson, Magrath & Bullingham, 2016). More recently, the conversation of inclusion has switched from that of lesbian, gay and bisexual athletes, to that of transgender athletes.

Anderson (2002) discussed, in the context of gay athletes in sport at the time, that a lack of visibility ought not to assume hostility from their heterosexual peers. In fact, Anderson's (2011b) work shows a progression toward heterosexual athletes being increasingly inclusive of sexual minorities. As a response to this attitudinal shift toward inclusivity, Anderson (2009) proposed Inclusive Masculinity Theory to understand the changing and softening of masculinity among young sporting men. He described a cultural zeitgeist of low homohysteria and homophobia, leading to the erosion of a hierarchy of masculinities into a broader ranged spectrum of acceptable masculinities. The aspects of Inclusive Masculinity Theory are evident from the ways in which young heterosexual men engage with other men, exhibiting a range of once-stigmatizing behaviors.

This type of inclusivity is demonstrated through the ways in which the participants of this research enthusiastically discussed the positive experiences they have had with their teammates during their transition and in their everyday athletic events. When discussing positive experiences, Alex passionately described a very special encounter he had with his cisgender male teammates:

> I had already come out to my teammates as a transman, and after a tournament we were offered a shower before the trip back home. I can pass reasonably well clothes, but my anatomy was unmistakable when naked. I feared being noticed, embarrassed, or worse, so I decided to load up on deodorant and bail. I turned to find my teammates standing around in towels awaiting me. Without words, they told me they were with me. Trembling and dizzy, I stripped, wrapped a towel around my waist and walked to the showers. No one noticed my tears mixing with the water. Their generosity of spirit strengthened me, and I still wear the confidence they shared.

The respect and support that his teammates showed him that day in the locker room inspired him to tell his story and fight for the rights of young transgender athletes to one day be able to play on the team of their choice and have these types of life changing experiences.

Showing some difference from research with participants has found coaches to be less inclusive than players (Adams, Anderson & McCormack, 2010), other participants discussed how positive and supportive their coaches have been through their transitions. For example, Blake said:

> None of my coaches have ever really cared. It's all about performance and being a good teammate and a team leader, as well as physical and mental preparedness and performance. I don't think that anyone has looked at me and expected me to perform differently, certainly not once they know me.

The CrossFit participant, Sam, also discussed how he has received support from his trainers and other CrossFit athletes at the gym that he trains at:

> My experiences with my CrossFit teammates have been amazing. My Box community is incredibly supportive. I have always felt welcome and a part of the community. My friends and coaches have supported me through surgery, as I've grown as an athlete, and in reaching out to other transgender athletes to join our Box. Most of the people I work out with know that I'm transgender and are incredibly respectful. They encourage me to do my best.

While some research on gay footballers has found that concern regarding how opposing players might treat gay athletes is a reason why some may not come out (Cashmore & Cleland, 2011). However, this did not appear to be an issue for these trans athletes. Participants have also commented on the ways in which opponents treat them, Alex said:

> It's part of my identity and it's not something that I keep secret at all, not even from my opponents. I don't think that in the hockey

community the teams that play against my team go in and say "oh, that's the trans goal keeper, he's not going to be as good as everyone else," if anything they just say "oh, that's the 5' 8" goal keeper, shoot high or shoot wide" as opposed to anything else.

In American football, Casey and Blake are open about their transgender identity to teammates and opponents; however, due to the amount of pads used for the sport, they are able to blend in completely with their team-mates. Casey said:

> When I'm playing, in my pads and helmet, no one knows that I'm transgender. Nobody treats me any different than anyone else.

The participants of this research stated that most of their experiences had been positive and inclusive in their respective sports. They are treated fairly, and judged on the quality of their performance and work ethic, rather than their gender identity. Teammates, coaches, and opponents accepted these transgender athletes as part of the athletic community; in fact, all five participants report that they have had far more positive experiences in sport since their transition than negative experiences.

When discussing the negative experiences that these athletes have had in their sporting careers, most of the athletes have reported that the majority of their negative experiences have either been at the institutional level or negative experiences pre-transition:

> Pre-transition, I went to a different Box. The vibe there was very 'bro.' The owner/head coach would routinely make homophobic or sexist remarks which turned me off to that entire community. I joined my new Box right before my transition and the coaches and community there have been awesome. Everyone has been supportive. In fact, almost all of my experiences since then have been positive, with the exception of the dust-up around CrossFit banning transgender competitors from the Open (and Regionals/the Games), but that's more of an organizational problem.

Although organizational issues persist to some degree, the positive experiences prevail over the negative experiences in the cases of these participants. The teammates, coaches and opponents discussed for this research have all demonstrated high levels of inclusivity toward transgender athletes.

Acknowledging a slight privilege

In 1977, American tennis player Dr. Renee Richards, a Male-to-Female transgender athlete, successfully challenged the right to compete in the women's draw at the US Open. Since this challenge, the United States Tennis Association and other sporting organizations have required athletes to undergo sex-verification testing in order to check hormone levels and to determine the chromosomal make-up of participating athletes. Although other forms of sex-verification tests have existed in the past, this mainstream event was the first event of its scale (Buzuvis, 2011). Richards was bombarded with essentialist arguments that support segregation of sport by sex, which claimed that MtF transgender athletes have a competitive advantage over cisgender women athletes. While the rules of transgender participation have changed in modern sport, the stigma on MtF athletes has not faded.

The FtM participants involved in this research spent ample time discussing their MtF community members, and their hardships in the world of athletics. All five participants made it clear that they wish to be portrayed as supportive of MtF athletes and their experiences. These participants were also not shy about acknowledging the privilege they have in this context. For example, Sam said:

> I think I have had a completely different experience compared to MtF transgender athletes. None of the men in my Box think that I am secretly trying to take hormones so I can beat them. I doubt if any of them are worried that I am going to outperform them. I think MtF athletes are always cast in a light as if they are just trying to gain some kind of competitive advantage over cis-gendered women. When people have debates about whether transgender athletes should be able to compete, it is always the MtF athletes who are under scrutiny. I can't imagine how hard that would be.

Similarly, Dylan said:

> Honestly, it is much easier for a transgender man in the world of athletics than it is for transgender women. So, that piece has been less challenging in some ways than being an openly queer woman was, and even that wasn't particularly difficult, nobody really cares. In a lot of ways, I'm just viewed as a normal teammate, and just judged on my own merits, which is kind of awesome.

These participants sympathize with MtF athletes, and point out that the world needs to be educated about the process of transitioning and what really happens biologically if this stigma is ever truly going to disappear. When discussing this, Alex said:

There is a great deal of myth that people believe about transgender athletes who were identified as female biologically or intersex athletes that have more male secondary characteristics than female, that these athletes are going to be stronger, faster, able to dodge bullets and leap tall buildings. There is a lot of ignorance around what happens as you transition hormonally, but really the only think that a transgender athlete keeps with them is whatever internal emotional structure they've acquired and any skeletal advantage or disadvantage that they bring to the sport. If you are talking about somebody who is transitioning from male to female, all she is going to take with her is however large her skeleton was. Even then there is some evidence that suggests that bone density and osteoarthritis will set in with transgender women just as it does with cis-gender women.

Additionally, Casey said:

I think there is a lot of ignorance around transgender women in sport, whereas in a lot of ways transgender men in sport get almost the advantage of people assuming that we are not going to be as strong, fast or capable or whatever because of our anatomy, which has not been the experience of most of the transgender guys that I know of that participate in any level of sport. It's not something that has been studied enough at all.

Being a FtM transgender athlete is certainly challenging at times; however, the participants of this study believe that there is greater discrimination and social stigma toward MtF transgender athletes.

Changing the rules

In January 2016, the International Olympic Committee created new guidelines that opened the door for more transgender athletes to compete internationally. Under these new guidelines, FtM transgender athletes became eligible to compete in the male category without restriction; however, MtF transgender athletes had to declare their gender identity as female and pass testosterone level tests routinely for 12 months prior to her first competition as well as throughout the period of competition. While these rule changes are a step in the right direction, the participants in this research have discussed short-term and long-term goals that they would like to see enacted by all sports organizations.

All five participants were excited about the progress that has been made in sport, thanks in large part to the Olympics' new guidelines; however, they are hopeful of progressing transgender athlete inclusion even further. Related to this, Sam said:

I would like to see all sporting organizations adopt the IOC guidelines on transgender athletes. I would also like to see CrossFit allow transgender competitors.

Others participants expressed a sense of uncertainty about the compliance of nations in regards to the new rules set forth by the Olympics Committee. Alex said:

The IOC just came out with a big statement about transgender athletes not having to have surgery to compete in the sport of their choice, but just because the IOC says that doesn't mean that nations or teams or organizations are going to follow through with that as their plan. So, right now I'd like to see those plans come to fruition and be respected by all participating nations.

Furthermore, participants wanted to see increased openness and support from other sporting institutions. On this point, Casey said:

I would love for transgender athletes to be able to be open and play on the team that they feel suits them best.

Additionally, Dylan said:

When I started to transition, there really was no social support structure, and there still isn't a lot. I'd like to see a support system for transgender athletes that creates a space for us to actually talk about our experiences.

As an extension from short-term goals, there were a number of goals discussed by participants that focus more on the bigger picture of transgender athletes in the future. In an interview, Blake states:

I think a bigger goal is to educate a bigger picture in the world view. I would like to see more of an understanding of what being transgender is all about.

Finally, Alex believes that the current structure of organized sport is not well equipped to handle transgender athletes properly.

I think we are still very trapped in a binary assumption of athletics and that is not necessarily going to serve us as long as we have gender variant athletes that want to participate in sports. If we have somebody that identifies as gender fluid or gender queer and is an athlete, there needs to be some understanding of how and why and where that person can and should be allowed to participate. I feel like, in general, most sports are totally unprepared for that, but those situations are coming. There are people that are going to identify with not fitting in the binary in any way, and they are going to want their place at the table. For me, that's much more important than trying to find a place for myself. I'm talking about people that are going to be competing at the highest level in their sports that deserve the ability to participate, and I don't think we are ready organizationally.

The athletes in this study have made it clear that being a transgender athlete competing in sports within the gender binary has been extremely challenging and disheartening. Educating the world about transgender individuals and changing the oppressive gender segregation of sport are important in making strides toward equality.

Thinking about the FtM athlete experience

As the world attempts to accommodate and understand transgender athletes in sport, it remains vital to understand the perspectives of these athletes and their everyday experiences as human beings. The concept of 'being an athlete' is a crucial part of the identity of transgender athletes, and it is a part of their identity that has transcended their gender transition, and shaped the core of their humanity. When discussing the topic, Sam said:

> I think being a FtM athlete is mostly about me pushing my boundaries and trying to redefine myself. Trying to break new ground, grow new muscles, and learn new skills. Sometimes, I feel held back by my body- by the years that I wasn't on testosterone, by my female frame, and the hips and knees that I inherited, but mostly I'm excited and ready to continue to redefine what I can do.

When interviewing the athletes about their transition, topics of identity were commonplace. I inquired about the ways in which embracing a new bodily identity might affect the ways in which they compete, both physic- ally and psychologically. The quote above illustrates just how important the identity of an 'athlete' is to transgender athletes. During the beginnings of their transitions, the league in which they competed was less important than the desire to compete and remain an athlete. Transgender athletes also understand that being an athlete is not only physical, it's mental and emotional as well. Regarding this topic, Sam said:

> The word 'athlete' defines more than just what you do, it defines your mind-set. An athlete is someone who thinks about sport, who analyses sport, who dreams about sport, and who is a happier person when

they're engaged in sport. Doing CrossFit is more than just exercise- it is the way that I have fun and the way that I stimulate that sport/team oriented part of my personality

When discussing identity, Alex highlighted how essential being an athlete is to his life. From his early days in his all girl school, being an athlete is what got him through the times of uncertainty, and it is through his identity as an athlete that he has gained a lot of the confidence that makes him the man that he is today. He said:

> For me, identifying as an athlete and being involved in athletics is very cornerstone to my life. Interestingly enough, if someone asked me 'how do you identify' being an athlete would be in the list, but it might take me a while to get there. But in fact, it is pretty critical to my being. If I take a small break from sport, I almost immediately notice that there's a gap in my life. I miss the team dynamic of sports. For me, I think team sports feed a part of me that I don't get in other aspects of my life. It's like my opportunity for socialization in a lot of ways. If I wasn't part of a team, I would simply be isolated further.

Conclusion

A small-scale exploratory study, such as this, cannot be generalized or representative of all or even most of the experiences of FtM transgender athletes. This study does, however, add to our understanding of some of the issues facing transgender athletes, as well as shedding insight on some of the experiences FtM transgender athletes might have with their teammates, coaches and opponents. While all five of the participants have documented many positive experiences with their sports and used their sport and teammates as a support system in many ways, they have also highlighted aspects of their sports, and the structure of sports in general, that need to change in order to be more accommodating to the multiplicities of gender identities in contemporary society. More research is required in order to fully understand the diversity of transgender athlete experiences and the nuances of the intersectionality between FtM transgender athletes and their sporting environments.

References

Adams, A., Anderson, E., & McCormack, M. (2010). Establishing and challenging masculinity: The influence of gendered discourses in organized sport. *Journal of Language and Social Psychology, 29*(3), 278–300.

Anderson, E. (2002). Openly gay athletes contesting hegemonic masculinity in a homophobic environment. *Gender & Society, 16*(6), 860–877.

Anderson, E. (2009). *Inclusive masculinity: The Changing nature of masculinities*. London; New York: Routledge.

Anderson, E. (2011a). Masculinities and sexualities in sport and physical cultures: Three decades of evolving research. *Journal of Homosexuality, 58*(5), 565–578.

Anderson, E. (2011b). Updating the outcome gay athletes, straight teams, and coming out in educationally based sport teams. *Gender & Society, 25*(2), 250–268.

Anderson, E. (2014). *21st century jocks: Sporting men and contemporary heterosexuality*. London: Palgrave.

Anderson, E., & McCormack, M. (2016). *The changing dynamics of bisexual men's lives*. New York: Springer.

Anderson, E., & McGuire, R. (2010). Inclusive masculinity theory and the gendered politics of men's rugby. *Journal of Gender Studies, 19*(3), 249–261.

Anderson, E., Magrath, R., & Bullingham, R. (2016). *Out in sport: The experiences of openly gay and lesbian athletes in competitive sport*. London: Routledge.

Bailey, R. (2005). Evaluating the relationship between physical education, sport and social inclusion. *Educational Review, 57*(1), 71–90.

Buzuvis, E. (2011). Transgender student-athletes and sex-segregated sport: Developing policies of inclusion for intercollegiate and interscholastic athletics. *Seton Hall Journal of Sports & Entertainment Law, 21*, 1.

Cashmore, E., & Cleland, J. (2011). Glasswing butterflies gay professional football players and their culture. *Journal of Sport & Social Issues, 35*(4), 420–436.

Cashmore, E., & Cleland, J. (2012). Fans, homophobia and masculinities in association football: Evidence of a more inclusive environment. *The British Journal of Sociology, 63*(2), 370–387.

Foddy, B. & Savulescu, J. (2011). Time to re-evaluate gender segregation in athletics? *British Journal of Sports Medicine, 45*(15), 1184–1188.

Hargreaves, J., & Anderson, E. (2014). *Routledge handbook of sport, gender and sexuality*. London; New York: Routledge.

Magrath, R. (2016). *Inclusive masculinities in contemporary football: Men in the beautiful game*. Routledge.

McCormack, M. (2011). Mapping the terrain of homosexually-themed language. *Journal of Homosexuality, 58*(5), 664–679.

McCormack, M., & Anderson, E. (2014). The influence of declining homophobia on men's gender in the United States: An argument for the study of homohysteria. *Sex Roles, 71*(3–4), 109–120.

Rosewater, A. (2009). Learning to play and playing to learn: Organized sports and educational outcome. *Education Digest: Essential Readings Condensed for Quick Review, 75*(1), 50–56.

Chapter 10

Media accounts of the first transgender person to work in the English Premier League

Rory Magrath

Introduction

A growing body of academic research has documented how contemporary football (soccer) has become an increasingly inclusive space for sexual minorities (Adams & Anderson, 2012; Cashmore & Cleland, 2012; Cleland, Magrath & Kian, 2016; Magrath, 2016, under review; Magrath, Anderson & Roberts, 2015). But while matters are improving for lesbian and gay athletes in the game – and indeed sport more broadly (Anderson, Magrath & Bullingham, 2016) – little scholarly attention has been paid to the experience of transgender individuals in football. The limited research that does exist on transgender involvement in sport highlights greater levels of discrimination than for lesbian and gay athletes (Buzuvis, 2011; Carroll, 2014; see also Sykes, 2006; McGuire, Anderson, Toomey & Russell, 2010). Indeed, as Adam Love outlines in Chapter 15 of this collection, transgender athletes have suffered a range of institutional barriers.

This is best evidenced by the *Stockholm Consensus*, the guidelines set forth and approved by the International Olympic Committee in 2004, which were subsequently adopted by a range of sport governing bodies – including the Football Association (FA), the governing body of English football. However, as Love outlines in Chapter XXX, these guidelines are concerning for a number of reasons. Most significantly, they rely on a "conservative, binary understanding of sex, which stands in opposition to reality, as was highlighted in the difficulties associated with sex-verification testing" (Love, 2014, p. 379). Moreover, implementing the *Stockholm Consensus* continues to exclude many transgender athletes from participation in sport (Sykes, 2006). However, despite this, recent high-profile cases of transgender people involved in sport – such as boxing promoter Kellie Maloney (known as Frank Maloney prior to her transition), and retired American decathlete Caitlyn Jenner (formerly known as Bruce Jenner) – has increased attention to the presence of transgender individuals in sport. Despite this, however, their experience remains significantly undertheorized.

This is particularly the case in English professional football. I have previously written about how the British tabloid media's almost obsessive yet – at the time of writing – unsuccessful attempts to uncover which English Premier League players are gay (see Magrath, 2016). But this interest is not replicated with respect to transgender involvement in football. Indeed, there has been no known transgender participation in an English professional football match. Moreover, although a wide range of English Premier League clubs are now actively involved in various LGBT-inclusion schemes (Magrath & Anderson, 2017) – many even have officially-recognized, affiliated fan groups – these have primarily been concerned with homophobia, rather than transphobia. Thus, transgender involvement and coverage in professional football continues to be marginalized. Indeed, there exists no empirical, academic research dedicated solely to the experiences of the transgender community in English professional football.

However, in the summer of 2015, this silence was interrupted by the story of English Premier League club AFC Bournemouth's official club photographer Sophie Cook, who subsequently became the first transgender woman to work in professional football. In this chapter, I outline the response to her gender reassignment. To do so, this chapter is structured into three main sections: first, I review the current literature focusing on football and sexual minorities; second, I review the current literature focusing on the experiences of transgender individuals in football, and sport more broadly; finally, using a wide range of English print media, I contextualize the overwhelmingly positive response to Sophie Cook's gender reassignment, before concluding with some directions for future research.

Football, society and "LGB"

Until the most recent decade, homophobia has received limited academic attention from sociologists of football. Instead, it has been assumed as a culture of extreme hostility for lesbian, gay and bisexual (LGB) people – hence the lack of openly gay active professional footballers. Following the coming out of former English Premier League player Thomas Hitzlsperger (see Cleland et al., 2016), journalist Owen Jones (2014) claimed that football remains "one of the greatest fortresses of homophobia," while Hughson and Free (2011, p. 118) argue that: "To acknowledge that the national game is played at the highest level by men who contravene the conventions of ideal, heterosexual manhood is to acknowledge that there are 'traitors' in the rank."

In recent years, however, there has been a significant liberalizing of attitudes toward sexual minorities in Western cultures (Clements & Field, 2014; Twenge, Sherman & Wells, 2016) – a shift which has also been reflected in football, among both players and fans. In their pioneering, large-scale research on British football fans, Cashmore and Cleland (2012, pp. 377–378) present what they describe as "a new and surprising image: the exact opposite to one which has been characterized ... [as being] 'steeped in homophobia'" – 93 percent of fans would welcome the presence of openly gay players in English football. Footballers' playing ability was deemed the most important factor on which to judge them; everything else was secondary. This has been a consistent finding among other recent research with football fans: Cleland (2015), for example, documented the inclusion of homosexuality on 48 football fan forums, while Cleland et al. (2016) found high levels of support among fans when former English Premier League player Thomas Hitzlsperger announced that he was gay in 2014.

Elsewhere, other research has shown that footballers themselves are also becoming increasingly supportive of LGB issues. Due to professional football's existence as a closed and almost impenetrable culture, no academic research currently exists based on either current or former players' attitudes toward LGB people. Instead, we must base our judgments on anecdotal evidence. In October 2016, for example, Southampton FC's Player Liaison Officer Hugo Schekter reported that he had received nothing but support from the players after he came out of the closet. Moreover, other players – such as English football's oft-claimed villain Joey Barton – are willing to exhibit outspoken support for the LGB community. However, it is Magrath's (2016) research with the *next* generation of professional players in English football that is most telling. Here, footballers from English Premier League academies exhibit positive and inclusive attitudes, and would even go to extreme lengths to defend the honor of a hypothetically gay teammate. While a small number of participants espoused a more conservative response to LGB teammates – typically those with strong religious ties (see also Magrath, 2015) – these findings suggest that "this hypothetical inclusivity ... serves as a roadmap for when one of their teammates does come out" (Magrath, 2016, p. 169).

Even professional football clubs are, it seems, becoming increasingly likely to align their brand to one of LGB-friendliness. Indeed, in the 2015–2016 season, a record number of English Premier League clubs supported the *Football v Homophobia Initiative*, as well as participating in events like the *Rainbow Laces* campaign and having official representation at various pride events (see also Magrath & Anderson (2017) for a more detailed overview of clubs' LGB-friendly involvement). But despite the ever-increasing acceptance of the presence of the LGB community in British football, support for the T in the LGBT acronym, is missing, as the voices, experiences and involvement of transgender individuals are largely sidelined. The next section of this chapter focuses on the existing literature relating to transgender involvement in sport.

Football, society and "T"

The previous section of this chapter focused on the growing levels of acceptance, inclusivity and support of LGB athletes in football. However, there has been virtually no focus on the presence of transgender individuals in football – and little in sports research more broadly. While matters have significantly improved for the LGB community – both inside and outside of sport – this has not been consistently the case for transgender individuals. In the US, for example, Norton and Herek (2012) show that heterosexual adults adopt more discriminatory attitudes toward transgender people than they do toward LGB people. In the UK, comparable data is unavailable, though a recent poll conducted by Sky News found that 48 percent of Britons are supportive of those who desire to change gender[1] (Hirsch, 2015). Other research also shows that transgender people experience high levels of discrimination and harassment – particularly youth (Grossman & D'Augelli, 2006; McGuire et al., 2010; Rankin, Weber, Blumenfeld & Frazer, 2010; Robinson & Espelage, 2011).

In the US, the establishment of "bathroom bills" – which seek to regulate access to public facilities for transgender people – have been criticized as transphobic, and an attempt to eliminate transgender people from public spaces. Transgender people also face other significant barriers, such as the inaccessibility of healthcare for those from lower socioeconomic backgrounds – particularly in the US (e.g., Clark, Landers, Linde & Sperber, 2001). In the UK, the National Health Service (NHS) offers a range of treatments and care for transgender people, though they have been recently criticized for long delays before offering treatment.

In sport, transgender athletes have faced comparable barriers to their participation, in addition to significant hostility. Anderson et al. (2016, p. 10), for example, wrote: "The lives of transgendered people ... are found to be much more difficult than are the lives of sexual minorities ... Put simply, people are far more transphobic than they are homophobic." Hargie, Mitchell and Somerville (2015) support this line of argument, highlighting the existence of four interconnected themes that impact transgender participation in sport: issues with changing rooms – what Halberstam (1998, p. 365) describes as "the bathroom problem"; negative sporting experiences at school (see also Buzuvis, 2011); difficulties with appearing in public; and the overall impact of their exclusion from sport. This has resulted in a number of barriers governing the social exclusion of transgender people in sport. In similar research, Lucas-Carr and Krane (2012, p. 39) also illustrate issues with the "variance and fluidity" surrounding transgender experience in sport, and call for greater understanding of multiple transgender identities.

However, contrasting research – notably that of Travers (2006) and Travers and Deri (2011) – have documented what they describe as the potentially "radical transinclusive" space (Travers & Deri, 2011, p. 16) of select North American lesbian softball leagues. In these spaces, they argue, the prominence of transgender athletes has challenged the previously rigid women-only guidelines. This, according to Travers (2006) and Travers and Deri (2011), is evidence of a cultural shift toward one of inclusivity for transgender athletes' participation in sport – or at least in minority sports leagues. This is further supported by the growing number of transgender athletes achieving sporting success, including tennis player Renee Richards, golfer Mianne Bagger, and NWHL player Harrison Browne. In 2011, American Samoan footballer Jaiyah Saelua became the first – and, to date, only – transgender player to compete in a FIFA World Cup qualifying match, though, interestingly, this received little media attention (see Smith, 2014). These athletes play a significant role as, according to Mahoney, Dodds and Polasek (2015, p. 45), they "serve as role models and inspiration to transgender youth." Indeed, Outsports.com tells of numerous transgender athletes in non-elite sport, such as American footballer Kennedy 'Kenny' Cooley, who have been unanimously welcomed and accepted by various sports teams.

Recent years have also seen the reduction of the institutional barriers that transgender athletes have faced (Sykes, 2006). Love (2014, p. 381), for example, documented that a "growing number of sport governing bodies have adopted policies ostensibly intended to include transgender athletes." Most notably, the National Collegiate Athletic Association (NCAA) has adopted a trans-inclusion policy, as well as developing materials to help member schools create more inclusive environment within their athletic departments. In football, the FA updated their policy on transgender participation in football in 2014. Having previously adhered to the *Stockholm Consensus*, the FA included a more complex and inclusive range of regulations, as well as encouraging clubs to promote a positive environment for people of all backgrounds.[2]

Despite this, however, there have been recent controversies that have undermined these trans-inclusion policies. In 2014, for example, an amateur transgender footballer, Aeris Houlihan, was banned from participating in women's football, two years after undergoing gender reassignment therapy – even though she had provided the required medical documentation. And in May 2015, the annual *Football v Homophobia* event, due to be held at the University of Nottingham in the UK, was cancelled amid allegations of transphobia. Specifically, Luke Hutchinson, an amateur transgender footballer, was prevented from participating in the tournament unless he paid for specific medical tests to prove his affirmed gender. Thus, although football has made great strides for the inclusion of transgender players, such examples illustrate the complications and bureaucratic barriers they often continue to face – particularly when they are often regulated by a conservative, categorical gender binary system.

Sophie's story

While evidence in the previous section suggested attitudinal improvement toward the transgender community in football, their presence remains somewhat invisible – especially in the otherwise diverse world of the English Premier League. However, as outlined earlier in this chapter, Sophie Cook made history by becoming the first transgender person to work in the English Premier League, following her transition in the summer of 2015. Prior to her gender reassignment, she had been known as Steve Cook: a 300-pound former Royal Air Force (RAF) jet engine technician and newspaper editor. Residing in the city of Brighton and Hove, UK, she has been the official club photographer of English Premier League club AFC Bournemouth for the past two years, as well as being associated with the British rock band, The Libertines. She has also worked closely with other British music artists, such as Pete Doherty, Stereophonics, and Oasis.

On her website, Cook writes of her gender identity crisis – something she was aware of from a young age – and the problems associated with it. "My first memory of being 'trans' was at seven ... I knew something was wrong. When I went to see the GP in my twenties, he wasn't sympathetic," she said in an interview[3] with *The Times* (Syed, 2016). Other attempts to locate trans affirming healthcare had similar results. In recalling the high levels of transphobia she faced, Cook explained that "They [London healthcare clinic] saw it as their job to beat it out of you" (Syed, 2016). Accordingly, Cook began to live in a state of denial and depression, frequently self-harming and experiencing suicidal thoughts: life as a man was "mental torment" (Smith, 2016).

Eventually, in what she described as a "lightbulb moment," Cook decided that something needed to change. She said: "Living with the burden any longer would have killed me, so it was time to be true to myself. I couldn't keep living in the shadows" (Matthews, 2016). She attributed this desire for change to the sustained suppression of her true gender identity, something which began to dissolve after she made her decision. "I could no longer live a lie," she added. Despite this, she maintained a level of apprehension about what her decision would mean for her role as AFC Bournemouth's club photographer. Realizing the complexity of the situation, Cook said that, "I was living in Brighton and had hair extensions. It wasn't as if I could go back to Bournemouth, take my wig off and pretend I was still Steve. I was Sophie" (Crick, 2016). In an interview with Patricia Murphy for the *Irish Independent* newspaper, Cook recalled her fear in more detail:

> The end of last season [2014–15] we were promoted to the Premier League ... It was the most amazing day in the history of my football club but I was terrified because I knew that during the summer I was

going to tell them [the players and staff of the club] I was transgender and I thought I'd never work in football again ... The fear was real.

Cook's fear of social and legal reprisal is a common theme among transgender individuals undergoing gender reassignment therapy: Grossman and D'Augelli (2006), for example, show that transgender youth fear constant verbal harassment and discrimination.

Earlier in this chapter, I outlined how extensive contemporary research highlights that football is more acceptant of sexual minorities than ever before (Adams & Anderson, 2012; Cashmore & Cleland, 2012; Cleland *et al.*, 2016; Magrath, 2016, under review; Magrath *et al.*, 2015). The fact that Cook was becoming the first transgender person to work in the English Premier League – and indeed English professional football more broadly – made her experience even more unique. But the reaction toward Cook was one of positivity and inclusivity. Prior to the commencement of the 2015–2016 English Premier League season, the chairman and coaching staff of AFC Bournemouth called a meeting with the players. Here, she was introduced as Sophie Cook. She recalled:

The assistant manager [Jason Tindall] called the players together and said: "You'll probably notice our photographer has changed a little from last season, lost a bit of weight, and grown her hair out a bit. I'd like you all to meet Sophie." I had no idea how they would react but suddenly the captain started clapping and the rest of the boys joined in. I haven't looked back. It feels amazing.

(Matthews, 2016)

She added that she feels like she has been "totally accepted by players and fans" (Bellamy, 2016). While some may claim that this positive inclusive response could be as a result of social desirability and pressure from the club's hierarchy – indicative of the prominent nature of English Premier League footballers' media training – Cook then continued: "Some of the guys came up afterwards and showed their support for me. They [the players] have been amazing" (Murphy, 2016). Thus, the response of a group of professional footballers toward a transgender woman is congruent with general attitudes toward sexual minorities in the game: that of positivity and acceptance.

But football is a multi-layered industry, and there are several groups of people with significant interest in the game. Most notably, the English Premier League commands national and international attention from fans. Previous research has also highlighted that, despite significant improvements in the contemporary game, football fans have often engaged in discriminatory chanting – particularly related to racism, homophobia and misogyny (Collinson, 2009; Pearson, 2012). In forthcoming research,

Magrath (under review) shows that British football fans are likely to target anything they deem to be a weakness, ensuring that they can in some way impact the success of their team.

Consequently, there were fears that fans would be abusive toward Cook, and engage in a range of negative chants. However, these fears have not been realized:

> Some of my friends feared all sorts of chants and abuse shouted at me … It hasn't been like that at all though and I've been totally accepted by the players and fans and I am so grateful to just be me.
>
> (Crick, 2016)

There have also been no known incidents of transphobia since this initial interview. In short, much like Cashmore and Cleland's (2012) research – which showed high levels of support for sexual minorities in football – it appears that football fans are also becoming accepting of transgender involvement in the game, at least preliminarily. It is likely, however, that greater transgender involvement in the game will be required before these attitudes can be determined on a wider scale.

Despite this widespread acceptance and support, Cook has faced some hostility outside of football. "I get some people stop and stare, snigger and point and call me 'sir' … I've had a group of teenagers shout out 'that's a man' pointing at me," she said in an interview with the *Daily Mirror* (Corless, 2016). One particular incident even led to a threat of physical violence: "I was abused on the train back from London last night. A drunk youth shouted: 'Oi, manwoman, oi you!' He squared up to me. It was terrifying" (Syed, 2016). Academic research highlights that transgender people in the U.S. "…experience multiple acts of violence or intolerance on a daily basis" (Stotzer, 2009, p. 177). However, this research is inconsistent with Cook's experience, perhaps indicating the acceptance of transgender individuals is greater in the UK. Indeed, while she has received occasional threats – such as the one outlined above – these are infrequent (c.f. Grossman & D'Augelli, 2006; Norton & Herek, 2012; Stotzer, 2009). As she wrote in a recent article in the *Daily Telegraph:* "Like the bigots of the past … the anti-transgender lobby is gradually fading" (Cook, 2016).

The (only) transgender English Premier League role model

Since Cook's gender reassignment in 2015, her role in football has extended beyond simply being AFC Bournemouth's club photographer. She has become an outspoken activist against bigotry and discrimination in football – and also wider society, too. She has spoken at prestigious events such as the FA's LGBT History at Wembley Stadium, and the Pride Sport campaign at Liverpool FC's Anfield Stadium. Moreover, she was the first and currently only transgender Ambassador for UK football's primary equality and inclusion organization *Kick it Out*, as well as the first transgender Patron of *Just a Ball Game?* She also holds several other non-sporting roles with organizations that include Stonewall, the Dorset LGBT Network and Sussex Police. She is also the Head of Diversity for Brighton's local television channel *Latest TV*, becoming the first transgender news anchor in Europe in the process.

Accordingly, she is a central figure for the transgender community. Further evidencing this, Cook became a central figure in advising Brighton College on their strict uniform codes – which had gone back 170 years – to ensure the inclusion of transgender pupils (Cook, 2016). She was also nominated for the LGBT Role Model at the National Diversity Awards in March 2016. Perhaps more importantly for the sporting world, she is the only transgender woman currently involved in English football. Thus, she is widely recognized as an important role model in football – the only transgender person to have ever worked in the English Premier League. Consequently, her positive experiences speak loudly of the growing acceptance of transgender involvement in sport (Travers & Deri, 2011), particularly for those considering a career in professional football.

Conclusion

In this chapter, I have outlined how contemporary football culture in the UK has become increasingly accepting of LGB involvement in the game (Adams & Anderson, 2012; Cashmore & Cleland, 2012; Magrath, 2016). Transgender experiences in football, however, had been afforded little academic attention. Previous research illustrates that transgender people face considerable hostility and discrimination (Hargie *et al.*, 2015; Lucas-Carr & Krane, 2012). Moreover, institutional barriers were also prohibitive for transgender involvement in sport. Consequently, Anderson *et al.* (2016, p. 4) write that: "Considerable research has shown that the experiences of … transgendered individuals are *far worse* than gays and lesbians in American and Western European countries."

However, the experience of Sophie Cook challenges this assumption. Cook became the first-ever transgender person to work in the English Premier League, following her gender reassignment in the summer of 2015. Despite fearing rejection and discrimination, Cook's experience has been one of positivity and acceptance, characterized by strong support from both players and fans. She has seemingly been unanimously accepted in the game and, at the time of writing, there have been no instances of discrimination against her by anyone in the game. Thus, although she is *only* a club photographer – not a member of the playing or coaching staff – Cook can be described as a trendsetter; something to inspire future transgender involvement in English football. Despite this, transgender footballers should approach the professional game with caution. Previous literature, which illustrates higher levels of discrimination, should not be overlooked and ignored. Moreover, despite the adoption of trans-inclusion policies in football, the examples of Aeris Houlihan and Luke Hutchinson illustrate the ongoing barriers that transgender footballers must face.

Thus, this chapter highlights two significant points that affect football. First, the positive experience of Sophie Cook suggests that football culture may also be inclusive of transgender people in the game, as well as sexual minorities. Although it is likely that greater transgender involvement will illustrate this further, there has been a positive preliminary response to Cook – suggesting that the same response is possible for transgender players. Second, it also highlights a dearth of academic research on transgender experiences in football. This is likely attributable to the lack of high-profile transgender players at the professional levels of the game. Indeed, there has only been one known case – the relatively unknown American Samoan player Jaiyah Saelua. Trans-inclusion policies have been implemented to regulate transgender inclusion – some of which have moved away from the IOC's rigid policies – yet, still, little is known about their experience. Moreover, although a now significant body of academic research has focused on attitudes toward lesbian and gay footballers (Cashmore & Cleland, 2012; Magrath, under review), we know nothing of the experience of transgender football fans.

I therefore call for academic scholars to extend this knowledge base, and not to exclude transgender experiences from their theorizing. Future research projects in this field should consider what is occurring among this minority group in numerous capacities: there is a story to tell by transgender players, fans, coaches, or even any other form of employment. Currently, however, there is nobody to tell it.

Notes

1 This is compared to approximately 70 percent of Britons who show no objection to homosexuality (see Clements & Field, 2014).
2 Information about The FA's *Policy on Trans People in Football* can be found here: www.thefa.com/news/governance/equality/2014/nov/fa-launches-transgender-policy.
3 Cook's gender reassignment commanded some media attention in the British and Irish press, and I rely on these articles to inform the majority of this chapter.

References

Adams, A. & Anderson, E. (2012). Exploring the relationship between homosexuality and sport among the teammates of a small, Midwestern Catholic college soccer team. *Sport, Education and Society, 17*, 347–363.
Anderson, E., Magrath, R. & Bullingham, R. (2016). *Out in sport: The experiences of openly gay and lesbian athletes in competitive sport*. London: Routledge.

Buzuvis, E. (2011). Transgender student-athletes and sex-segregated sport: Developing policies of inclusion for intercollegiate and interscholastic athletics. *Seton Hall Journal of Sports and Entertainment Law*, *21*, 1.

Carroll, H. J. (2014). Joining the team: The inclusion of transgender students in United States school-based athletics. In J. Hargreaves & E. Anderson (eds.), *Routledge handbook of sport, gender and sexuality* (pp. 367–375). London: Routledge.

Cashmore, E. & Cleland, J. (2012). Fans, homophobia and masculinities in association football. *British Journal of Sociology*, *63*, 370–387.

Clark, M. E., Landers, S., Linde, R. & Sperber, J. (2001). The GLBT Health Access Project: A state-funded effort to improve access to care. *American Journal of Public Health*, *91*, 895–896.

Cleland, J. (2015). Discussing homosexuality on association football fan message boards: A changing cultural context. *International Review for the Sociology of Sport*, *50*, 125–140.

Cleland, J., Magrath, R. & Kian, E. T. M. (2016). Masculinity and sexuality in association football: An online response to the coming out of Thomas Hitzlsperger. *Men and Masculinities* (Online First).

Clements, B. & Field, C. D. (2014). Public opinion toward homosexuality and gay rights in Great Britain. *Public Opinion Quarterly*, *78*, 523–547.

Collinson, I. (2009). Singing songs, making places, creating selves. *Transforming Cultures eJournal*, *4*, 15–27.

Cook, S. (2016, 21 January). Why I advised Brighton College over its "trans uniforms". All schools should follow suit. *Telegraph*. Retrieved from www.telegraph.co.uk, accessed October 1, 2016.

Corless, L. (2016, 4 January). Premier League's first transgender woman reveals players applauded when she was first introduced as Sophie. *Daily Mirror*. Retrieved from www.mirror.co.uk, accessed September 30, 2016.

Crick, A. (2016, 4 January). First transgender woman in Premier League tells of pride after being accepted by players and fans. *The Sun*. Retrieved from www.thesun.co.uk, accessed 15 April, 2016.

Grossman, A. H. & D'Augelli, A. R. (2006). Transgender youth: Invisible and vulnerable. *Journal of Homosexuality*, *51*, 111–128.

Halberstam, J. (1998). *Female masculinity*. Durham, NC: Duke University Press.

Hargie, O. D. W., Mitchell, D. H. & Somerville, I. J. A. (2015). "People have a knack of making you feel excluded if they catch on to your difference": Transgender experiences of exclusion in sport. *International Review for the Sociology of Sport* (Online First).

Hirsch, A. (2015). Trans people: Poll reveals changing attitudes [online]. Retrieved from www.skynews.com, October 10, 2016.

Hughson, J. E. & Free, M. (2011). Football's "coming out": Soccer and homophobia in England's tabloid press. *Media International Australia, Incorporating Culture and Policy*, *140*, 117–125.

Love, A. (2014). Transgender exclusion and inclusion in sport. In J. Hargreaves & E. Anderson (eds.). *Routledge handbook of sport, gender and sexuality* (pp. 376–383). London: Routledge.

Lucas-Carr, C. & Krane, V. (2012). Troubling sport or troubled by sport? *Journal for the Study of Sports and Athletes in Education*, *6*, 22–44.

Magrath, R. (2015). The intersection of race, religion and homophobia in British football. *International Review for the Sociology of Sport* (Online First).

Magrath, R. (2016). *Inclusive masculinities in contemporary football: Men in the beautiful game*. London: Routledge.

Magrath, R. (under review). "To try and gain an advantage for my team": Homophobic and homosexually-themed chanting among English football fans. *Sociology*.

Magrath, R. & Anderson, E. (2016). Homophobia in men's football. In J. Hughson, K. Moore, R. Spaaij & J. Maguire (eds.), *Routledge handbook of football studies* (pp. 314–324). London: Routledge.

Magrath, R. & Anderson, E. (2017). Football, homosexuality and the English Premier League: A changing cultural relationship. In R. Elliott (ed.), *The English Premier League: A socio-cultural analysis*. London: Routledge, pagination to be determined.

Magrath, R., Anderson, E. & Roberts, S. (2015). On the door-step of equality: Attitudes toward gay athletes among academy-level footballers. *International Review for the Sociology of Sport, 50*, 804–821.

Mahoney, T. Q., Dodds, M. A. & Polasek, K. M. (2015). Progress for transgender athletes: Analysis of the School Success and Opportunity Act. *Journal of Physical Education, Recreation and Dance, 86*, 45–47.

Matthews, A. (2016, 4 January). Football team's photographer who went from Steve to Sophie becomes the first trans person working in the Premier League. *Daily Mail*. Retrieved from www.dailymail.co.uk, accessed October 1, 2016.

McGuire, J. K., Anderson, C. R., Toomey, R. B. & Russell, S. T. (2010). School climate for transgender youth: A mixed method investigation of student experiences and school responses. *Journal of Youth Adolescence, 39*, 1175–1188.

Murphy, P. (2016, January 5). First transgender woman to work as a Premier League photographer – "I thought I'd never work in football again." *Irish Independent*. Retrieved from www.independent.ie, accessed October 8, 2016.

Norton, A. T. & Herek, G. M. (2012). Heterosexuals' attitudes toward transgender people: Findings from a national probability sample of US adults. *Sex Roles, 68*, 738–753.

Pearson, G. (2012). *An ethnography of English football fans: Cans, cops and carnivals*. Manchester: Manchester University Press.

Rankin, S., Weber, G. N., Blumenfeld, W. J. & Frazer, S. (2010). *2010 state of higher education for LGBT people*. Charlotte, NY: Campus Pride.

Robinson, J. P. & Espelage, D. L. (2011). Inequities in educational and psychological outcomes between LGBTQ and straight students in middle and high school. *Educational Researcher, 40*, 315–330.

Smith, P. (2014). Jaiyah Saelua: If I experience transphobia I just tackle harder. *Guardian*. Retrieved from www.theguardian.com, accessed October 18, 2016.

Stotzer, R. L. (2009). Violence against transgender people: A review of United States data. *Aggression and Violent Behavior, 14*, 170–179.

Syed, M. (2016, April 6). Should Caitlyn Jenner compete with women? *The Times*. Retrieved from www.thetimes.co.uk, accessed October 2, 2016.

Sykes, H. (2006). Transsexual and transgender policies in sport. *Women in Sport and Physical Activity Journal, 15*, 3–13.

Travers, A. (2006). Queering sport: Lesbian softball leagues and the transgender challenge. *International Review for the Sociology of Sport, 41*, 431–466.

Travers, A. & Deri, J. (2011). Transgender inclusion and the changing face of lesbian softball leagues. *International Review for the Sociology of Sport*, 46, 488–507.

Twenge, J. M., Sherman, R. A. & Wells, B. E. (2016). Changes in American adults' reported same-sex sexual experiences and attitudes, 1973–2014. *Archives of Sexual Behavior*, 45, 1713–1730.

Part III

When policy and identity clash

Chapter 11

Subjective sex

Science, medicine and sex tests in sports

Vanessa Heggie

The maintenance of sex-segregated sports in the twentieth century has been based on two assumptions: that human beings come in two sexual forms, male and female, and that one of these forms has significant biological advantages in terms of sporting performance. From the 1930s sports organisations have increasingly turned to biomedical experts to provide 'objective' scientific tests to maintain segregation in sports, an activity nearly always justified by an appeal to the notion of fair competition. Ironically, through the same period a range of scientific disciplines – including genetics, endocrinology and forensic psychology – as well as social sciences such as anthropology and sociology, began to describe human gender identities as flexible and continuous, and identified not a binary sex system, but a complex identity built of many kinds of sex (e.g. Fausto-Sterling, 1992).

This chapter outlines the medical and scientific tests used to determine whether athletes were eligible to compete in women's sporting events in the twentieth century. Variously called tests for 'sex', 'gender' and 'femininity', these surveillance regimes had to satisfy competing and often contradictory demands from sports organising bodies, scientific professionals, advocacy groups and the athletes themselves. Such tests were discussed by sports organisations and medical professionals in the early 1930s, and were relatively common in Western sports by the 1940s, undergoing significant political and procedural changes throughout the second half of the twentieth century. Examining these tests demonstrates the shifting balance of power and authority in sports sciences, as well as highlighting clear conflicts between biological, social and cultural ways of understanding bodily difference.

Histories of sex testing in sports have tended to localise the origins of the tests in the games of the 1950s, where in the shadow of a Cold War successful female athletes from behind the iron curtain were accused of gender fraud. More recent studies have shown that this gender anxiety was in fact clearly present as early as the 1930s, leading to systematic requirements for female athletes to prove they were eligible to compete in women's events (Heggie, 2010). These concerns matched broader social fears about the apparent mutability of biological sex, fed by popular understandings of newly-discovered sex hormones. In particular it was the phenomenon of the female-to-male transition that provoked popular coverage and interest, and several examples were drawn from the world of sport. Through the twentieth century the concern within sport remained fixed on this transformation, from female into male; whereas in the worlds of sexology, endocrinology and reassignment technologies quite the opposite happened, with the male-to-female transition becoming the focus of attention (Meyerowitz, 2002). The on-going demand for a binary sex system, and a focus on female transgression, meant that the needs of sports were not well met by the scientific sex and gender tests that were introduced, since these were the products of quite different understandings of biology and psychology, as this chapter will show.

The most well known cases of gender ambiguity in the first third of the twentieth century are Stella Walsh (born Stanisława Walasiewicz in Poland, Walsh's family emigrated to the US when before she was a year old) and the German-born Heinrich Ratjen. Ratjen is the only documented case of straight-forward gender fraud; the dramatic version of his story that he was compelled by corrupt Nazi sports officials to compete fraudulently is almost certainly a myth, rather his story seems to be one of gender confusion at birth and an on-going inability to negotiate a new sexual or gender identity once he had mistakenly been registered as female (Heggie, 2010). Ratjen's case was resolved in 1938 when he was given new papers and a new identity as a man. Walsh, on the other hand, lived her entire life as a woman, and only had her gender questioned after her violent death, when in 1980 an autopsy revealed some ambiguous sexual features. The autopsy had no effect whatsoever on the introduction of sex tests, and her frequent appearance in articles relating to the topic of sex testing was driven more by authors' senses of dramatic irony than a desire to explain a chain of causes and consequences (Claims that Walsh was 'suspected' of 'being a man' during her years as a competitive athlete appear to be an invention by modern authors) (Heggie, 2010).

Walsh took second place in the women's 100 m race at the 1936 Olympic Games in Berlin; first place went to the American Helen Stephens. Questions were raised – by whom it is not clear – about Stephens' gender, and she was subject to an unspecified sex test by the German authorities, who confirmed her eligibility and her right to the gold medal. Outraged by this accusation, chair of the US Olympic Committee, Avery Brundage – who disapproved of women's competitive athletics in general – complained bitterly about the indignity of an accusation of manliness followed by an intrusive test, and argued that female competitors should bring their own certificates to events to prove their eligibility. He pointed, not to Walsh, but to two other successful female athletes who had undergone surgical procedures and were now living as men, as evidence that there was a gender problem in modern sports. Zdenek Koubkov had competed as Zdenka Koubkova for Czechoslovakia, and Mark Weston had won world records competing as Mary Weston for Britain. To this short list of widely-known sporting transsexuals we should also add the famous case of Willy (Elvira) de Bruyne, a Belgian cyclist who transitioned in 1935 (Meyerowitz, 1998).

By the 1930s Germany had become the centre of expertise for those wanting to transition from one sex to another, using a combination of hormone therapy and surgical intervention – and the first account of a case of surgical transition was published by a German surgeon in 1931, a few years before Koubkov, Weston and de Bruyne transitioned (Abraham, 1931). While doctors and scientists talked of restoring 'true' sex or of 'fixing nature's mistakes', as if there were underlying gender identities that could be confidently medically established, this work took place in an era when hormonal and endocrinological theories of sex promoted more mutable notions of sexual identity, which had strong cultural penetration. From the scandalous claims of Charles Eduard Brown-Séquard in 1889 that extracts of guinea-pig testicles were returning his lost virility, the use of 'gland extracts' (the specific hormones of progesterone, oestrogen and testosterone were only identified in 1929, 1934 and 1935 respectively) was widely discussed in Europe and North America. Gland therapy and its extraordinary – and usually sexual – effects was used by popular writers, such as Conan Doyle, in the 1929 Sherlock Holmes story *The Adventure of the Creeping Man*. It was also covered in popular newspapers, for example, in the late 1930s the coach of the Wolverhampton Wanderers' football club announced that he was giving 'gland extracts' to his players to improve their performances (Heggie, 2011, p. 81).

While titillating, the use of 'male hormones' to augment male performance – sexual or sporting – did not seem particularly problematic (in the case of Wolverhampton Wanderers, media coverage was concerned for the health of the players, but ambivalent about cheating). Similar attitudes did not extend to women. Female sport, already a transgressive activity, by the early twentieth century had its strong supporters, including social reformers, doctors and politicians, although female participation in vigorous or competitive exercise was still limited by gender expectations. Whether it was the political danger of publicly visible, independent women (particularly associated with cycling), or the medical danger of vigorous exercise to the more fragile female organism, or the social danger of encouraging women to be competitive and aggressive, limits were put on women's right to participate in sport (Hargreaves, 1994).

By the 1930s mainstream biomedical authorities appear to have been, in general, more positively disposed towards female sport (and female robustness) than sports organisations themselves – particularly the International

Olympic Committee (IOC). Nonetheless, the internationally-reported presence of female-to-male transsexuals in sport certainly contributed to popular and sporting suspicions that even if sport did not 'make' women into men, the sorts of women who were successful in sports might 'really' be men, or manly. The earliest 'sex tests' were therefore generally physical, phenotypical,[1] or physiological tests – that is, sex was determined by the possession of a certificate of femininity signed by a doctor, usually one's family doctor (team doctors were still not common for sports organisations in the 1930s). This requirement was brought in by the International Amateur Athletics Federation in the late 1930s (Rule 17 Paragraph 3) and adopted by the IOC, so that the first post-war Games, in 1948 in London, were the first to include this requirement for female athletes.

Gender controversies at mid-century make more sense when we see them in the longer context. Focusing on the Ukranian sisters Irina (1939–2004) and Tamara Press (b. 1937), sports coverage sometimes suggested that they were 'really' men, but as frequently discussed, it was more likely that 'substances', possibly hormones, were used to create male-like body types and high-level sporting success. This was explicitly the way the IOC saw the problem, as an article in its *Bulletin* in 1961 makes clear: "a particularly revolting form of doping ... [involves taking] male hormones which lead[s] to castration of the functional cycle of women amount[ing] sometimes to an atrophy of the ovaries which may cause a chronic disease in the long run" (Eyquem, 1961, p. 50). The associations between hormonal doping and gender anxiety continued into the twenty-first century – as Davis and Delano (1992) have shown, anti-doping campaigns focusing on steroids act to reinforce the binary nature of gender, representing gender-transgressive or gender-ambiguous bodies as evidence/consequence of drug use.

Crucially, though, at mid-century science could not yet offer an effective test for the use of hormones; what it could offer was a test for *sex* (Shackleton, 2008). Although the IOC had specifically highlighted the problem of doping with sexual hormones, the preventive measures it introduced examined only the problem of *naturally occurring* transgressive bodies. This ambiguity was admitted by the IOC

> ... certain medicasters have not hesitated to render women champions ... more *virile* in order, that during international competitions, they may achieve results which are over and above their normal capacities ... However dangerous this may be for the feminine organism and however reprehensible it may be from a moral point of view, these "treatments" in no way change the basic sexual characteristics, for it has been scientifically proved that hermaphroditism does not exist. One is born a man or a woman and one remains of that sex.
>
> (Berlioux, 1967, p. 1)

Instead of introducing tests for substances that increased 'virility', the IOC attempted to find tests that would provide a simple, comprehensive, *objective* measure of someone's birth sex, that is, their unchangeable, natural gender identity.

Accusations of gender fraud increased through the 1950s – importantly, not just aimed at the women we remember, such as the Press sisters, but also to other, forgotten athletes. One member of the British team at the 1960 Rome Olympics was charged by two other teams with being a man. In response, an indignant Jack Crump, secretary of the British Amateur Athletic Board, insisted that all his team had the "proper form", signed by both himself and a medical practitioner, "[i]t would be unthinkable" he argued "for us and for anybody else to challenge the integrity and capability of a registered practitioner" (Anon, 1960). But such a challenge is exactly what occurred in the 1960s, as the level of suspicion, and the stakes of competition, meant that the word of medical practitioners from athletes' home nations were no longer to be trusted in international competition.

The first *systematic* at-event sex testing was introduced at the 1966 European Athletics Championship, held in Budapest, and then taken up widely at other international sports events. Initially these tests were a continuation of the practices of the 1930s and 1940s, that is a physical and phenotypical test. But what might have been acceptable when practised by one's family doctor, or a familiar team doctor, was quite a different experience when practised by unsympathetic strangers. Participants in women's sports in the 1960s later gave highly critical accounts of the processes. Maren Siedler, an American shot putter said that at the 1967 Pan-American Games in Winnipeg

> [t]hey lined us up outside a room where there were three doctors sitting in a row behind desks. You had to go in and pull up your shirt and push down your pants. Then they just looked while you waited for them to confer and decide if you were OK.
>
> (Larned, 1976, p. 8)

At other events even more invasive systems of testing were chosen, for example sex-testing at the 1966 Commonwealth Games in Jamaica, was described by British pentathlete Mary Peters:

> [it was] the most crude and degrading experience I have ever known in my life … [I was] ordered to lie on the couch and pull my knees up. The doctors then proceeded to undertake an examination which, in modern parlance, amounted to a grope. Presumably they were searching for hidden testes. They found none and I left.
>
> (Larned, 1976, p. 8)

The unpleasantness and invasiveness of the test meant it was not going to be a sustainable practice; in addition, it also appeared alarmingly arbitrary. Ewa Kłobukowska, a Polish sprinter, passed the test in Budapest in 1966, but then failed it in 1967 at the European Cup Track and Field Event in Kiev. Clearly the phonotypical test for sex was too subjective – different panels of doctors might reach different decisions. Since, as the IOC had insisted, we were all born either male or female, and could not change over our lifetime, a test was sought which could distinguish between men and women conclusively. The test chosen was the Barr Body test – used on Kłobukowska in 1967 after she failed a "close up visual inspection of the genitalia", and which she also 'failed', leading to her disqualification for life from women's sports (Anon, 1967).

The Barr Body test had been developed in the 1950s by Canadian microanatomist Murray Barr. He and a research student first spotted this deeply staining cellular artefact whilst studying cats in the late 1940s, and published on the topic in *Nature* in 1949 (Barr and Bertram, 1949). The Barr Body was only present in the cells of female cats, and Barr developed a theory that this artefact was actually stained heterochromatin[2] (that is the material that makes up chromosomes) and therefore evidence of two condensed X chromosomes. If that were the case, then the fairly easily visualised Barr Body could be used as a proxy for establishing chromosomal sex, at a time when more extensive karyotyping was difficult and unreliable. In mammals, at least, a Barr Body could be taken as evidence of an XX sex-chromosome karyotype, and therefore femininity, while its absence indicated the organism was XY, and therefore male.

To prove this was the case Barr and his assistants engaged in a series of experiments with hormones and the removal and transplant of sexual organs, in an attempt to prove that the Barr Body was an indicator of chromosomal sex at conception, rather than being an artefact produced by, say, high levels of female hormones. By the early 1950s he had concluded that these experiments were a success, and that Barr Bodies were proxies for female chromosomal sex. By the 1950s, the prevailing understanding of sex determination assumed that male identity was the default for mammalian foetuses, controlled by the non-sex chromosomes (the autosomes). It was only where a 'double dose' of 'female-making' sex chromosome was present – that is in XX individuals – that an embryo would shift course and become female instead of male. In this reading the Y chromosome was generally considered inert and inactive.

Barr's team wrote in 1953 that "[o]ur hope is that the chromosomal sex will prove to be a reliable indicator of the dominant sex of the patient as a whole" (Moore *et al.*, 1953, p. 641). However, before the end of the decade flaws in the system had already been discovered, most notably through studies of people with various sex chromosome disorders, i.e. those whose sex chromosomes are XXY (Barr Body female, phenotypically male) or XO (Barr Body male, phenotypically female). Two of Barr's assumptions were also overturned, first, that the Barr Body itself was formed of both X chromosomes. Instead it was found to be a single X chromosome; since only one X chromosome is necessary to fulfil genetic functions, in people with two copies of the X one becomes inactivated and appears as the dense ball that constitutes the Barr Body. Second, it was discovered that the Y chromosome was not inert, but played a role in sex determination and development.

Despite this, it was the Barr Body test that the IOC chose as its 'femininity test' of choice in the late 1960s. As the article, quoted above, in the IOC's own Bulletin-cum-Newsletter (later the *Olympic Review*) goes on to say: "[t]he chromosome formula indicates quite definitely the sex of a person and, some years ago, it was discovered that a simple saliva test will reveal its composition" (Berlioux, 1967, p. 1). This is a significant overstatement of the competencies of the Barr Body test, and it is not clear from the published sources why this, already critiqued, test for sex was so eagerly taken up by the IOC. I would suggest three factors may have played a role in this choice: first, the test seemed both scientific and objective, and gave a straightforward negative or positive outcome, which meant it had significant advantages over the apparently subjective, human process of assessing phenotypical and physical sex. Second, the test was largely non-invasive, involving initially a cheek swab (buccal smear) and later a hair sample, reducing the need for the deeply unpopular and unpleasant visual and manual tests. Third, the committee tasked with organizing sex testing was not a specialist committee, but a sub-committee of the newly-formed Committee on Doping. No permanent Medical Committee was formed by the IOC until 1967, and as Alison Wrynn (2004) has shown, this organisation was riven in its early years by disputes about authority, remit and funding.

It is clear that many of those tasked with organizing and carrying out early sex testing – including doctors and scientists – had very poor understandings of the clinical and psychological consequences. For example, this rather naïve quotation comes from a report to the IOC, drawn up by the doctor in charge of the trials of the Barr Body test at the Winter Games in 1968 (which disqualified one downhill skier):

> I do not exactly know why some personages are unwilling to tolerate this examination; the main obstacle would seem to be the fear of seeing the young adolescent's psychism [*sic*] traumatized. Considering the harmless nature of the swab, I fail to understand where the traumatism comes in.
>
> (Thiebault, 1957, no pp.)

Meanwhile, geneticists and other scientists were actively criticizing the choice of the Barr Body test. It is worth quoting at length from one critique, as it was written by Dr Keith Moore, who was supervised through his MSc and PhD by Barr himself, and had been a co-author on some of the papers relating to the Barr Body in the 1950s:

> The question of whether certain female athletes are in fact female will certainly arise during medical examinations at the Olympics, even though the obviously doubtful cases will likely remain at home. The rapid advances registered during the last decade in our understanding of sex and its aberrations have resulted in confusion in the minds of some, however, concerning the contribution of various factors (genetic, gonadal, hormonal) towards the sexual identity of an individual. As a result, females have been declared ineligible for athletic competition for no other apparent reason than the presence of an extra chromosome ... [these tests] cannot be used as indicators of 'true sex'.
>
> (Moore, 1968, p. 787)

Despite these protests, the IOC stuck with the Barr Body test; in Part I would suggest because the internal struggles over the role and responsibility of the Medical Committee left little time for high-tech or psychosociological discussions of issues as complicated as sex testing. Since many sports organisations followed the lead of the IOC in terms of eligibility and the organisation of competition, the consequence was that tests for chromosomal sex were used widely as a means of establishing an athlete's eligibility to compete as a woman – despite scientific opposition. The only significant change in the 1970s was a switch to hair samples rather than buccal smears, and in some cases the use of a fluorescent dye test for the presence of the Y chromosome (in part to deal with the possibility of XXY and XO competitors).

The consequences of the use of this test are impossible to measure, because although some records are kept of at-event tests, and scandals are well known, thousands of women were tested quietly, secretly, 'at home'. In 1970 the British Association of Sport and Medicine (later the British Association of Sport and Exercise Medicine) funded a 'sex test' and a 'chromatin count service' for the use of any British governing bodies of sport who wanted to check their athletes' chromosomes before attending a major sporting event and it did not fund counselling or medical support for athletes found to be chromosomally 'abnormal' (Anon, 1970).

The first significant challenge to these testing regimes came in the 1980s. Spanish hurdler, Maria Martinez-Patino, underwent a sex test at the 1983 World Track and Field Championships in Helsinki, passed, and was given a certificate of eligibility. In 1985 she went to Kobe, Japan, to compete in the World University Games. She forgot her certificate and the authorities insisted on re-testing her. This time she failed, and her coach advised her to fake an injury and go home, which she did. When she tried to compete again the following year her story was leaked to the press; she was banned from her teams, her medals and records were revoked, and her fiancé left her (Patino, 2005).

Patino began a three-year campaign for reinstatement. She found sympathetic Spanish doctors willing to write reports about her medical condition, and was championed by Finish geneticist Albert de la Chapelle, who challenged routine sex testing on ethical and human rights grounds. Chapelle had received a PhD in human genetics from the University of Helsinki in 1962, and spent much of that decade investigating the phenomenon of XX males; that is people who are chromosomally 'female', but physiologically and hormonally 'male'. At exactly the time that Patino was mounting a challenge to the use of chromosomal sex tests, Chapelle was effectively developing a test for *genetic* sex. Between 1984 and 1987 he and colleagues published a series of papers in extremely high profile journals (including *Nature* and *Science*) demonstrating that the Y chromosome plays a crucial role in sex determination.

In this reworked understanding of sex determination in mammals, the female is now the 'default' developmental pathway for a foetus. Instead of a 'double dose' XX signal directing female development, a signal from a specific region of the Y chromosome (later known as the Sex Determining Region, or SDR) starts a cascade of events, which lead to male phenotypical development. Further, the X and the Y chromosomes can sometimes exchange genetic material through a process of 'crossing over' during cell division (meiosis)[3] which means that the SDR can end up on an X chromosome, hence the phenomenon of XX males.

With this support, Patino was reinstated in 1988, on the grounds that she had Androgen Insensitivity Syndrome; that is a fault in the testosterone receptors in the body such that, as a foetus, the signals for male development had no effect, and she continued through a near-normal female developmental pathway. In the same year the IAAF dropped chromosomal testing, reverting instead to a reliance on the physical examination conducted by the team doctor (in other words, a reversion to the 1940s system of sex testing). The IAAF abandoned all forms of systematic sex testing in 1992, arguing that because athletes had to pass urine in front of witnesses for drugs testing, and because of the revealing nature of tight sports clothes, it did not consider sex fraud a genuine threat to sport.

The IOC did not drop its testing protocols; it remained steadfast in its assertion that this was the right way to ensure fair competition, and "remov[e] scandal and innuendo from international sport" (Ferguson-Smith and Ferris, 1991, p. 20). By 1991 official objections to the IOC's testing regime had been issued by the American Medical Association, American College of Physicians, ACP Division of Internal Medicine, American College of Obstetrics and Gynaecology, the Endocrine Society, the American Society of Human Genetics, the genetic societies of Canada and

Australia, and many other organisations. In 1992 the IOC switched from tests for chromosomal sex to tests for genetic sex. A new sex test was introduced, looking for two specific regions of DNA usually found in the SDR on the Y chromosome. Although this test used cutting-edge research, rather than something a decade old (as had been the case for the Barr Body test), it still did not give the precision and the objective answers the IOC needed; all eight women who 'failed' the test at Atlanta in 1996 were reinstated after a physical examination. Finally, under increasing pressure from scientists and other lobby groups, the IOC announced in 1999 that it would no longer routinely test for sex at the Olympic Games.

Of course, sports organisations – including the IOC and IAAF – have reserved the right to insist on sex testing for athletes if specific accusations are made, or suspicions raised about their 'true' sex. Despite the growing scientific evidence that gender and sex are multifaceted and graduated identities, not binaries, and despite growing social acceptance of transgender and intersex identities, sport still functions on a principle of binary, simple, sexual identity. It is hardly surprising that biomedicine failed to provide an adequate testing regime; not only was there no consensus on which 'sort' of sex (genetic, nuclear, chromosomal, phenotypical, hormonal, genital, psychological) really mattered, but the IOC and other sports organisations also had competing aims for sex testing.

On the one hand, the IOC and others talked about the need to ensure fairness in competition; an ethically complicated aim, given that competitive sport itself depends upon inherent differences between athlete's abilities. The need to divide into gender categories was a social need, not a sporting or scientific one – tests were not introduced for any other hormonal, physiological or genetic sporting advantage, and we do not segregate by height, race or possession of any of dozens of gene variants which have significant impacts on peoples' potential performance. On the other hand, a great deal of concern was also expressed about the need to protect female athletes from public criticism or negative evaluations of their physical appearance. It is quite clear that no testing regime has solved the problem that the successful athletic body often does not neatly match contemporary Western cultural ideals of femininity. Attempts to rely on scientific authority to 'prove' an athlete's 'true' sex, regardless of appearance, have failed. If anything, the current system emphasises this clash of goals; selective gender testing, that is testing only of 'suspicious'-looking athletes, can only act to reinforce a hegemonic vision of acceptable, heterosexually attractive, female appearances.

> It comes into everybody's mind ... that when a woman takes advantage of her size and her body build in sports and gets national recognition, she must be more of a man than a woman.
>
> (Larned, 1976, p. 41)

Notes

1 Phenotypical. An organism's phenotype is the sum of its observable characteristics, physical and behavioural. This is used in contrast to its 'genotype', which is simply the genetic code of the organism that does not include the possible effects of environment, variations in the process of development, etc.
2 Heterochromatin. Chromatin is the collective name for the material that forms chromosomes, consisting of DNA and associated proteins. It can come in two forms, euchromatin, which is the most common, and the more unusual heterochromatin, which is particularly dense.
3 Meiosis. Meiosis is the term given to the first cell division after conception. Unlike normal cell division (mitosis), in meiosis the chromosomes – one set from each parent – exchange genetic material. This 'shuffling' process ensures that children are not clones of their parents, and maintains genetic diversity in a population.

References

Abraham, F. (1931) Genitalumwandlung an zwei männlichen Transvestiten. *Zeitschrift Für Sexualwissenschaft und Sexualpolitik* 18: 223–226.

Anon (1960) Olympic Women 'have medical certificates'. *Times* (London) 22 Aug, 4.

Anon (1967) Girl athlete to have new sex tests. *Daily Mirror* (London) 20 Sept, 6.

Anon (1970) Minutes of the Executive Committee of the BAS(E)M, 7 Mar. Wellcome Library Archives, SA/BSM.

Barr, M. L. and Bertram, E. G. (1949) A morphological distinction between neurones of the male and female, and the behaviour of the nucleolar satellite during accelerated nucleoprotein synthesis. *Nature* 163: 676–677.

Berlioux, M. (1967) Feminity [*sic*]. *Olympic Review* 3: 1–2.

Davis, L. R. and Delano, L. C. (1992) Fixing the boundaries of physical gender: side effects of anti-drug campaigns on athletics. *Sociology of Sport Journal* 9: 1–19.

Eyquem, M. T. (1961) Women sports and the Olympic Games. *Bulletin du Comite International Olympique.* 73: 48–50.

Ferguson-Smith, M. A. and Ferris, E. A. (1991) Gender verification in sport: the need for change. *British Journal of Sports Medicine* 25: 17–20.

Fausto-Sterling, A. (1992) *Myths of Gender: Biological Theories about Men and Women.* New York: Basic Books.

Hargreaves, J. (1994) *Sporting Females: Critical Issues in the History and Sociology of Women's Sport.* London; New York: Routledge.

Heggie, V. (2010) Testing sex and gender in sports; reinventing, reimagining and reconstructing histories. *Endeavour* 34: 157–163.

Heggie, V. (2011) *A History of British Sports Medicine.* Manchester: Manchester University Press.

Larned, D. (1976) The femininity test: a woman's first Olympic hurdle. *Womensports* 3: 8–11.

Meyerowitz, J. (1998) Sex change and the popular press: historical notes on transsexuality in the United States, 1930–1955. *GLQ: A Journal of Lesbian and Gay Studies* 4: 159–187.

Meyerowitz, J. (2002) *How Sex Changed: A History of Transsexuality in the United States*. Cambrudge, MA: Harvard University Press.

Moore, K. L. (1968) The sexual identity of athletes. *Journal of the American Medical Association* 205: 787–788.

Moore, K. L. *et al.* (1953) The detection of chromosomal sex in hermaphrodites from a skin biopsy. *Surgery, Gynecology and Obstetrics* 96: 641–648.

Patino, M. M. (2005) A woman tried and tested. *Lancet*, 366s: 38–39.

Shackleton, C. (2008) Steroid analysis and doping control 1960–1980. *Steroids* 74: 288–295.

Thiebault, M. (1967) Medical Commission of the International Olympic Committee Reports. IOC Historical Archives, Olympic Studies Centre, Lausanne.

Wrynn, A. (2004) The human factor: science, medicine and the International Olympic Committee, 1900–70. *Sport in Society* 7: 211–231.

Chapter 12

Including transgender students in United States' school-based athletics

Helen J. Carroll

Introduction

An increasing number of young people in schools are identifying as transgender; meaning that their internal sense of gender identity is different from the gender they were assigned at birth. These students challenge many parents and educators to rethink their understanding of gender as universally fixed at birth, simultaneously challenging them to create educational institutions that value and meet the needs of all students. Educators must ensure that these students have equal access to opportunities in all academic and extracurricular activities in safe and respectful school environments.

It is particularly important for school sports to be open to transgender students. School sport programmes are integral parts of the high school and college experience, particularly in the United States. The benefits of school athletic participation include many positive effects, and participation in high school sport improves chances of acceptance into college. For some students, playing on high school teams leads to future careers in athletics, either as competitors or in ancillary occupations. All students, including those who are transgender, deserve access to these benefits. Thus, schools must identify effective and fair policies to ensure equal access.

Though the needs of transgender students in high school and college have received some attention in recent years, this issue has not been adequately addressed in the context of athletics. Few high school or collegiate athletic programmes, administrators, or coaches are prepared to fairly, systematically, and effectively facilitate a transgender student's interest in participating in a sport. The majority of school sport programmes have no policy governing the inclusion of transgender student athletes. In fact, most school athletic programmes are unprepared to address even basic accommodations such as knowing what pronouns or names to use when referring to a transgender student, where a transgender student should change clothes for practice or competition, or what bathroom or shower that student should use.

In response to this need, the National Center for Lesbian Rights Sports Project and the Women's Sports Foundation initiative "It Takes a Team! Education Campaign for Lesbian, Gay, Bisexual and Transgender Issues in Sport" convened a national think tank in October 2009 called "Equal Opportunities for Transgender Student Athletes". Think tank participants included leaders from the National Collegiate Athletic Association (NCAA) and the National High School Federation, transgender student athletes, and an impressive array of experts on transgender issues from a range of disciplines – including law, medicine, advocacy, and athletics (Griffin and Carroll, 2010).

Think tank participants were committed to a set of guiding principles based on core values of inclusion, fairness, and equal opportunity in sport. The think tank goals were to develop model policies and identify best practices for high school and collegiate athletic programmes to ensure the full inclusion of transgender student athletes.

In October 2010, the think tank released a report titled *On the Team: Equal Opportunity for Transgender Student Athletes*. In August 2011, the National Collegiate Athletic Association (NCAA) published an organizational policy and best practices guide about the inclusion of transgender collegiate student athletes, which it distributed to its 1,200 member institutions across the country. It is important for school-based athletic leaders to learn about the basic issues facing transgender students so they can adopt and implement inclusive policies).

What does 'transgender' mean?

'Transgender' describes an individual whose gender identity (one's internal psychological identification as a boy/man, girl/woman, or neither) does not match the person's sex at birth. For example, a male-to-female (MTF) transgender woman or girl is someone who was born with a male body, but who identifies as a girl or a woman. A female-to-male (FTM) transgender man or boy is someone who was born with a female body, but who identifies as a boy or a man (Gender Spectrum: 2). Some transgender people choose to share the fact that they are transgender with others. Other transgender people prefer to keep the fact that they are transgender private.

It is important that other people recognize and respect a transgender person's identification as a man or a woman. In order to feel comfortable and express their gender identities to other people, transgender people may take a variety of steps, including: changing their names and self-referencing pronouns to better match their gender identity; choosing clothes, hairstyles, or other aspects of self-presentation that reflect their gender identity; and generally living and presenting themselves to others in a manner consistent with their gender identity. Some, but not all, transgender people take hormones or undergo surgical procedures to change their bodies to better reflect their gender identity.

An increasing number of high school and college-aged young people are identifying as transgender or another gender identity that does not conform to typical notions of gender as fixed or binary. For example, some young people identify as gender fluid, meaning that their gender identity may change from day to day; genderqueer or non-binary, meaning they do not identify themselves according to the typical gender binary; or agender, meaning that they do not identify with any gender. These students challenge educators to rethink an understanding of gender as binary or fixed at birth. Educators must be open to this challenge to create educational institutions that value and meet the needs of all students. Once we recognize that these young people are part of school communities across the United States, educational leaders have a responsibility to ensure that they have access to equal opportunities in all academic and extracurricular activities in a safe and respectful school environment.

Some people are confused by the difference between transgender people and people who have intersex conditions. Apart from having a gender identity that is different than their bodies, transgender people are not born with physical characteristics that distinguish them from others. In contrast, people with intersex conditions (which may also be called 'Differences of Sex Development'), are born with physically mixed or atypical bodies with respect to sexual characteristics such as chromosomes, internal reproductive organs and genitalia, and external genitalia (Intersex Society of North America, 2008). An estimated one in 2,000 people are born with an anatomy or chromosome pattern that does not fit typical definitions of male or female. The conditions that cause these variations are sometimes grouped under the terms 'intersex' or 'DSD' (Disorders of Sex Development) (Advocates for Informed Choice: 1).

Most people with intersex conditions clearly identify as male or female and do not experience confusion or ambiguity about their gender identities. In fact, most intersex conditions are not visible, and many intersex people are unaware of having an intersex condition unless it is discovered during medical procedures or as part of 'gender verification testing' for female athletes. Though there may be some similar issues related to sports participation between transgender and intersex individuals, there are also significant differences. This chapter will focus on the participation of transgender people in sports.

Why address transgender issues in school sport programmes?

Core values of equal opportunity and inclusion demand that educational leaders adopt thoughtful and effective policies that enable all students to participate fully in school athletic programmes. Schools have learned over the past years the value and necessity of accommodating the sport participation interests of students of colour, girls and women, students with disabilities, and lesbian, gay, and bisexual students. These are all issues of basic fairness and equity that demand the expansion of our thinking about equal opportunity in sports. The right of transgender students to participate in sports calls for similar considerations of fairness and equal access.

Addressing the needs of transgender students is an important, emerging equal opportunity issue that must be taken seriously by school leaders. Because a more complex understanding of gender may be new and challenging for some people, there is a danger that misinformation and stereotypes will guide policy decisions rather than accurate and up-to-date information. Athletic leaders who are charged with policy development need guidance to avoid creating policies based on misconceptions and misinformation that, ultimately, create more problems than they solve.

Why focus on high school and college sport?

Providing equal opportunities in all aspects of school programming is a core value in education. As an integral part of educational institutions, high school and college sport programmes are responsible and accountable for reflecting the goals and values of the educational institutions of which they are a part. It follows that school athletic programmes must reflect the value of equal opportunity in all policies and practices.

Sport programmes affiliated with educational institutions have a responsibility, beyond those of adult amateur or professional sports programmes, to look beyond the value of competition to promote broader educational goals of participation, inclusion, and equal opportunity. Because high schools and colleges must be committed to those broader educational goals, they should not unthinkingly adopt policies developed for adult Olympic and highly elite athletes. Recognizing the need to address the participation of transgender athletes, a few leading international and professional sport-governing organizations had developed policies based on overly stringent, invasive, and rigid medical requirements. These policies were not workable or advisable for high school and college athletes for a number of reasons.

For example, in 2004 the International Olympic Committee (IOC) developed a policy addressing the eligibility of transgender athletes to compete in IOC sanctioned events (International Olympic Committee, 2003: 1). While the IOC deserved credit for its pioneering effort to address the inclusion of transgender athletes, medical experts have since identified serious flaws in the IOC policy, especially its requirement of genital reconstructive surgery, which lacks a well-founded medical or policy basis. The IOC policy was reviewed and updated in 2015 to remove the surgery requirement and require one year of hormone treatment for the male to female transgender participant instead of the two-year regulation. Most transgender people – even as adults – do not have genital reconstructive surgery, which can be very costly and is rarely covered by insurance (Grant *et al.*, 2011). In addition, whether a transgender person has genital reconstructive surgery has no bearing on his or her athletic ability. The IOC policy also fails to provide sufficient protections for the privacy and dignity of transgender athletes. Because of these serious flaws, high schools and colleges should not adopt or look to the IOC policy as a model (Dreger, 2010).

High school and college student athletes have needs that differ from those of adults. A core purpose of high school and college is to teach students how to participate and be good citizens in an increasingly diverse society, as well as how to interact respectfully with others. In addition, high school and college sporting programmes impose limits on how many years a student athlete can compete that do not exist in adult sporting competitions, where athletes can compete as long as their performances are viable or, in the case of most amateur sports, as long as they wish to.

High school and younger transgender students are also subject to different medical protocols than adults because of their age and physical and psychological development (Brill and Pepper, 2008). The World Professional Association for Transgender Health (WPATH) has established guiding medical protocols for transitioning – the process by which transgender people live consistent with their gender identities, and which may include treatments to have the person's physical presentation more closely align with his or her identity (2001). Those protocols vary based on the age and psychological readiness of the young person. For children and youth, transition typically consists entirely of permitting the child to dress, live, and function socially consistently with the child's gender identity. For youth who are approaching puberty, hormone blockers may be prescribed to delay puberty in order to prevent the youth from going through the traumatic experience of acquiring secondary sex characteristics that conflict with his or her core gender identity. For older youth, cross-gender hormones or even some sex-reassignment surgeries may be prescribed. Given these different stages of emotional and physical development, it is essential that policies related to transgender athletes are tailored to the ages of the participants.

Should the participation of transgender student athletes on school teams raise concerns about competitive equity?

Concern about creating an 'unfair competitive advantage' on sex-separated teams is the primary reason administrators provide when they resist policies ensuring equal participation of transgender student athletes. This concern is cited most often in discussions about transgender women or girls competing on a women's or girls' team. Some advocates for gender equality in high school and college sports are concerned that allowing transgender girls or women – that is, male-to-female transgender athletes who were born male, but who identify as female – to compete on women's teams will take away opportunities for other girls and women, or that transgender girls or women will have a competitive advantage over other non-transgender competitors.

These concerns are based on three assumptions: One, that transgender girls and women are not 'real' girls or women and therefore do not deserve an equal competitive opportunity; two, that being born with a male body automatically gives a transgender girl or woman an unfair advantage when competing against non-transgender (cisgender) girls and women; and three, that boys or men might be tempted to pretend to be transgender in order to compete in competition with girls or women.

These assumptions are problematic for several reasons. First, the decision to transition from one gender to the other – to align one's external gender presentation with one's internal sense of gender identity – is a deeply significant and difficult choice that is made only after careful consideration and for the most compelling of reasons. Gender identity is a core aspect of a person's identity, and it is just as deep seated, authentic, and real for a transgender person as for others. For many transgender people, gender transition is a psychological and social necessity. It is essential that educators in and out of athletics understand this.

Second, while some people fear that transgender women will have an unfair advantage over non-transgender women, it is important to place that fear in context. When examined carefully, the realities underlying this issue are more complex than they may seem at first blush. The basis of this concern is that transgender girls or women who have gone through male puberty may have an unfair advantage due to the growth in long bones, muscle mass, and strength that is triggered by testosterone. However, a growing number of transgender youth are undergoing medically guided hormonal treatment prior to puberty, thus effectively neutralizing this concern. Increasingly, doctors who specialize in treating transgender people are prescribing hormone blockers to protect children who clearly identify as the other gender from the trauma of undergoing puberty in the wrong gender and acquiring unwanted secondary sex characteristics. When the youth is old enough to make an informed decision, he or she can choose whether to begin cross-gender hormones. Transgender girls who transition in this way do not go through a male puberty, and therefore their participation in athletics as girls does not raise the same equity concerns that might otherwise be present.

In addition, even transgender girls who do not access hormone blockers or cross-gender hormones display a great deal of physical variation, just as there is a great deal of natural variation in physical size and ability among non-transgender girls and boys. Many people may have a stereotype that all transgender girls and women are unusually tall and have large bones and muscles. But that is not true. A male-to-female transgender girl may be small and slight, even if she is not on hormone blockers or taking oestrogen. It is important not to over-generalize: the assumption that all male-bodied people are taller, stronger, and more highly skilled in a sport than all female-bodied people is not accurate and is often based on sex stereotyping. This assumption is especially unreliable when applied to youth, who are still developing physically and who therefore display a significantly broader range of variation in size, strength, and skill than older youth and adults.[1]

It is also important to know that any athletic advantages a transgender girl or woman arguably may have as a result of her prior testosterone levels dissipate after about one year of oestrogen therapy. According to medical experts, the belief that a transgender girl or woman competing on a women's team has a competitive advantage outside the range of performance and competitive advantage (or disadvantage) that already exists among female athletes is simply not supported by medical evidence (Wagman, 2009). As one survey of the existing research concludes, 'the data available does not appear to suggest that transitioned athletes would compete at an advantage or disadvantage as compared with physically born men and women' (Devries, 2008). Dr. Nick Gorton (2010) also found that 'transgender student athletes fall within the spectrum of physical traits found in athletes of their transitioned gender, allowing them to compete fairly and equitably' (Griffin and Carroll, 2010).

Dr. Nick Gorton, medical-legal consultant for transgender health care

Finally, fears that boys or men will pretend to be female to compete on a girls' or women's team are unwarranted given that in the entire 40-year history of 'sex verification' procedures in international sport competitions, no instances of such 'fraud' have been revealed (Buzuvis, 2011). Instead, 'sex verification' tests have been misused to humiliate and unfairly exclude women with intersex conditions (Simpson *et al.*, 2002). The apparent failure of such tests to serve their stated purpose of deterring fraud – and the terrible damage they have caused to individual women athletes – should be taken into account when developing policies for the inclusion of transgender athletes.

Rather than repeating the mistakes of the past, educators in high school and collegiate athletics programmes must develop thoughtful and informed policies that provide opportunities for all students, including transgender students, to participate in sports. These policies must be based on sound medical science, which shows that male-to-female transgender athletes do not have any automatic advantage over other women and girls. These policies must also be based on the educational values of sports and the reasons why sports are included as a vital component of the educational environment: promoting the physical and psychological well-being of all students, and teaching students the values of equality, participation, inclusion, teamwork, discipline, and respect for diversity.

What are the benefits of adopting inclusive policies and practices regarding transgender student athletes?

All stakeholders in high school and collegiate athletics will benefit from adopting fair and inclusive policies that enable transgender student athletes to participate on school sports teams. School-based sports, even at the most competitive levels, remain an integral part of the process of education and development of young people, especially emerging leaders in our society. Adopting fair and inclusive participation policies will allow school and athletic leaders to fulfil their commitment to create an environment in which all students can thrive, develop their full potential, and learn how to interact with persons from diverse groups.

Many schools and athletic departments identify diversity as a strength and have included sexual orientation and gender identity/expression in their non-discrimination policies. Athletic departments and personnel are responsible for creating and maintaining an inclusive and non-discriminatory climate in the areas they oversee. Adopting inclusive participation policies provides school athletic leaders with a concrete opportunity to fulfil that mandate, and to demonstrate their commitment to fair play and inclusion.

Moreover, when all participants in sport are committed to fair play, inclusion, and respect, student athletes are free to focus on performing their best in athletic competition and in the classroom. This climate promotes the well-being and achievement potential of all student athletes. Every student athlete and coach will benefit from meeting the challenge of overcoming fear and prejudice about social groups of which they are not members. This respect for difference will be invaluable to all student athletes as they graduate and enter an increasingly diverse workforce that requires people to work effectively and closely with people of varied and wide-ranging backgrounds (Griffin and Carroll, 2010)

What are the harmful, potential consequences of failing to adopt transgender-inclusive policies and practices?

When schools fail to adopt inclusive participation policies, they are not living up to the educational ideals of equality and inclusion, and may reinforce the image of athletics as a privileged activity not accountable to broad institutional and societal ideals of inclusion and respect for difference. Moreover, this failure puts schools, athletic conferences, and sport governing organizations at risk of costly discrimination lawsuits and negative media attention.

Failure to adopt inclusive participation policies also hurts non-transgender students by conveying a message that the values of non-discrimination and inclusion are less important than values based on competition and winning. Schools must model and educate about non-discrimination values in all aspects of school programming, not only for students, but for parents and community members as well.

Last but not least, failure to adopt policies that ensure equal opportunities for transgender student athletes may also result in costly and divisive litigation. A growing number of states and localities are adopting specific legal protections for transgender students. In addition, state and federal courts are increasingly applying sex discrimination laws to prohibit discrimination against transgender people.

Several studies show that schools are often hostile places for transgender students and other students who do not conform to stereotypical gender expectations (Greytak *et al.*, 2009). These students are frequently subjected to peer harassment and bullying which stigmatizes and isolates them. This mistreatment can lead to feelings of hopelessness, depression, and low self-esteem. When a school or athletic organization denies transgender students the ability to participate in sports because of their gender identity or expression, it condones, reinforces and affirms the students' social status as outsiders or misfits who somehow deserve the hostility they experience from peers.

Finally, the absence of transgender-inclusive policies and practices reinforces stereotypes and fears about gender diversity. When transgender students are stigmatized and excluded, even non-transgender students may experience pressure to conform to gender-role stereotypes as a way to avoid being bullied or harassed themselves (Griffin and Carroll, 2010).

Policy recommendations for including transgender student athletes

The below policies are recommended for competitive athletic participation on teams and in organized extramural competition, comprised of leagues with state and national championships, among high school and collegiate schools. It is recommended that participation within schools (intramural and recreational participation) be open to participants without discrimination on the basis of race, colour, religion, age, sex, sexual orientation, gender identity, gender expression or national origin and without the requirement of any medical intervention for transgender participants. Bates College of Lewiston, Maine adopted a model intramural/recreational policy in 2011 that encompasses these values: People participating in any intramural sports or other athletic programmes, such as physical education courses, may participate in accordance with their gender identity, should that be relevant, regardless of any medical treatment.

Guiding principles

In addition to the organization's stated values, it is recommended that the following principles be included in any transgender student athlete policy statement:

1   Participation in interscholastic and intercollegiate athletics is a valuable part of the education experience for all students.
2   Transgender student athletes should have equal opportunity to participate in sports.
3   The integrity of women's sports should be preserved.
4   Policies governing sports should be based on sound medical knowledge and scientific validity.
5   Policies governing sports should be objective, workable, and practical; they should also be written, available and equitably enforced.
6   The legitimate privacy interests of all student athletes should be protected.
7   The medical privacy of transgender students should be preserved.
8   Athletic administrators, staff, parents of athletes, and student athletes should have access to sound and effective educational resources and training related to the participation of transgender and gender-variant students in athletics.
9   Policies governing the participation of transgender students in athletics should comply with state and federal laws protecting students from discrimination based on sex, disability, and gender identity and expression.

(Griffin and Carroll, 2010)

Recommended policy for high school athletics

A transgender student athlete at the high school level shall be allowed to participate in a sports activity in accordance with his or her gender identity irrespective of the gender listed on the student's birth certificate or other student records, and regardless of whether the student has undergone any medical treatment. This policy shall not prevent a transgender student athlete from electing to participate in a sports activity according to his or her assigned birth gender.

Recommended policy for college athletics within the United States

A transgender student athlete participating at the elite intercollegiate competitive level should be allowed to participate in any sex-separated sports activity so long as that athlete's use of hormone therapy, if any, is consistent with the National Governing Body's (NGB) existing policies on banned medications. Specifically, a transgender student athlete should be allowed to participate in sex-separated sports activities under the following conditions:

I Transgender student athletes who are undergoing hormone treatment

1 A male-to-female (MTF) transgender student athlete who is taking medically prescribed hormone treatment related to gender transition may participate on a men's team at any time, but must complete one year of hormone treatment related to gender transition before competing on a women's team.[2]

2 A female-to-male (FTM) transgender student athlete who is taking medically prescribed testosterone related to gender transition may not participate on a women's team after beginning hormone treatment, and must request a medical exception from the National Governing Body (NGB) prior to competing on a men's team because testosterone is a banned substance.

3 A female-to-male (FTM) transgender student athlete who is taking medically prescribed testosterone for the purposes of gender transition may compete on a men's team.

4 In any case where a student athlete is taking hormone treatment related to gender transition, that treatment must be monitored by a physician, and the NGB must receive regular reports about the athlete's eligibility according to these guidelines.

II Transgender student athletes who are not undergoing hormone treatment

1 Any transgender student athlete who is not taking hormone treatment related to gender transition may participate in sex-separated

sports activities in accordance with his or her assigned birth gender.

2   A female-to-male transgender student athlete who is not taking testosterone related to gender transition may participate on a men's or women's team.

3   A male-to-female transgender student athlete who is not taking hormone treatments related to gender transition may not compete on a women's team.

(Carroll and Griffin, 2011)

The recommended U.S. collegiate transgender policy for participation of skilled, elite student athletes, which requires a male to female transitional time of one year of hormonal therapy and no surgery, allows for the maximum number of participants to become eligible within their playing career. International competition, including the Olympics, will use these standards and achieve a level playing field for all competitors throughout the world.

Notes

1 Assuming that boys have an automatic advantage over girls is particularly false with respect to pre-pubescent children, where gender plays virtually no role in determining relative athletic ability. For that reason, we strongly recommend that school and recreational sports adopt the policy recommended by the Transgender Law and Policy Institute and endorsed by Gender Spectrum. Transgender Law and Policy Institute, *Guidelines for Creating Policies for Transgender Children in Recreational Sports* (2009).

2 Recent research indicates that most salient physical changes likely to affect athletic performance occur during the first year of hormone treatment making a longer waiting period unnecessary. See Louis Goorin and Mathijs Bunck, 'Transsexuals and competitive sports', *European Journal of Endocrinology* 151 (2004): 425–429 www.eje.org/cgi/reprint/151/4/425.pdf.

References

Buzuvis, E. (2011) 'Transgender Student-Athletes and Sex-Segregated Sport: Developing Policies of Inclusion for Intercollegiate and Interscholastic Athletics', *Seton Hall Journal of Sports and Entertainment Law* 21:1 (2011): 1–59 http://law.shu.edu/Students/academics/journals/sports-entertainment/upload/Buzuvis-Transgender-Athletes-3.pdf

Devries, M. (2008) 'Do Transitioned Athletes Compete at an Advantage or Disadvantage?' Available at: www.caaws.ca/e/resources/pdfs/Devries_lit_review(2).pdf

Goorin, L. and Mathijs, B. (2004) 'Transsexuals and Competitive Sports', *European Journal of Endocrinology* 151 (2004): 425–429. Available at: www.eje.org/cgi/reprint/151/4/425.pdf

Griffin, P. and Carroll, H. (2010) 'On the Team: Equal Opportunity for Transgender Students'. Available at: www.nclrights.org/wp-content/uploads/2013/07/TransgenderStudent...

Griffin, P. and Carroll, H. (2011) 'NCAA Inclusion of Transgender Athletes'. Available at: www.ncaapublications.com/p-4335-ncaa-inclusion-of-transgender...

IOC Consensus Meeting on Sex Reassignment and Hyperandrogenism – Guidelines for Transgender Athletes (2015). Available: document (pdf) posted on its website.

Transgender Law and Policy Institute (2009) 'Guidelines for Creating Policies for Transgender Children in Recreational Sports'. Available at: www.transgenderlaw.org/resources/TLPI_GuidlinesforCreatingPoliciesforTransChildreninRec-Sports.pdf

Wagman, B. (2009) 'Including Transitioning and Transitioned Athletes in Sport – Issues, Facts and Perspectives – Summary'. Available at: www.caaws.ca/e/resources/pdfs/Summary_Transition_Discussion_Paper_FINAL1%20(2).pdf

Women's Sports Foundation (2008) 'Participation of Transgender Athletes in Women's Sports: A Women's Sports Foundation Position Paper'. Available at: www.womenssportsfoundation.org/Content/Articles/Issues/Homophobia/T/Participation-of-Transgender Athletes.aspx

Chapter 13

Transgender athletes in elite sport competitions

Equity and inclusivity

Eric Vilain, Jonathan Ospina Betancurt, Nereida Bueno-Guerra and Maria Jose Martinez-Patiño

I Introduction

People who are both transgender and elite athletes represent a very small fraction of the total population. Although it is difficult to establish how many individuals identify as transgender, studies suggest a prevalence between 0.2 percent and 0.5 percent (California Department of Finance 2007; Conron *et al.* 2012; Gates 2011; Reed *et al.* 2009; Horton 2008). Although numbers are again difficult to determine, elite competition sport is an activity enjoyed by a very small number of individuals who exhibit both the talent and desire to pursue them. This makes the probability that a transgender person becomes an active elite athlete extremely small. Nevertheless, a number of visible transgender athletes have emerged, starting with American tennis player Renée Richards in the 1970s. Thus, policies need to address their inclusion.

Designing sports policies that address both issues of inclusion and equity is a complex challenge, however. The objective of this chapter is to analyze transgender participation in elite competition sports with special emphasis on Male-To-Female who have hormonally transitioned. While definitions vary widely, and transgender is an umbrella term; for purposes of this chapter when we say transgender it is this category of people to whom we refer. We select this population because these cases yield more issues from the perspective of equity principle in female competitions than others.

II Justification for sexual segregation in sports

Sport is an activity that takes place in a social framework and is therefore socially constructed, complete with stereotypes and assumptions about identity, behavior and rules from society (Anderson 2009). One of these rules is the principle of non-discrimination, which is recognized in the Universal Declaration of Human Rights and is reflected in the majority of the constitutions of the world. The Olympic Charter, in its Fundamental Principles of Olympism also sets that

The practice of sport is a human right. Every individual must have the possibility of practicing sport, without discrimination of any kind and in the Olympic spirit, which requires mutual understanding with a spirit of friendship, solidarity and fair play

(IOC 2015b)

This integrative spirit has not always been present and has certainly been unevenly practiced. One of the main manifestations of sexual discrimination in sport has been the prohibition or the social and cultural ban on women playing certain sports that were considered inappropriate for their gender. Indeed, women had to wait until the year 1900 and the Paris games to be allowed to participate in the Olympics, and even then in very few events. It would take another 84 years before they were permitted to run the Olympic marathon (Hargreaves and Anderson 2014). From a historical perspective, female participation in sports was groundbreaking in the fight against sexual discrimination if it is compared to the right to vote. Inclusion of women in sports was accompanied by a consensual sex segregation, where men and women compete separately (Anderson, 2008). An increasing number of scholars are asking if this separation constitutes a new form of discrimination (for example, Joseph and Anderson 2015; Travers 2008, 2013)

The underlying goal of sex-segregated competition is purportedly to establish a fair competition (term known as "fair play") given that the alternative of a competition without sex segregation would put women at a disadvantage. One alternative would be to establish different competition categories (Tännsjö 2000; Schneider 2000; Wiesemann 2011), selecting criteria and imposing handicaps that would place athletes in categories other than sex and compensate for a range of natural performance advantages relating to weight and height. Practically, this might be difficult to design a fair system with these characteristics; although fight sports, wrestling, and some youth team sports manage to do this successfully. Despite these examples, public opinion seems to dictate that there should be only two competition categories: male and female, and this division is falsely seen to ensure fairness in competition based on the difference in athletic abilities due to the different amount of lean body mass (LBM) for each sex.

However imperfect the division into male and female categories at elite competition level is, it implies that all competitors wishing to participate in these sporting events must be included in either of the two categories. A regulating mechanism therefore effectively guarantees that female competition only involves women and male competition only involves men. This regulatory mechanism clashes with the complexity of human sexual and gender diversity that makes it difficult to maintain a strict binary division in modern sports.

III The eligibility criteria to compete in the female category

Sex categorization, from a medical perspective, is simultaneously ideological in that there are vast differences between members of one sex; in that there exists a mean average difference between males and females. Regardless of its complexity, it was the first strategy used by international sports agencies when, in 1946, the first rules in this matter were established (Heggie 2010). The main obstacle of biological characterization of sex is that there is not one unique physiological marker that clearly defines sex. The emphasis can be put on chromosomes, gonads, hormones, secondary sexual characteristics or the appearance of external or internal genitalia. If one takes into account that gender is also a psychological, cultural and social concept, achieving a simplified definition that allows a clear distinction between subjects to meet the sexual binary concept is challenging.

The problem of such plurality of sex markers is that none of them is conclusive. The simplest solution would be to establish what should be the best criteria, and indeed that was what the international sports authorities have attempted to do. This approach is not without critique, but the goal has been to establish, in each historical time and according to the state of scientific knowledge, a different criterion to declare an athlete eligible for a female sports competition.

The International Olympic Committee (IOC) and the International Association of Athletics Federations (IAAF) were the pioneering agencies in establishing these policies. Both organizations adopted policies that until the year 1991 for the IAFF (Pieper 2016, 151) and until the year 1999 for the IOC (Simpson *et al.* 2000) established a definition of woman based on medical criteria, as explained by Yamaguchi *et al.* (1992). The evolution of the rules, defining criteria and techniques used in each verification is summarized in Table 13.1.

However, this initial regulatory framework was questionable. For years, the eligibility of the athletes based on genetic tests meant the exclusion of many women with XY chromosomes (paradoxically, it would have allowed men with XX chromosomes, a known condition, to compete with women). However, the chromosome testing did not take into account that, in many cases, XY women also displayed complete insensitivity to androgens, and because of that, did not have a clear advantage in their sports performance, since testosterone, a major factor contributing to athletic capability, was not functionally active. The fight to exclude the genetic marker as a single measure was complex and dramatic. Maria Patiño, a Spanish hurdler, and co-author of this chapter, was a passionate pioneer in this fight. Her determination against this policy led to the establishment of a new paradigm of eligibility that would respond to the principle of fairness and allow for sexual segregation in athletics based on markers

Table 13.1 Evolution of the sex testing and gender verification policy

Year	Event	Rule/policy	Description
1946	IAAF	Official IAAF Certificate	All athletes registering in an event regulated by the IAAF should submit a letter from their physician certifying the sex to which they belonged, making them eligible in the sport
1948	IOC	Identity Cards	
1966	European Athletics Championships	"Nude Parades"	All athletes should appear nude in front of a medical panel, who performed a visual inspection of their genitalia and decided if they were or were not eligible to compete
1967	European Cup Athletics	Sex chromatin test	Barr Body Test: Examination of cells from the buccal mucosa shows a chromatin mass and the Barr bodies, which probably represent an inactive X chromosome attached to the nuclear membrane in most female cells
1968	Olympic Games Mexico City	Women's Medical Examination	
1972	Olympic Games Munich	Sex control	
1976	Montreal Olympic Games	Femininity testing	
1980	Olympic Games Moscow	Femininity testing	
1984	Olympic Games the Angeles	Gender verification	
1988	Olympic Games Seoul	Gender verification	
1991	IAAF	**End of sex testing/gender verification from IAAF**	
1992	Olympic Games Barcelona	Gender control	Polymerase Chain Reaction (PCR Test):
1996	Olympic Games Atlanta	Gender verification	To check the presence or absence of the Y and chromosome
1999	IOC	**End of sex testing/gender verification from IOC**	

Source: Martínez Patiño *et al.* (2010), Sánchez *et al.* (2013).

relevant to sports, and not defining male or female identity (Martínez-Patiño 2005; Martínez-Patiño *et al.* 2016).

The shift, from a medical perspective, with a search for a genetic diagnosis to a sports-related perspective for the best biological marker eventually lead to the end of gender verification policies. The transition was neither easy nor quick. Sports authorities began a period of reflection that lasted for years.

Gender verification policies were not immediately replaced by others. There was indeed a no-policy gap after the IOC announced that, during the Olympic Games of Sydney 2000, there would be no gender verification (Lager 2011, 189). That decision was celebrated by the former President of the Medical Commission of the IOC and the IAAF, Arne Ljungqvist, in a letter written to his colleagues and researchers (eg Carlson, of la Chapelle, Ehrhardt, Ferguson-Smith, Ferris, Genel and Simpson), as Lindsay Parks Pieper remarked: "Victory is finally ours, the genetic based test for screening for female gender at the Olympic Games has gone into the history books!" (Pieper 2016, 179).

A path was opened for a new paradigm. If sex segregation in sports competition is justified in maintaining equity for the difference in performance between the sexes, then, rather than finding a marker linked to the medical definition of sex, the attempt of a solution was to determine the triggering factor for this difference in athletic performance, and to focus on the anabolic hormone testosterone. Thus, for example, in the "*IAAF Policy on Gender Verification*," prepared by the IAAF Medical and Anti-Doping Commission (IAAF 2006), this criterion was already underscored when pointing to the genetic conditions that do not represent any competitive advantage for women in comparison with other athletes: these conditions are: (i) Androgen Insensitivity Syndrome (AIS and PAIS); (ii) Gonadal dysgenesis; and (iii) Turner's syndrome.

This regulation established that certain conditions, which may mean some competitive advantage, were accepted: (i) Congenital adrenal hyperplasia; (ii) Androgen producing tumors; and (iii) Anovulatory androgen excess (polycystic ovary syndrome). During the long regulation gap after 1999, a new case resulted in a turning point. The South African athlete Caster Semenya was investigated in the 12th IAAF World Championships in Athletics in Berlin, in 2009, because her marks had been suspiciously superior to those of her rivals, and because her physical appearance was perceived as too virile. Accordingly, she was temporarily suspended from competition. The results of a subsequent investigation were not disclosed to the public, but some information leaked to the Australian media suggested that her androgens levels, i.e., testosterone, were above the range average for women (Wells and Darnell 2014). The suspension was subsequently lifted and a new approach to eligibility started to be analyzed.

Even though there is scientific recognition that the difference in performance between men and women responds to multiple biological, environmental and socio-economic factors, a major factor was deemed responsible: functional testosterone (Handelsman and Gooren 2008; Tucker and Collins 2010; Sánchez et al. 2013). Before puberty, both sexes have similar levels of testosterone and also a similar body composition. At the onset of puberty, however, the male body produces significant amounts of testosterone (mostly from the testicles), while the female body produces considerably smaller amounts, from the adrenal glands and ovaries. The increase of testosterone levels at male puberty (up to ten times more than in female puberty) causes boys to acquire significantly more muscle mass than girls, which results in a significant physical advantage for men. This laid down the foundations for the new regulations on "hyperandrogenism" (cases of women who have increased levels of testosterone) and was used by IAAFs in their 2011 Regulations, by IOC for the Olympic Games in London in 2012 (IOC 2012) and in Sochi 2014 (IOC 2014). These regulations established that eligibility would depend on the level of androgens naturally produced by the athlete and their sensitivity to these androgens. High levels of androgens crossing the male range, that the IAAF set at 10 nmol/L, and a full sensitivity to them, which would imply the absence of inhibition of its potential effects on sport performance, determined that the athlete will become ineligible for female competition. This ineligibility would last as long as those levels remained in the male range. This new paradigm was also used later in the design of specific sports policies on transgender eligibility.

IV The eligibility of MTF transgender athletes: regulations on sex verification of the consensus of Stockholm (2003) and gender reassignment (2015)

While the controversy over the best marker to distinguish men and women was raging, sports authorities faced a new challenge: the case of transgender athletes. Let's begin with Female-to-Male (FTM) transgender athletes who have typically not posed a real eligibility problem in male competitions, since their natal body does not have an increased muscle advantage on their future male competitors. Therefore, there were no formal eligibility tests for male competitions and no sports equity problems have arisen in terms of access of FTM athletes. However, it is a different picture from the anti-doping perspective.

The hormone treatment for the transition of woman to man involves the supply of exogenous androgens, a prohibited substance in sports. The World Anti-Doping Agency (WADA) allows Therapeutic Use Exemptions (TUE) and has addressed the case of athletes who make the transition from Female to Male: "Medical Information to Support the Decisions of TUECs

– Female to Male Transsexual Athletes" (WADA 2016). In order not to interfere with a personal process of sex change, WADA has established that the substances reducing the levels of testosterone supplied to the athletes who make the MTF transition (e.g., estrogen and antiandrogens) are not prohibited in sport, and do not require authorization or monitoring from WADA.

In these cases, WADA authorizes testosterone treatment to FTM athletes since its use is fundamental for improving the quality of life of these athletes as well as their health, preventing the decrease of bone density. Dose and method of administration should be regulated or supervised by staff physicians and all records should be available for a possible review at any time. In this case, the TUE ensures that FTM athletes have similar androgen levels to those of eugonadal men, (the TUE application form can be found at www.wada-ama.org/en/resources/therapeutic-use-exemption-tue/tue-application-template).

Thus, transgender FTM individuals can typically be granted a TUE and use testosterone, and there are no grounds for restriction on their eligibility. However, the case of transgender MTF athletes is different. The verification of sex based on chromosomal testing would render any MTF athlete ineligible, which was historically the case. However, in 2003, a specific policy for the eligibility of transgender MTF athletes was adopted by the IOC, which convened a group of seven experts (mainly geneticists, physiologists and endocrinologists) who signed the "Statement of the Stockholm Consensus on Sex Reassignment in Sports" (IOC 2003). This document established the conditions that should be met by MTF trans athletes to participate in elite competition. These requirements were different depending on whether the sex reassignment happened before or after puberty, since in the former, the athlete would not have developed and trained with a male body, which could not have conferred advantages in competing with other women. For these athletes, it stated that "individuals undergoing sex reassignment of male to female before puberty should be regarded as girls and women." For the latter, on the other hand, the demands were that

> (i) surgical anatomical changes have been completed, including external genitalia changes and gonadectomy; (ii) legal recognition of their assigned sex have been conferred by the appropriate official authorities; and (iii) appropriate for the assigned sex hormone therapy has been administered in a verifiable manner and for a sufficient length of time to minimise gender-related advantages in sport competitions.

The IAAF, meanwhile, approved in 2006 the "IAAF Policy on Gender Verification," prepared by the IAAF Medical and Anti-Doping Commission, established for cases of "reconstructive surgery and sex reassignment" that

(i) sex change operations as well as appropriate hormone replacement therapy are performed before puberty then the athlete is allowed to compete as a female; (ii) if the sex change and hormone therapy is done after puberty then the athlete has to wait two years after gonadectomy before to physical and endocrinological evaluation is conducted (The crux of the matter is that the athlete should not be enjoying the benefits of natural testosterone predominance normally seen in a male).

These policies were both considered social progress, allowing a path along which transgender athletes could compete, but they were also quite restrictive, with some conditions very difficult to achieve (e.g., a legal change of sex is impossible in many countries, and surgical sex reassignment is not the only way to lower levels of androgens). Despite the strict framework of the regulations, some transgender athletes were able to make the transition, and be admitted for competition at national and international levels. Kye Allums was the first publicly transgender person to play NCAA Div. 1 college basketball (Zeigler 2010).

Limitations of the Stockholm Consensus of 2003 and the IAAF Policy of 2006 were overcome in the IOC Medical & Scientific Commission experts' meeting of 2015 upon approval of the "IOC Consensus Meeting on Sex Reassignment and Hyperandrogenism" (IOC 2015a). The meeting was attended by 20 experts, including for the first time, a former athlete and transwoman, Dr. Joanna Harper, who had not stopped training and competing after her transition (Harper 2015). In the year 2015, the regulation on hyperandrogenism had already been consolidated regarding the eligibility for female competitions and was exclusively based on functional (i.e., active) testosterone levels. This new paradigm was used in improving the MTF transgender participation rules in elite sports competitions.

The IOC Consensus Meeting of 2015 tried to find a balance between the demands of equity in sport and the exclusion and discrimination situation endured by transgender athletes, including the impossibility of legal recognition of their change of gender in many countries of the world. The spirit of sports equity led to include a sole requirement for eligibility as a testosterone level below the natal male range, setting it below 10 nmol/L. To increase inclusiveness and relevance to performance, the surgical requirement of reassignment was removed, as well as the legal requirement.

The recommendations of the IOC Consensus Meeting on Sex Reassignment and Hyperandrogenism in 2015 read as follows:

1   Those who transition from female to male are eligible to compete in the male category without restriction.

2   Those who transition from male to female are eligible to compete in the female category under the following conditions:

2.1 The athlete has declared that her gender identity is female. The declaration can not be changed, for sporting purposes, for a minimum of four years.

2.2 The athlete must demonstrate that her total testosterone level in serum have been below 10 nmol/L for at least 12 months prior to her first competition (with the requirement for any longer period to be based on to confidential case-by-case evaluation, considering whether or not 12 months is a sufficient length of time to minimize any advantage in women's competition).

2.3 The athlete's total testosterone level in serum must remain below 10 nmol/L through out the period of desired eligibility to compete in the female category.

2.4 Compliance with these conditions may be monitored by testing. "In the event of non-compliance, the athlete's eligibility for female competition will be suspended for 12 months.

V The bases of the transgender eligibility criteria

Just as in the regulation on hyperandrogenism, the underlying rationale of the specific recommendations on eligibility for MTF transgender athletes is based on the identification of testosterone as the decisive factor to differentiate sports performance between men and women; although there is an ongoing debate about whether there is enough direct evidence of the effect of *endogenous* testosterone on sports performance.

The evidence underlying these recommendations can be found in several studies. Gooren and Bunk (2004) have shown that the hormone treatment supplied to patients who want to make MTF transition (i) decreased their levels of testosterone in plasma to castration levels, in such a way that MTF Serum testosterone (nmol/L) before treatment 21.5 +/-5.8 and MTF Serum testosterone (nmol/L) after treatment 1.0 +/-0.0; and (ii) significantly reduced muscle mass of the patient after one year of treatment (see Table 1 in Gooren and Bunck 2004). Major changes in serum testosterone level in the Gooren and Bunck study happened only after one year of hormone treatment and without performing sex reassignment surgery. This may be one of the reasons why the new recommendations established for MTF transgender eligibility, requested that levels of testosterone lower than 10 nmol/L be maintained in the last 12 months only.

The results of low testosterone levels in MTF transgender undergoing hormone therapy are shown in other studies (T'Sjoen *et al.* 2008). In a cross-sectional study with 50 individuals who made the transition from MTF with the SRS, the results of serum testosterone levels were

33 +/– 12 ng/dL (33 ng/dL = 1.1451 nmol/L) (see Table 1 of the study). The T'Sjoen study shows that anti-androgen hormone therapy supplied to MTF individuals produces: (i) loss of muscle mass, (ii) increase in fat mass, and (iii) decrease in bone mineral density. Research ensures that all these changes in the MTF transgender are produced in the first phase of the hormonal treatment (from month 6 to month 12). In addition, it shows that they are comparable to those changes produced in patients with treatments for the prostate cancer or after castration (T'Sjoen et al. 2008). In other words, a period of two years is not necessary to bring hormonal levels into compliance. Given that athletic careers are short, a year is more reasonable.

VI How does the suspension on hyperandrogenism regulations affect the rules on transgender athletes' eligibility?

The new paradigm for female competitions eligibility was that the level of functional testosterone in blood be below the male range. This is the base for the regulations on hyperandrogenism – IOC 2012 and 2014 and IAAF 2011 – and also the IOC Consensus Meeting on Sex Reassignment and Hyperandrogenism in 2015.

This paradigm was recently challenged however. Hyperandrogenism regulations were applied to the Indian athlete Dutee Chand in 2014, who was declared ineligible because of having androgens functional levels above 10 nmol/L. The matter was taken to the Court of Arbitration for Sport (CAS), with a request to declare the regulation on hyperandrogenism of the IAFF of 2011 invalid and null because it (i) was a discriminatory regulation targeting only women athletes; (ii) it is based on the false premise that there is a relationship between testosterone and athletic performance; and (iii) is disproportionate with regard to any legitimate objective of equity to attain.

CAS, in the Interim arbitral award of July 24 of 2015-CAS 2014/A/3759, Dutee Chand v. Athletics Federation of India (AFI) and The International Association of Athletics Federations (IAAF), argued that the rules on hyperandrogenism was not in proportion to the legitimate goal of maintaining equity in female sport. CAS agrees that an athlete with a functional testosterone level above 10 nmol/L has a competitive advantage over the other female athletes. That advantage, however, is derived from natural production of hormones for her body. Therefore, what is relevant for her ineligibility is not that greater level of testosterone produces greater performance, but that it does so in levels comparable to those enjoyed by male athletes above female athletes, which in the end is what justifies sexual segregation in sport. CAS concluded that there is not enough evidence that a functional level of testosterone in women of 10 nmol/L or more generates sport performance equivalent to that of a man, (i) "the Hyperandrogenism

Regulations are suspended for a period of not longer than two years from the date of this Interim Award"; and (ii)

> the International Association of Athletics Federations may, at any time within two years of the date of this Interim Award, submit further written evidence and expert reports to this Panel addressing the Panel's concerns concerning the Hyperandrogenism Regulations as set forth in this Interim Award and, in particular, the current degree of athletic performance advantage sustained by hyperandrogenic female athletes as compared to non-hyperandrogenic female athletes by reason of their high levels of testosterone

> (CAS 2015)

One controversial aspect of this decision of CAS, resulting in the suspension of the hyperandrogenism rule, is that it is based partly on the argument that the rule had failed to demonstrate that the *entirety* of the 10–12 percent performance difference between male in female athletes in track and field was caused by the difference of levels in testosterone between men and women. This part of the ruling is based on an improvable request of evidence. One would have to compare athletes for whom everything else than testosterone level is being equal (e.g., height, nutrition, socioeconomic status, geographical location, training), and show that only a difference of testosterone level will make a difference in performance.

The suspension is effective only for the regulation of the IAAF, and not for other federations nor the Olympics, but the IOC has decided to suspend the hyperandrogenisn rule while the CAS ruling comes to a conclusion after the two-year suspension. It also exclusively refers to the eligibility of the athletes with hyperandrogenism. It is not applicable to the MTF transgender athletes since these regulations were not subject to challenge. However, the reasoning behind the CAS ruling makes it difficult to differentiate, from a sports perspective, between a female-identified athlete who has testosterone in the male range because of an intersex condition or because she is a trans woman. For example, an XY athlete with 5 alpha reductase deficiency (and no androgen resistance), having gone through biologically male puberty, having levels of testosterone well in the male range, having other male characteristics (such as osteological parameters) and identifying as a women, would be able to compete in the male category. A MTF trans woman, who also has XY sex chromosomes, who also went through male puberty, would still have to abide by a different rule that is there just for transgender athletes, requiring them to have levels of testosterone less than the male range for at least a year. Both rules seem incompatible with each other. In other words, if the hyperandrogenism rule becomes invalid, there is little legitimate reason to keep the rule on MTF trans athletes, which is solely based on hyperandrogenism. The

CAS decision is therefore likely a prelude to a challenge to the rules on eligibility of the MTF transgender athletes, leaving only the declaration of gender as the sole criteria, without the need for any biological marker.

At the time writing, and despite the expectation generated in the 2016 Rio Games, there is no evidence of any self-identified transgender athlete who has reached the Olympic sport elite. The closest cases (who eventually did not qualify) are of two British MTF athletes who were about to become part of the British Olympic team (Manning and Gallagher 2016) and the Colombian transgender athlete Yanelle Zape Mendoza (Diaz Sanchez 2016). However, this is likely a reflection of, as stated at the beginning of the chapter, a nexus of both a low percent of the population that is trans, and a low percent of the population that is capable of elite level athletic performances. This is not to say that we will not be, eventually, faced with an Olympic medalist who has declared him/herself transgender.

VII Conclusion: sport equity and transgender inclusivity

The worlds of transgenderism and elite sports competition have not crossed paths historically. The social exclusion that transgender individuals have suffered remains very deep, and their relationship with elite competition is no exception. Social and legal discrimination of transgender individuals and the legal restrictions on the recognition of the change of sex prevented any transgender athlete from being eligible by sports authorities for a sexual category that was not congruent with the biological one.

However, recent regulations have opened the possibility for transgender individuals to participate in elite level sports. From a sporting point of view, this chapter highlights that it is difficult to always balance inclusiveness and fairness. Would a transgender (MTF) athlete whose reassignment has occurred after puberty be able to compete fairly after a one-year testosterone level reduction? The question is not simple and it can give rise to controversy in certain situations in which the MTF trans athlete has had an intensive athletic training, developed in accordance with their biological sex. Studies show that lower testosterone will result in a significant reduction of muscle mass after a year of treatment. However, the recent challenge to the hyperandrogenism rule may lead to an eligibility based exclusively on gender declaration, leaving the door open for anatomically and biologically male athletes to compete in the female category, which would raise questions of fairness vis à vis other natal female athletes.

Sports authorities will thus continue to face the difficult challenge of balancing the values of equity and inclusiveness in an increasingly gender diverse world.

References

Anderson, E. "'I Used To Think Women Were Weak': Orthodox Masculinity, Gender-Segregation and Sport." *Sociological Forum*, 2(23) (2008): 257–280.

Anderson, E. *Sport Theory and Social Problems: A Critical Introduction.* Routledge: London, 2009.

California Department of Finance. "Race/Ethnic Population with Age and Sex Detail, 2000–2050." (2007) (accessed September 10, 2016).

Conron, K., G. Scott, G. Stowel and S. Landers. "Transgender Health in Massachusetts: Results From a Household Probability Sample of Adults." *American Journal of Public Health* 102(1) (2012): 118–122.

Court of Arbitration for Sports. "CAS 2014/A/3759 Dutee Chand v. Athletics Federation of India (AFI) & The International Association of Athletics Federations (IAAF)." July 24, 2015. www.tas-cas.org/fileadmin/user_upload/award_internet. pdf (accessed August 13, 2016).

Díaz, S. W. "Primera Transexual En Juegos Olímpicos Podría Ser Colombiana." El Colombiano. February 23, 2016. www.elcolombiano.com/deportes/otros-deportes/ en-su-segundavida-yanelle-persigue-un-hito-AE3633417 (accessed August 13, 2016).

Dörner, G., W. Rohde, I. Poppe, R. Lindner, R. Weltrich, L. Pfeiffer and H. Peters. "Aspectos etiogénitocos de la homosexualidad y de la transexualidad." In La evolución de la sexualidad y los estados intersexuales, by J. Botella Llusía and A. Fernández de Molina, 340. Madrid: Ediciones Díaz de Santos, S. A., 1998.

Gates, G. J. "How Many People Are Lesbian, Gay, Bisexual, And Transgender?" The Williams Institute, UCLA School of Law. April 2011. http://williams institute.law.ucla.edu/wp-content/uploads/Gates-How-Many-People-LGBT-Apr-2011.pdf (accessed August 20, 2016).

Gooren, L. J. G., C. Mathijs and M. Bunck. "Transsexuals and Competitive Sports." *European Journal of Endocrinology* 151 (2004): 425–429.

Handelsman, D. J. and L. J. Gooren. "Hormones and Sport: Physiology, Pharmacology & Forensic Science." *Asian Journal of Andrology* 10(3) (2008): 348–350.

Hargreaves, J. and E. Anderson (eds.). *Routledge Handbook of Sport Gender and Sexuality.* Routledge: London, 2014.

Harper, J. "Do Transgender Athletes Have An Edge? I Sure Don't." *Washington Post.* April 1, 2015. www.washingtonpost.com/opinions/do-transgender-athletes- have-an-edge-i-sure-dont/2015/04/01/ccacb1da-c68e-11e4-b2a1-bed1aaea2816_ story.html?utm_term=.8321b6d09970 (accessed August 12, 2016).

Heggie, V. "Testing Sex and Gender in Sports; Reinventing, Reimagining and Reconstructing Histories." *Endeavour* 34(4) (2010): 157–163.

Horton, M. A. "The Incidence and Prevalence of SRS among US." September 2008. www.tgender.net/taw/thb/THBPrevalence-OE2008.pdf (accessed September 10, 2016).

"IAAF Regulations Governing Eligibility of Females Athletes with Hyperandrogenism to Compete in Women's Competition." May 1, 2011. www.iaaf.org/news/iaaf- news/iaaf-to-introduce-eligibility-rules-for-femal-1 (accessed August 12, 2016).

International Association of Athletics Federations. "IAAF Policy on Gender Verification." November 12, 2006. https://oii.org.au/wp-content/uploads/2009/01/ iaaf_policy_on_gender_verification.pdf (accessed August 14, 2016).

International Olympic Committee (IOC). "Statement of the Stockholm Consensus on Sex Reassignment in Sports." October 28, 2003. https://stillmed.olympic.org/AssetsDocs/importednews/documents/en_report_905.pdf (accessed August 12, 2016).

"IOC Regulations on Female Hyperandrogenism." Games of the XXX Olympiad in London, 2012. June 22, 2012. https://stillmed.olympic.org/Documents/Commissions_PDFfiles/Medical_commission/2012-06-22-IOC-Regulations-on-Female-Hyperandrogenism-eng.pdf (accessed August 12, 2016).

"IOC Regulations on Female Hyperandrogenism." 2014. https://stillmed.olympic.org/Documents/Commissions_PDFfiles/Medical_commission/IOC-Regulations-on-Female-Hyperandrogenism.pdf (accessed August 21, 2016).

"IOC Consensus Meeting on Sex Reassignment and Hyperandrogenism." November 2015a. https://stillmed.olympic.org/media/Document%20Library/Olympic Org/IOC/Who-We-Are/Commissions/Medical-and-Scientific-Commission/EN-IOC-Consensus-Meeting-on-Sex-Reassignment-and-Hyperandrogenism.pdf#_ga =1.173370785.382628396.1465732304 (accessed August 12, 2016).

International Olympic Committee. "Olympic Charter." 2015b. https://stillmed.olympic.org/Documents/olympic_charter_en.pdf (accessed August 12, 2016).

Joseph, L. and E. Anderson. "The Influence of Gender Segregation and Teamsport Experience on Occupational Discrimination in Sport-based Employment." *Journal of Gender Studies* (2015) (online first).

Lager, G. *Doping's Nemesis: Arne Ljungqvist.* Cheltenham: Sports Books Limited, 2011.

Manning, S. and I. Gallagher. "Transgender British Athletes Born Male Set to Make Olympic History by Competing in the Games as Women." *The Daily Mail.* July 3, 2016. www.dailymail.co.uk/news/article-3671937/Transgender-British-athletes-born-men-set-make-Olympic-history-competing-gameswomen.html (accessed August 10, 2016).

Martínez, P., M. José *et al.* "An Approach to the Biological, Historical and Psychological Repercussions of Gender Verification in Top Level Competitions." *Journal of Human Sport and Exercise* 5(3) (2010): 307–321.

Martinez-Patiño, M. J. "Personal Account: A Woman Tried and Tested." *Lancet* 366 (2005): S38.

Martínez-Patiño, M. J., E. Vilain and N. Bueno-Guerra. "The Unfinished Race: 30 Years of Gender Verification in Sport." *The Lancet* 388(10044) (2016): 541–543.

Parliament of the United Kingdom. "Gender Recognition Act 2004." July 1, 2004. www.legislation.gov.uk/ukpga/2004/7/contents (accessed August 12, 2016).

Pieper, L. P. *Sex Testing: Gender Policing in Women's Sports.* Urbana: University of Illinois Press, 2016.

Reed, B., S. Rhodes, P. Schofield and K. Wylie. "Gender Variance in the UK: Prevelance, Incidence, Growth, and Geographic Distribution." June 2009. www.gires.org.uk/assets/Medpro-Assets/GenderVarianceUK-report.pdf (accessed September 10, 2016).

Sánchez, F. J., M. J. Martínez-Patiño, and E. Vilain. "The New Policy on Hyperandrogenism in Elite Female Athletes Is Not about Sex Testing." *Journal of Sex Research* 50(2) (2013): 112–115.

Schneider, A. J. "On the Definition of 'Woman' in the Sport Context." In *Values in Sport: Elitism, Nationalism, Gender Equality, and the Scientific Manufacturing of Winners*, C. M. Tamburrini and T. Tännsjö, 123–138. New York: Taylor & Francis, 2000.

Simpson, J. L. *et al.* "Gender Verification in the Olympics." *Journal of the American Medical Association* 284(12) (2000): 1568–1569.

Sullivan, C. F. "Gender Verification and Gender Policies in Elite Sport: Eligibility and 'Fair Play'." *Journal of Sport and Social Issues* 35(4) (2011): 400–419.

Tännsjö, T. "Against Sexual Discrimination in Sports." In *Values in Sport: Elitism, Nationalism, Gender Equality and the Scientific Manufacture of Winners*, by T. Tännsjö and C. M. Tamburrini, 101–115. New York: Taylor & Francis, 2000.

The World Professional Association for Transgender Health. "Standards of Care for the Health of Transsexual, Transgender, and Gender Nonconforming People." 2012. https://s3.amazonaws.com/amo_hub_content/Association140/files/Standards%20of%20Care%20V7%20-%202011%20WPATH%20(2)(1).pdf (accessed August 20, 2016).

T'Sjoen, G., S. Weyers, Y. Taes, B. Lapauw, G. S. Toye and J-M. Kaufman. "Prevalence of Low Bone Mass in Relation to Estrogen Treatment and Body Composition in Male-To-Female Transsexual Persons." *Journal of Clinical Densitometry* 12(3) (2008): 306–313.

Tucker, R. and M. Collins. "The Science of Sex Verification and Athletic Performance." *International Journal of Sports Physiology and Performance* 5 (2010): 127–139.

Wells, C. and S. C. Darnell. "Caster Semenya, Gender Verification and the Politics of Fairness in an Online Track & Field Community." *Sociology of Sport Journal* 31 (2014): 44–65.

Wiesemann, C. "Is There a Right Not to Know One's Sex? The Ethics of 'Gender Verification' in Women's Sports Competition." *Journal of Medical Ethics* 37 (2011): 216–220.

World Anti-Doping Agency. "Medical Information to Support the Decisions of TUEC's – Female to Male Transsexual Athletes." March 2016. www.wada-ama.org/en/resources/science-medicine/medical-information-to-support-the-decisions-of-tuecs-female-to-male (accessed August 19, 2016).

World Health Organization. "International Statistical Classification of Diseases and Related Health Problems 10th Revision." 2008. http://apps.who.int/classifications/icd10/browse/2008/en#/F64.0 (accessed August 13, 2016).

Yamaguchi, A., M. Fukushi, Y. Kikuchi, J. Aparicio and A. Wakisaka. "A Simple Method for Gender Verification Based on PCR Detection of Y-Chromosomal DNA and its Application at the Winter Universiade 1991 in Sapporo City, Japan." *International Journal of Sports Medicine* 13 (1992): 304–307.

Zeigler, C. "Fallon Fox Comes out as Trans Pro MMA Fighter." Outsports. March 5, 2013. www.outsports.com/2013/3/5/4068840/fallon-fox-trans-pro-mma-fighter (accessed August 12, 2016).

Zeigler, C. "Kye Allums: First Transgender Man Playing NCAA Women's Basketball." Outsports. November 1, 2010. www.outsports.com/out-gay-athletes/2013/2/21/4015388/kye-allums-first-transgender-man-playing-ncaa-womens-basketball (accessed August 12, 2016).

Part IV

Challenging the system

Chapter 14

From transsexuals to transhumans in elite athletics

The implications of osteology (and other issues) in leveling the playing field[1]

Michelle A. B. Sutherland, Richard J. Wassersug and Karen R. Rosenberg

In May 2004, the International Olympic Committee (IOC) announced a landmark decision that transsexual athletes, who had been sexually reassigned after puberty, could compete in the Olympic Games in their self-identified gender category as long as certain stipulations were fulfilled (Ljunqvist *et al.* 2003):

> The group recommends that individuals undergoing sex reassignment from male-to-female after puberty (and the converse) be eligible for participation in female or male competitions, respectively, under the following conditions:
>
> - Surgical anatomical changes have been completed, including external genitalia changes and gonadectomy.
> - Legal recognition of their assigned sex has been conferred by the appropriate official authorities.
> - Hormonal therapy appropriate for the assigned sex has been administered in a verifiable manner and for a sufficient length of time to minimize gender-related advantages in sport competitions.

The IOC was advised by an ad hoc group convened by the IOC Medical Commission. In their opinion, eligibility to compete should begin no sooner than two years after gonadectomy. They stipulated that in the event that the gender [*sic*] of a competing athlete is questioned, the medical delegate, or equivalent, of the relevant sporting body should have the authority to take all appropriate measures to determine the gender of a competitor.[2]

More recently in January 2016, the IOC's medical advisory board revisited the guidelines listed above. In anticipation of the Rio Olympics – and challenged by cases of Caster Semenya and Dutee Chand (Genel *et al.* 2016) – they relaxed the requirement for internal or external sexual reassignment surgery. At the time of this writing, the IOC requires two years of hormonal therapy and may require blood work to verify hormone levels.

There have been many iterations of sex assignment for elite athletics over the past century. Sixty years ago, Olympic competitors were sorted into categories based on sex as assessed by genital appearance. However, as genetic testing became available, athletes were separated based on the presence or absence of a Y chromosome. Once Androgen Insensitivity Syndrome was recognized and accepted, athletes were sorted by the endocrinological influences on their bodies during development and their resultant adult phenotype (Reeser 2005). With its 2004 ruling, one might argue that the IOC returned to giving primacy to external genitalia in assessing the gender of an athlete provided it is concordant with their current hormonal status. In 2016, however, they flipped back again to giving primacy to hormone levels. In this chapter, we explore the implications of these rulings, and the history of sexual dimorphism in elite athletics.

Olympic history

Between 1968 and 1998, the Olympic Committee conducted various genetic "gender [*sic*] authentication tests" to discourage and eliminate any male imposters competing in the women's events. This was probably tied to the rising number of female athletes accused of being men because of their impressive achievements, and Hermann Ratjen's confession of fraud in 1957. Ratjen won fourth place in the 1936 Olympic women's high jump under the pseudonym 'Dora' and is the only well-documented Olympic male imposter (Stephenson 1996). It is possible that the implementation of the Gender Authentication process scared other imposters both off of and out of the field. For example, the Ukrainian Olympic champions, Tamara and Irena Press, were suspected of being XY males. They disappeared from competition in 1968, right before the Mexico City Olympics, where genetic testing was to be conducted for the first time in Olympic history. Beyond these examples, there is little evidence from before 1968 that any female Olympics competitors were actually biological males. Neither the Barr Body test nor the PCR chromosomal test has discovered a 'normal' genetic male among the female competitors since the implementation of this testing (Cavanagh and Sykes 2006).

However, the implementation of genetic testing did reveal a number of self-identified female competitors who, although genotypically male, were phenotypically female due to various genetic or endocrinological conditions. In fact, data suggests that 1 in 500–600 athletes are genetically "abnormal," compared to the 1 in 5000 individuals in the general population (Stephenson 1996). These conditions included Androgen Insensitivity Syndrome (AIS), a condition in which XY males develop as females because they cannot respond to the testosterone they are producing. Complete AIS (CAIS) women do not have a uterus or ovaries, but they do have female external genitalia and many of the Olympic athletes that failed the

IOC's Gender Authentication tests were previously unaware of their AIS status. In terms of morphological differences, the average CAIS woman was 1.7 meters tall instead of the 1.65 meters average for women overall, but had no obvious muscular advantages over XX females (Hughes and Deeb 2006).

Initially, AIS women were disqualified or prevented from competing (Lemonick 1992). Less than twenty years later, at the Atlanta Olympic Games in 1996, all eight of the female athletes that 'failed' the genetic test were allowed to compete. Seven of them failed the test because of Androgen Insensitivity. The eighth athlete failed because she had a 5α-reductase deficiency, which blocked the conversion of testosterone to the more potent dihydrotestosterone, and thus having suppressed the body's masculinization (Simpson *et al.* 2000).

The acceptance of AIS women was one of the reasons the IOC abandoned the gender authentication tests after the 1998 winter Olympics. Another important reason was the implementation of the drug-doping test that requires athletes to urinate in front of an official. This practice catches any individuals who claim to be female, but possess male external genitalia. Thus, implicitly, if not explicitly, the criteria for distinguishing males from females reverted from genetic markers to the phenotypic expression of the external genitalia. The new IOC medical guidelines, which do not require genital reconstruction, avoid this regressive and embarrassing practice of genital examination.

Transsexuals in sports

The first major international decision that allowed transsexuals to compete in sporting events as their self-identified gender came in 1990, when the International Association of Athletics Federation (International Association of Athletics Federations 2006) ruled that transsexuals, who had completed prepubescent sexual reassignment surgery (SRS) could compete. The case of post-pubescent SRS transsexuals posed a much more complex problem, and the IAAF decided that it should be discussed on a case-by-case basis (Ljunqvist 2004). More than a decade later, the IOC finally announced its decision to allow post-pubescent male-to-female (MtF) transsexuals to compete as females, the first ruling of its kind by any major sports organization. This declaration corresponded with the first of the six fundamental rules set down in the 2004 Olympic Charter that declared, "The practice of sport is a human right. Every individual must have the possibility of practicing sport, without discrimination of any kind and in the Olympic spirit which requires mutual understanding of … fair play" (International Olympic Committee 2004).

Since 2004, a large number of sports organizations have used the IOC policy as a basis for their own policies on transsexual participants. These include, but are not limited to, the Ladies European Golf Tour, the United States Golf Association, USA Track and Field, and the Gay and Lesbian International Sports Association (Griffin 2016). The response from Vanessa Edwards Foster, chair and co-founder of the National Transgender Advocacy Coalition, was, "We've existed in some sort of twilight zone, being neither male nor female. This ruling allows transsexuals to compete as men and women" (Letellier 2004). The impact of the most recent IOC ruling will likely result in changes to the rules in other sports organizations.

The IOC rules nevertheless assume that transsexuals can be categorized precisely into the gender binary of male and female. They continue to avoid the confounding facts that both culturally and biologically sex is often much more complicated than a simple male/female binary (Fausto-Sterling 2000). However, there are anatomical and biomechanical reasons to believe that a post-pubertal MtF transsexual, who is fully female according to the laws of her country, may still be outside the range of normal variation for phenotypical females. If MtF transsexuals actually retain an advantage on average over biological females after sexual reassignment surgery, it seems that in order to honor the fair play directive and avoid unacceptable discrimination, an alternative solution must be developed to incorporate these women.

Here we make the case that, on average, osteological males have a competitive advantage over osteological females, regardless of their surgical or hormonal status. This leads to the ethical problem of attempting to eliminate discrimination while trying to create a fair play environment. With this problem in mind, we consider a solution for how transsexuals may still be able to compete in Olympic level athletics without unfairly disadvantaging genetic females.

Additionally we proffer the idea that a post-pubertal MtF transsexual's advantage constitutes an enhancement of human functionality, much like those proposed by followers of the transhumanist movement (Bostrom 2003b; Butryn 2003). We explore this in the context of the broader problem of maintaining fair competition conditions as surgical procedures to improve human performance become available.

The osteological advantage

An analysis of skeletal growth and development suggests that, while the hormonal manipulations core to gender reassignment (i.e., the androgen deprivation) will reduce muscle mass and impede an MtF transsexual's performance as a male, they will not change the osteology (or the geometry of their muscle attachments) that distinguishes the average adult male from the average adult female.

Granted, the current hormone-based Olympic gender categories allow significant variation among the competitors' osteology. So, if a transsexual's osteological structure falls within the osteological range of genetic females, it may still be considered fair that the MtF compete as a female. However, if a transsexual's osteology falls outside of that range, the MtF will have a bio-mechanical advantage over the average genetic female. This would be true whether we are looking at the overall range of variation for the population at large or the increasingly specialized morphologies that have come to characterize elite athletes in particular sports (such as basketball; Olds 2016). Under the current hormone-based system, genetic females and the MtF transsexual with a male-typical osteological structure outside the feminine range characteristic of particular sports, will not be able to compete fairly.

According to the World Records, overall, men run and swim faster, jump higher and farther, and throw objects longer distances than do females (International Association of Athletics Federations 2016). While this generalization is occasionally inaccurate – most notably when Janet Evans swam an Olympic record in the women's 400 meter free-style swimming event in 1988 that was faster than the men's record – such occurrences are rare. In the majority of athletic events that require absolute power, the male body is physiologically superior and are in accord with males holding the vast majority of world records in athletics (Genel 2000).

Male average higher performance is mostly due to the influence of testosterone during development, which causes males to develop larger muscles and a different osteology, such as larger jaws, brow ridges, and tuberosities on bones where muscles attach (Sheridan 2000). Genetic males also have relatively narrower hips, as estrogen at puberty causes a relative widening of the hips in females. The absence of testosterone in post-pubertal MtF transsexuals, while reducing muscle mass, does not reverse the developmental effects of high levels of testosterone and low level of estrogen on the skeleton. Therefore, the osteological advantages that males typically acquire by puberty are retained even after transsexual transition (Reeser 2005). This allows MtF transsexuals to retain an average advantage over biological females in the generation of power in certain specific actions.

The closest the medical literature has come to directly discussing the athletic implications of the osteological differences between genetic females and MtF transsexuals is a review by Reeser in the *British Journal of Sports Medicine* (2005). Reeser recognized that some physical features that distinguish post-pubertal males and females (height being the most obvious) are not reversed with sexual reassignment. He points out that "gender discrepancy in height might itself be construed as offering an unfair performance advantage to self-identified female transsexual athletes who participate in sports for which height is thought to be an asset, such as volleyball, basketball and netball." However, he goes on to show that for volleyball, at least, the tallest teams in the Olympics rarely win; that is, the "gold medal winning women's team in every Olympic Games since 1968 has (with one exception) not been the tallest team in the tournament." Thus, Reeser concludes that there appear to be "factors more critical to individual performance and team success than average player height." Reeser does not discuss any other typical, gender-specific, osteological differences. Those differences in the skeletal system are easily identifiable and may, in fact, be more critical to performance than height alone.

It is unclear exactly what information the IOC committee used in 2004 to arrive at its decision on transsexuals and to what extent they discussed osteology. The explanatory note attached to the policy suggests that they considered the effects of testosterone on muscle mass as their primary, if not only, physiological feature that gave males an advantage (Ljungqvist 2004). The half-life of residual testosterone after surgical or chemical castration is short, and can be measured in days to weeks (McGriff *et al.* 2001). The effects of androgen deprivation on muscle mass became clear in the subsequent months. Two years after androgen deprivation has begun, the muscle mass of a genetic male approximates on average that of a genetic female. Data of this sort seemed to have persuaded the IOC that two years after hormonal treatment, MtF transsexuals would be physically comparable to genetic females and thus would be fair competitors to those females. Upon closer inspection, however, it is clear that the effects of androgen deprivation merely eliminate the possibility of a muscular advantage. The osteological differences between genetic males and genetic females do not appear to have been incorporated in the IOC ruling.

The IOC seems to have ignored or downplayed the fact that sex differences in bone structure become largely fixed at or shortly after puberty and insensitive to crossed sex hormonal treatment. The average osteological differences between male and female skeletons are substantial and not simply one of height or bone length (Ivkovic *et al.* 2007). Size independent sex differences occur in both the axial and appendicular skeleton (e.g., Wunderlich and Cavanagh 2001), such that forensic anthropologists can often assign bones to male or female with a high level of certainty even when the overall height of the individual is more difficult to estimate.

By adulthood, osteological sexual dimorphism is solidified and resistant to hormone treatments later in life.[3] In fact, once developed, the bone size and alignment of the extremities cannot be substantially altered using any method short of reconstructive surgery, and those procedures are not included in SRS (Sohn and Bosinski 2007). A MtF transsexual, therefore, will retain the bone structure that she developed growing up as a male. As shown below, all other things being equal, this gives her an athletic advantage, even though she may have low androgen titers and may be taking exogenous estrogen.

Seen in one light, the retention of the bone structure may appear to be a disadvantage because the smaller, feminine, muscles have to move larger, masculine, bones. In fact, Kristen Worley, a transitioned transsexual female, who was a 2008 Olympic cycling hopeful, admitted that she still retains her masculine skeleton, but claims that she needed to "work out so hard to build muscles to move the larger skeleton" (Morris 2006). In contrast, our analysis of sexual dimorphism in certain joints, demonstrates how the retention of a masculine skeleton may confer a biomechanical advantage to MtF transsexuals, just as it does on average for biological and hormonal males. The key is not the size of the bones, per se, but the mechanical advantage that may come with particular morphologies.

Specific osteology and biomechanical advantage: the case of the knee

The most dimorphic feature of the knee joint is the Q-angle, where "Q" refers to the quadriceps muscle group, made up of the four large extensor muscles at the front of the thigh (Figure 14.1). The common tendon of the

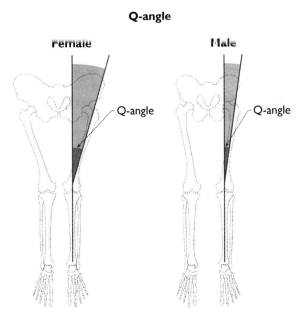

Q-angle

Female   Male

Q-angle   Q-angle

Figure 14.1 The Q-angle is the angle between the vector that represents the force of the quadriceps muscles and the direction of pull of the patellar tendon. The Q-angle at the knee (exaggerated in these figures) is typically greater for females than males. That reflects the fact that females commonly have wider hips for their height than do males. Because of their smaller Q-angle, all else being equal, males can generate more force upon extension at the knee than can females. Males also are less likely to sustain knee injuries than females. Here and in the remaining figures, the terms "female" and "male" refer to the typical morphology of genetic (i.e., cisgender) human females and males.

quadriceps extends down past the patella, or kneecap, to attach to the front of the tibia, or shin bone. This arrangement allows the quadriceps to use the patella as a pulley to extend, or straighten the leg, as happens when one stands from a squatting position, kicks a soccer ball, or pushes down on the pedal of a bicycle. Knee extension against resistance is a motion used in virtually all athletic activities that involve full body resistance to gravity in the upright posture. The Q-angle is defined as the angle between the vector force of the quadriceps and the direction of the patellar tendon (Hungerford and Barry 1979).[4]

The dimorphism of the Q-angle has been well documented (Ferber *et al.* 2003; Conley *et al.* 2007). In a review on the subject, Livingston (1998) reported overwhelming evidence that on average women have greater Q-angles than males. Woodland and Francis (1992) found the average standing Q-angles to be 14 degrees in men and 17 degrees in women. The increased Q-angle in women is likely responsible, in part, for their increased incidence of a variety of knee injuries, notably non-contact anterior cruciate ligament (ACL) injuries (Moul 1998; Sutton and Bullock 2013). Indeed, young and otherwise healthy females are up to seven times more likely to suffer a non-contact ACL injury than a male of similar age and health (McLean *et al.* 2005). This osteological difference has important implications for athletic performance. Simply put, the same tensile force from quadriceps contraction exerted by males and females will allow the male leg to push harder down on the pedal or off the ground.

The trigonometry behind this difference in the extensor force is illustrated in Figure 14.2. In both men and women, the exerted force generated by the quadriceps is broken down into two components, an extensor force vector and a lateral force vector. In order to extend the knee, the extensor force runs parallel to the patella tendon. The lateral force vector deflects the patella laterally. Because the lateral vector is using part of the exerted force, not all of the force generated by the quadriceps muscle group can be used to extend the leg. When the Q-angle is larger, the lateral force will be larger and the extensor force vector smaller than in individuals with otherwise equal length femurs and identical quadriceps muscle mass.

Because this difference is a product of osteology, not muscle mass, a transitioned MtF, is more likely than genetic females to possess this osteological advantage in spite of having lost the muscular mass advantages she may have had as a male. Such an advantage will allow her to push harder than her osteologically female counterparts and with less risk of knee injury (Hsu *et al.* 1990; Ferber *et al.* 2003).

All told, the average genetic woman loses approximately 1.4% more of her quadriceps force in leg extension than the average genetic male of equal stature and muscle mass (Figure 14.2). While, this may not seem like much, it could make all the difference for a world-class athlete. In the 2004 Sydney Olympics female 100-meter sprint, the difference between first and

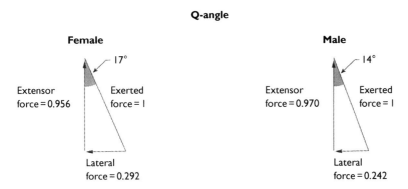

Q-angle

Female

Extensor
force = 0.956

17°

Exerted
force = 1

Lateral
force = 0.292

Male

Extensor
force = 0.970

14°

Exerted
force = 1

Lateral
force = 0.242

Figure 14.2 Because of the average difference in the Q-angles between males and females, the force available for the extension of the knee differs even if they have identical musculature. In the example here, we have used average Q-angles of 14 degrees for men and 17 degrees for women (taken from Woodland and Francis 1992), which is a conservative estimate of the average difference between males and females (cf. Livingston 1998). Assuming equal muscle strength, the difference in the Q-angle between the male and female with this modest Q-angle difference of 3 degrees creates a 1.4 percent advantage in the extensor force for the male.

second place was 0.3 percent of the winner's total time. In many track and field events, where the competitors are scored on the times taken to complete the event, differences between gold and silver performances are less than 1.4 percent.

One would have predicted that a sport in which MtF transsexuals competing as females would have the clearest advantage would be an event such as cycling, which depends massively on powerful extension at the knee. Indeed, MtF transsexuals seem to thrive in this particular sport. Michelle Dumaresq, for example, who underwent sexual reassignment over two decades ago, subsequently took up mountain bike racing in 2001, dominating the Canadian field for several years (Billman 2004). In 2002, a year into her racing career, she won the Canada Cup Mountain Bike Series. There were several demands for her removal from female competition before she eventually retired (Reifer 2002). After her success in 2002 and a number of complaints from other riders, the Canadian Cycling Association suspended her license. She was eventually reinstated and went on to win the 2006 UCI Masters World Championships but not without objections and public protests from her competitors. As part of an appeal motion in 2002, Michelle's former mentor and competitor, Sylvie Allen, wrote that she was "too suspiciously impressive for a woman" (Billman 2004).

In 1996, when Dumaresq was completing her transition, Kristen Worley was beginning down the same path. She completed SRS in 2001. Worley competed as a track cyclist before her SRS and continued in the sport as a female. Her desire to compete as a female quickly engendered controversy (McIlroy 2007). That controversy continued right up to 2016 with legal challenges from Worley against the IOC about the appropriate gonadal hormone levels for male and female Olympians, transsexual or otherwise (Cutler 2016).

While neither of these transsexual women have a hormonal advantage, they are still likely to have an osteological advantage. Under the current IOC regulations, the osteological differences at the knee provide an advantage for MtF transsexuals competing against biological females in any events that utilize powerful leg extensions.

The case of the elbow

Sexual dimorphism at the elbow may give transsexuals a similar advantage in events that require powerful extension of the forearm. As with the Q-angle at the knee, there is a carrying angle at the elbow (Figure 14.3).

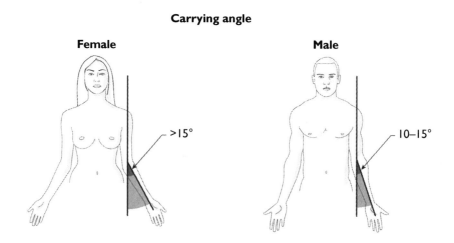

Figure 14.3 Males and females also differ in the average carrying angle at the elbow, which is due to the fact that the humerus and ulna (like the femur and tibia in the lower limb) are not in a straight line. As with the knee, females have a greater angle at the elbow. Again, the larger the angle, the lower the force that can be generated with extension at the elbow, even when the extensor muscle (the triceps brachii) mass is identical. This has implication to all sports that require throwing a ball or other object with the arm. Males have on average a mechanical advantage due just to the alignment of their bones.

When the elbow is fully extended and the palm turned forward, the forearm deviates laterally from the long axis of the upper arm, slightly but significantly more so in females than males. This is known as the "carrying angle" and its morphological correlates can be used to determine sex in forensic contexts (Atkinson and Elftman 1945; Rogers 1999; Falys *et al.* 2005).

On average, males have a mean carrying angle of 14.4 degrees and females of 16.2 degrees (Atkinson and Elftman 1945), leading to a difference of 1.8 degrees. However, the carrying angle is also subject to population differences and may also be dependent on the height, and relative length of the arm and forearm than on the biological sex of an individual (Atkinson and Elftman 1945; Khare *et al.* 1999).

Powerful extension at the elbow is achieved by contraction of the triceps brachii muscle. Using the same trigonometric analysis that was used for the Q-angle, males and females with identical triceps, but a carrying angle difference of 1.8 degrees, will have a difference of 0.9 percent in the maximum power that can be generated. Once again the advantage is to the individuals with the smallest carrying angle – in general this goes to males.

One implication of a larger carrying angle at the elbow is that women throw differently to men.[5] No study appears to have closely examined whether there is a correlation between either the power or accuracy with which people throw and the carrying angle at the elbow. However, given the data on the Q-angle and quadriceps force, one might assume that throwing efficiency (distance and speed, if not accuracy) would be enhanced with a lower carrying angle at the elbow. Thus, again, a MtF transsexual may be likely to have an advantage over the genetic females of similar stature and muscle mass in sports that require powerful extension at the elbow, such as softball, javelin, discus, shot-put, and possibly even racket sports. It may indeed be more than a coincidence that the first publicly recognized MtF athlete was the tennis player Richard Raskind (Kraus 2002).

In parallel with the sex differences reported above for lower extremity injuries, females have a significantly higher prevalence than men for a variety of musculoskeletal disorders involving the shoulder (Vafadar *et al.* 2015) and elbow (Ivković *et al.* 2007).

The extent to which the shoulder problems can be attributed to sex differences in scapular osteology is not known, but such differences do exist in the shape of the glenoid fossa (Merrill *et al.* 2006). The triceps crosses and thus acts upon both the elbow and shoulder joints putting both joints at risk.

The pelvis

The pelvis is the part of the skeleton that is most distinctively different between males and females. In contrast to the rest of the human body, in which males are generally larger than females, the birth canal in the human pelvis shows a reverse sexual dimorphism in which females generally have larger dimensions than males. Anthropologists have traditionally interpreted this sexual dimorphism as reflecting competing selective forces coming from locomotion, in which a compact pelvis would be most efficient, and obstetrics, where selection would favor a capacious pelvis. These conflicting demands are known as the "obstetrical dilemma" (Washburn 1960; Lovejoy 1988; Rosenberg 1992; Rosenberg and Trevathan 2002) and suggest that females are on average less efficient in locomotion than males by virtue of their mammalian commitment to giving birth. The relatively broad hips of females reflect our species' need for females to be able to bear children of large head size (Lovejoy 1988, 2005; Tague 1992).

The sexual dimorphism in the hips, knees, and elbow are interrelated. The greater angle at the elbow and the knee in genetic females is understood to be related to the fundamentally broader hips that females have relative to their height. The Q-angle at the knee allows women to have broad hips and walk efficiently with their legs and feet close to their midline. The carrying angle at the elbow similarly allows for the hands to deviate laterally enough that a female can walk without her forearms and hands bumping into her hips with each step.

Recent experiments have however failed to document sexual dimorphism in selective measures of locomotor efficiency in humans (Dunsworth

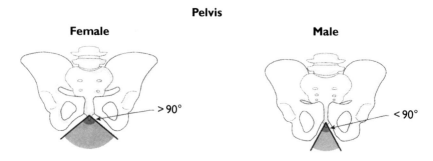

Pelvis

Female   **Male**

$>90°$ $<90°$

Figure 14.4 The largest average osteological differences between males and females are in the pelvis. This is due to the fact that, for their height women have a wider pelvis than do males. This is necessary to permit safe passage of the infant during birth. These differences in shape may reduce the locomotor efficiency of the female musculoskeletal compared to males and the resultant compromise between locomotor and obstetric functions has been called the "obstetrical dilemma".

et al. 2012; Warrener *et al.* 2015). This has led to the suggestion that the selective advantage of male pelvic morphology comes predominantly from a far lower rate of injury as noted above for the knee. A proportionately smaller pelvis in males helps align the femur with the tibia, reducing the Q-angle and limiting the lateral vector forces at the knee that are associated with high injury rates in females. A narrower pelvis in males relative to females contributes to a lower rate of bone and joint injury and lowers the amount of force that the female skeleton can endure without catastrophic failure. All told, a male skeletal design can bear greater loads for a longer time than a female skeleton of comparable mass.

Fairness in the field

So where does this leave talented MtF athletes, who should neither be discriminated against nor deprived of the opportunity to compete at the Olympic level? A parsimonious solution would be to offer a separate MtF category, since the bodies of MtF transsexuals would have more in common with each other than with either natal male or female bodies. However, an obvious drawback to this particular solution is the limited number of athletes that would fall into this category. It would also likely be challenged by transsexual athletes and sports authorities alike, who share a strong commitment to a gender/sex binary.

Additionally, this solution ignores an underlying problem: Between all individuals, male, female, or otherwise, there is a natural range of Q-angles, carrying angles and pelvic dimensions. When the IOC was evaluating the participation of the AIS women, Dr. Jean Wilson, the editor of *Harrison's Principles of Internal Medicine* summed up the dilemma, "It is also true that people are not equal in athletic prowess in regard to height, weight, coordination or any other parameters, and it follows that [androgen sensitivity] is just another way in which athletes would not be equal" (Kraus 2002). Having narrower hips and smaller Q-angles might be an example of 'other parameters' of significance.

Success in athletic competition relies on many factors, including hormone levels, mental status, training regime, technique, nutrition, myology, osteology and cultural factors, such as expectations and opportunities. The current Olympic rules match athletes according to only the first category, allowing the athletes to acquire advantages in other categories. Factors, such as mental status, training regime, and technique are modifiable by the competitors and a fair competition assumes that the winner will be the one who has mastered these areas. What cannot be substantially modified or "mastered" is adult osteology.

In order to achieve a true spirit of fair play this innate biomechanical advantage needs to be taken into account. One possible solution would be to separate the Olympic athletes first by their hormonal status and then by their osteology. Due to the large number of factors that could be taken into account, an "Osteological Index" could be designed. Such an index could be calculated by multiplying specific osteological parameters (e.g., height, Q-angle, carrying angle at elbow, relative hip width to height ratio, etc.) by their influence on one's ability to succeed in a specific sport. One could imagine different sports using different parameters in calculating such an index to reflect the importance of specific body segments in various sports.

Such an Osteological Index could be of two forms, both of which would reflect the spectrum from the andromorphic to gynecomorphic skeletal types. In its simplest form, it could incorporate the single most conspicuous, sex specific osteological factor of the ratio of hip and shoulder widths. In a more robust form, it could also be built around pelvic breadth, the Q-angle at the knee and the carrying angle at the elbow. The male and female categories could then be broken down into classes specific for different ranges of "Osteological Indexes." Each class would have its own medal winners, minimizing the skeletal advantages and disadvantages to any group, independent of the chromosomal or gender identity.

This solution, in permitting more than two categories based on a range of morphology rather than a simple sex/gender binary, may be complex, but it is not novel. Boxers, wrestlers, and Paralympic athletes are all separated into more than two competitor categories that reflect physical criteria beyond just genital anatomy and hormonal status. Wrestlers and boxers are sorted by weight to eliminate size advantages, while the Paralympics committee goes even further to separate functional ability into many subcategories, such as blindness or paralysis (International Paralympic Committee 2006). For instance, wheelchair track and field athletes are separated into twelve categories based on the level of trunk, leg and arm function. By following their example, the IOC could keep the current gender categories, based primarily on hormonal status, but open up subcategories based on osteology, or they could even eliminate the gender categories altogether and use categories that reflect advantages conferred by phenotype. By accounting for natural variation within the male and female categories, such "Osteological Indexes" would ensure that none of the athletes, including MtF transsexuals, possess a major osteological advantage.

Adding competitive categories beyond (or instead of) a binary would help reduce controversies about fairness on the playing field like those that plagued Caster Semenya and Dutee Chand (Genel *et al.* 2016). Our proposal that the IOC use categories beyond males and females, could even be expanded to allow the Paralympics to be incorporated into the Olympics proper. In that case more categories would be needed, as sorting on osteology alone could not take into account varying levels of ability, such as intellectual handicaps (International Paralympic Committee 2006).

The addition of osteological categories for athletic competitions may be deemed impractical. There is no denying that adding competitor categories would make competitions more complex, expensive, and time consuming. In response to this, there is an alternative solution. Instead of rearranging the structure of the competitions, an Osteological Index could be used to proportionally handicap athletes. Although a committee would have to determine the mathematical details, an amount of time proportional to the additional force that an athlete's gender-specific skeletal structure allows them to generate could be subtracted from their final score, in either units of time or distance. For team sports, team averages could be used. If only the data from the typical gender difference in Q-angle were used and all other differences between typical genetic males and females were ignored, a somewhat more level playing field would be one in which the finishing times for MtFs were reduced proportionally to their osteological advantage.

Competitive categories that reflect biomechanically relevant yet largely non-plastic morphology makes fundamentally more sense than sorting individuals on genetic or current hormonal status. It recognizes that normal human variation confers advantages to some individuals by virtue of their phenotype. However, it accepts that some traits (e.g., muscle mass, coordination) are plastic and prone to change with training, while others, like the design of joints, less so.

Transsexuals as pioneer transhumanists

Expanding the binary gender system to include additional categories based on osteology or some other handicapping scheme are potential solutions that would allow the IOC to reconcile their concurrent desire to be non-discriminatory yet promote a fair play environment. Additionally, such solutions would prepare the Olympics for future body modifications, be they surgical, chemical, genetic or bionic. Transhumanist philosophy is based on the idea that the human body and its natural abilities are only a starting point and that with "applied reason" humans can greatly change and improve themselves (Bostrom 2003a). Transhumanists' theories emphasize "morphological freedom" (Sanberg 2001). According to the World Transhumanist Association co-founder Nick Bostrom (2003b), "Transhumanists hope that by responsible use of science, technology, and other rational means humans shall eventually manage to become post-human beings with vastly greater capacities than present human beings have."

Transhumanist thinkers deal, for the most part, with enhancements; i.e., those body alterations meant to improve the basic human condition. In considering transhumans, one must recognize that legitimate training and chemical enhancements are not the only ways to improve human performance. The "enhancement" for the MtF transsexual athlete is one that indirectly gives a female a male skeleton. Under the current IOC policy this osteological advantage can be achieved with hormonal manipulations alone and does not require surgical intervention.

The general idea that surgeries could bring transhumanism to elite athletics is not new (cf. Butryn 2003). From a transhumanist perspective, the "cyborgian border" was crossed when the IOC decided that individuals without fully formed or functional lower extremities could compete in the Olympics using carbon-fiber "blade" prostheses (Greenemeier 2016). The IOC's current policy advanced that substantially in requiring neither surgical nor cyborgian manipulations. Under current rules, hormonal status alone can allow for an individual to compete in a different category than their natal sex, with varying amounts of osteological advantage depending on the sport.

In looking toward the future one can imagine surgeries that add tissues for further embellishment. There already exist, for example, orthopedic procedures for lengthening long bones in the lower body to compensate for leg length discrepancies (Jochymek and Gal 2007). To the best of our knowledge no one has undertaken such surgery in order to gain an athletic advantage, but the mere existence of such procedures suggests that transhumanist options are not so futuristic as to be solely science fiction. Practically, of course, it may be impossible to tell whether an athlete is undergoing modification because of a transhumanist philosophy or a simple desire to gain an advantage in elite competition. The original intent however is arguably irrelevant.

Athletic ruling bodies could perhaps differentiate between surgical procedures that add tissue versus those that remove tissue. Removing testicles is an ablation, whereas lengthening bones is an augmentation. Athletic committees might decide that the former does not constitute an advantage to the extent that the latter does. This distinction may falter if one considers some simple modifications that could be done to the hands or the feet. Conceivably, the surface area in the hands and feet may be enhanced by congenital disorders like polydactylism or incomplete syndactyly (i.e., webbed fingers). While this may produce an advantage in swimming, there are no reports of swimmers being banned or dismissed for such minor anatomical variants. One could also conceive of a transhumanist, who has his hands surgically altered to increase the surface area in a similar way. It would be a relatively minor surgical procedure to fuse the skin between neighboring fingers and this procedure could be seen as an ablation procedure, which limits the autonomy of individual finger movements. Currently, such surgeries would probably disqualify a swimmer from the Olympics, even if their advantage would be no greater than someone who had been born with incomplete syndactyly.

The admission of transsexuals into elite athletics for their elected gender, forces us to recognize the inevitability of enhancements for increased athletic performance. Transsexuals may unwittingly be at the vanguard of the transhumanist movement. Their medical treatment was first and foremost undertaken to provide therapy for individuals with a Gender Identity Disorder (American Psychiatric Association 1994; now called Gender Dysphoria in the 2013 DSM-5). However, it has also given those same individuals a potential advantage in certain athletic events. The IOC, in its rulings on MtFs, has opened the way for other transhumanist athletes to compete.

Conclusion

The history of transsexuals in elite athletics has closely followed that of AIS women. They were ignored at first, later discriminated against, and finally accepted into the normal Olympic categories from which they had once been excluded. The same trajectory may be followed by (other) transhumanists, as they continue to push the bounds of what a modified human body is capable of.

Notes

1 An abbreviated version of this chapter was previously published as: "Getting a Leg Up on the Competition: The Importance of Osteology in Elite Athletics," Michelle Brett Sutherland, Benjamin Langer and Richard Wassersug (eds.) (2012) *American Journal of Bioethics* 12(7): 25–27.
2 Although the IOC documents used the term gender, it is clear from the kinds of tests that they performed, such as karyotyping, that they were striving to classify according to sex.
3 Interestingly, a recent study (Huseynov *et al.* 2016) suggests that later in life, after menopause, hormonal changes cause a subtle reversion of female pelvic morphology in the direction of males. The implications of this for athletics may be minor since such changes would normally take place after the age when most athletes would have stopped competing.
4 A related measure is the bicondylar angle of the femoral shaft, which is the angle between the sagittal plane perpendicular to the infracondylar plane and the longitudinal axis of the femoral diaphysis (Tardieu and Trinkaus 1994; Heiple and Lovejoy 1971). Both sets of authors found a significant sex difference in the majority of samples they studied, with females having a larger angle than males. However, Waxenbaum and Stock (2016) found that, although females had greater bicondylar angles than males in all of the samples they studied, the differences were generally not statistically significant.
5 There is feminist sociological literature exploring this gender difference in throwing that endorses the idea that it is linked to the "ambiguous transcendence and inhibitive intentionality of women" (Young 1990). Indeed one study suggested that women who are more concerned about their appearance are less accurate in throwing, suggesting that the gender difference in throwing is enculturated (Fredrickson 2005). However, that hypothesis does not rule out that both the osteological difference and the tendency toward self-objectification may both be linked to hormonal influences during development.

References

American Psychiatric Association. 1994. *Diagnostic and statistical manual of mental disorders, 4th edition.* Washington, DC: American Psychiatric Association.

Atkinson, W. B. and H. Elftman. 1945. The carrying angle of the human arm as a secondary sex character. *Anatomical Record* 91(1): 49–52.

Billman, J. 2004. Michelle raises hell: The hottest transgender talent in professional sport is making competition see pink. *Outside Magazine* (April). Available online at www.outsideonline.com/1822371/michelle-raises-hell (accessed October 12, 2016).

Bostrom, N. 2003a. *The Transhumanist FAQ, v. 2.1.* World Transhumanist Association. Available online at www.nickbostrom.com/views/transhumanist.pdf (October 12, 2016).

Bostrom, N. 2003b. Human genetic enhancements: A transhumanist perspective. *The Journal of Value Inquiry* 37(4): 493–506.

Butryn, T. M. 2003. Posthuman podiums: Cyborg narratives of elite track and field athletes. *Sociology of Sport Journal* 20(1): 17–39.

Cavanagh, S. L., and H. Sykes. 2006. Transsexual bodies at the Olympics: The International Olympics Committee's policy on transsexual athletes at the 2004 Athens summer games. *Body & Society* 12(3): 75–102.

Conley, S., A. Rosenberg and R. Crowninshield. 2007. The female knee: Anatomic variations. *Journal of the American Academy of Orthopaedic Surgeons* 15: S31–S36.

Cutler, T. 2016. Meet the Canadian athlete changing sports' attitude to gender. Newsweek, www.newsweek.com/meet-canadian-athlete-changing-sports-attitudes-gender-423405 (accessed October 10, 2016).

Dunsworth, H. M., A. G. Warrener, T. Deacon, P. T. Ellison and H. Pontzer. 2012. Metabolic hypothesis for human altriciality. *Proceedings of the National Academy of Sciences* 109: 15212–15216.

Falys, C. G., D. A. Weston and H. Schutkowski. 2005. The distal humerus-a blind test of Rogers' sexing technique using a documented skeletal collection. *Journal of Forensic Science* 50(6): JFS2005171–5.

Fausto-Sterling, A. 2000. *Sexing the body: Gender politics and the construction of sexuality.* New York: Basic Books, 2000.

Ferber, R., I. McClay Davis and D. S. Williams, III. 2003. Gender differences in lower extremity mechanics during running. *Clinical Biomechanics* 18: 350–357.

Fredrickson, B. L. 2005. Throwing like a girl: Self-objectification predicts adolescent girls' motor performance. *Journal of Sport & Social Issues* 29(1): 79–101.

Genel, M. 2000. Gender verification no more? *Medscape Women's Health* 5(3): 7218.

Genel, M, J. L. Simpson and A. de la Chapelle. 2016. The Olympic games and athletic sex assignment. *JAMA* 316(13): 1359–1360.

Greenemeier, L. 2016. Blade runners: Do high-tech prostheses give runners an unfair advantage? *Scientific American.* Available online at www.scientific american.com/article/blade-runners-do-high-tech-prostheses-give-runners-an-unfair-advantage/ (accessed October 9, 2016).

Griffin, P. 2007. Chalk talk: Inclusion of transgender athletes on sports teams. Available online at www.caaws-homophobiainsport.ca/e/pdfs/coaches_chalk_talk_e.pdf (accessed October 12, 2016).

Heiple, K. G. and C. O. Lovejoy. 1971. The distal femoral anatomy of *Australopithecus*. *American Journal of Physical Anthropology* 35: 75–84.

Hsu, R. W., S. Himeno, M. B. Coventry and E. Y. Chao. 1990. Normal axial alignment of the lower extremity and load-bearing distribution at the knee. *Clinical Orthopaedics and Related Research* 255: 215–227.

Hughes, I. A. and A. Deeb. 2006. Androgen resistance. *Best Practice & Research Clinical Endocrinology & Metabolism* 20(4): 577–598.

Hungerford, D. and M. Barry. 1979. Biomechanics of the patellofemoral joint. *Clinical Orthopaedics and Related Research* 144: 9–15.

Huseynov, A., C. P. Zollikofer, W. Coudyzer, D. Gascho, C. Kellenberger, R. Hinzpeter and M. S. P. de León. 2016. Developmental evidence for obstetric adaptation of the human female pelvis. *Proceedings of the National Academy of Sciences* 113: 5227–5232.

International Association of Athletics Federations. 2006. *IAAF Records*. Available online at www.iaaf.org/statistics/records/index.html (accessed September 12, 2007).

International Association of Athletics Federations. 2016. IAAF World Records. Available online at www.iaaf.org/records/by-category/world-records (Accessed Oct 18, 2016)

International Olympic Committee. 2004. *Olympic Charter*. International Olympic Committee. Available online at www.olympic.org/uk/utilities/reports/level2_uk.asp?HEAD2=26&HEAD1=10 (Accessed August, 26, 2007).

International Paralympic Committee. 2006. *IPC Athletics Classification Handbook*. Available online at www.paralympic.org/.../Athletics/About_the_sport/Rules/IPC_Athletics_Classification_Handbook_2006.pdf (Accessed September, 12, 2007).

Ivković A., M. Franić, I. Bojanić and M. Pećina. 2007. Overuse injuries in female athletes. *Croatian Medical Journal* 48(6): 767–778.

Jochymek, J., and P. Gal. 2007. Evaluation of bone healing in femurs lengthened via the gradual distraction method. *Biomedical Papers of the Medical Faculty of the University Palacky, Olomouc, Czech Republic* 151(1): 137–141.

Khare, G. N., S. C. Goel, S. K. Saraf, G. Singh and C. Mohanty. 1999. New observations on carrying angle. *Indian Journal of Medical Science* 53(2): 61–67.

Kraus, C. 2002. Sports: Transgender issues. *GLBTQ: An Encyclopedia of Gay, Lesbian, Bisexual, Transgender, and Queer Culture*, ed. C. J. Summers. Chicago, IL: glbtq, Inc. Available online at www.glbtqarchive.com/arts/sports_transgender_issues_A.pdf (accessed October 12, 2016).

Lemonick, M. D. 1992. Genetic tests under fire. *TIME Magazine* 139(8): 65.

Letellier, P. 2004. Olympics to let transsexuals compete. *PlanetOut Network*, May 18. Available online at www.planetout.com/news/article.html?2004/05/18/3 (accessed August, 26, 2007).

Livingston, L. A. 1998. The quadriceps angle: A review of the literature. *The Journal of Orthopaedic and Sports Physical Therapy* 28(2): 105–109.

Ljunqvist, A. 2004. *Explanatory note to the recommendation on sex reassignment and sports*. International Olympic Committee. Available online at https://stillmed.olympic.org/Documents/Reports/EN/en_report_904.pdf (accessed October 12, 2016).

Ljunqvist, A., O. Cohen-Haguenauer, M. Genel, J. L. Simpson, M. Ritzen, M. Fellous and P. Schamasch. 2003. *Statement of the Stockholm consensus on sex reassignment in sports.* International Olympic Committee. Available online at https://stillmed.olympic.org/Documents/Reports/EN/en_report_905.pdf (accessed August, 26, 2007).

Lovejoy, C. O. 1988. Evolution of human walking. *Scientific American* 259(5): 118–125.

Lovejoy, C. O. 2005. The natural history of human gait and posture: Part 1. Spine and pelvis. *Gait & Posture* 21(1): 95–112.

McGriff, N. J., G. Csako, M. Kabbani, L. Diep, G. P. Chrousos and F. Pucino. 2001. Treatment options for a patient experiencing pruritic rash associated with transdermal testosterone: A review of the literature. *Pharmacotherapy* 21(11): 1425–1435.

McIlroy, A. 2007. I'm a woman on the move. *The Globe and Mail* September 7. Available online at www.theglobeandmail.com/sports/im-a-woman-on-the-move/article1081665/?page=all (accessed October 12, 2016).

McKeon, J. M. M. and A. T. C. Hertel. 2009. Sex differences and representative values for 6 lower extremity alignment measures. *Journal of Athletic Training* 44(3): 249.

McLean, S. G., K. Walker and A. J. Van Den Bogert. 2005. Effect of gender on lower limb kinematics during rapid deceleration changes: an integrated analysis of three sports movements. *Journal of Science and Medicine in Sport* 8: 411–422.

Merrill A, K. Guzman and S. L. Miller. 2006. Gender differences in glenoid anatomy: Anatomic study. *Surgical and Radiologic Anatomy* 31(3): 183–189.

Morris, J. 2006. *Transgender mountain biker says she was shocked by comments directed at her.* Canadian Press. Available online at: www.canada.com/topics/sports/story.html?id=15313f56-0f72-4054-9ddd-dd51939ece93&k=11910&p=2 (accessed August 26, 2007).

Moul, J. L. 1998. Differences in selected predictors of anterior cruciate ligament tears between male and female NCAA Division I collegiate basketball players. *Journal of Athletic Training* 33(2): 118.

Olds, T. 2016. Survival of the fittest: the changing shapes and sizes of Olympic athletes. *The Conversation.* Available online at: http://theconversation.com/survival-of-the-fittest-the-changing-shapes-and-sizes-of-olympic-athletes-63184 (accessed, October 8, 2016).

Reeser, J. C. 2005. Gender identity and sport: Is the playing field level? *British Journal of Sports Medicine* 39(10): 695–699.

Reifer, S. 2002. Switching gears. *Sports Illustrated Women*, 4(7): 21–23.

Rogers, T. L. 1999. A visual method of determining the sex of skeletal remains using the distal humerus. *Journal of Forensic Science* 44(1): 57–60.

Rosenberg, K. R. 1992. The evolution of human childbirth. *American Journal of Physical Anthropology* 35, no. S15: 89–124.

Rosenberg, K. and W. Trevathan. 2002. Birth, obstetrics and human evolution." *BJOG: An International Journal of Obstetrics & Gynaecology* 109(11): 1199–1206.

Sanberg, A. 2001. *Morphological Freedom – Why we don't just want it, but need it.* Transvision. Available online at www.nada.kth.se/~asa/Texts/Morphological-Freedom.htm (accessed, October 12, 2016).

Sheridan, S. G. 2000. New life the dead receive: The relationship between human remains and the cultural record for Byzantine St. Stephen's. *Revue Biblique* 106(4): 574–611.

Simpson, J. L., A. Ljungquvist, M. A. Ferguson-Smith, A. de la Chapelle, L. J. Elsas, A. A. Ehrhardt, M. Genel, E. A. Ferris and A. Carlson. 2000. Gender verification in the Olympics. *The Journal of the American Medical Association* 284(12): 1568–1569.

Sohn, M. and H. A. G. Bosinski. 2007. Gender identity disorders: Diagnostic and surgical aspects. *Journal of Sexual Medicine* 4(5): 1193–1208.

Standring, S., ed. 2005. *Gray's Anatomy*. Toronto, ON: Elsevier Churchill Livingstone.

Stephenson, J. 1996. Female Olympians' sex tests outmoded. *The Journal of the American Medical Association* 276(3): 177–178.

Sutherland, M. B., B. Langer and R. Wassersug. 2012. Getting a leg up on the competition: The importance of osteology in elite athletics. *American Journal of Bioethics* 12(7): 25–27.

Sutton, K. M. and J. Montgomery Bullock. 2013. Anterior cruciate ligament rupture: differences between males and females. *Journal of the American Academy of Orthopaedic Surgeons* 21(1). 11 50.

Tague, R. G. 1992. Sexual dimorphism in the human bony pelvis, with a consideration of the Neandertal pelvis from Kebara Cave, Israel. *American Journal of Physical Anthropology* 88: 1–21.

Tardieu, C. and E. Trinkaus. 1994. Early ontogeny of the human femoral bicondylar angle. *American Journal of Physical Anthropology* 95: 183–195.

Warrener, A. G., K. L. Lewton, H. Pontzer and D. E. Lieberman. 2015. A wider pelvis does not increase locomotor cost in humans, with implications for the evolution of childbirth. *PloS one* 10.3 (2015): e0118903.

Vafadar, A. K., J. N. Côté and P. S. Archambault. 2015. Sex differences in the shoulder joint position sense acuity: A cross-sectional study. *BMC Musculoskeletal Disorders* 30(16): 273.

Washburn, S. L. 1960. Tools and human evolution. *Scientific American* 203: 62–75.

Waxenbaum, E. B. and M. K. Stock. 2016. Variation in the human bicondylar angle. *American Journal of Physical Anthropology* 160(2): 334–340.

Woodland, L. H. and R. S. Francis 1992. Parameters and comparisons of the quadriceps angle of college-aged men and women in the supine and standing positions. *American Journal of Sports Medicine* 20(2): 208–211.

Wunderlich R. E. and P. R. Cavanagh. 2001. Gender differences in adult foot shape: Implications for shoe design. *Medicine & Science in Sports & Exercise* (4): 605–611.

Young, I. M. 1990. *Throwing like a girl and other essays in feminist philosophy and social theory*. Bloomington, IN: Indiana University Press.

Chapter 15

The tenuous inclusion of transgender athletes in sport

Adam Love

Introduction

Few institutions adhere to a sex-segregated structure more strictly than sport. A system based on a static and binary understanding of sex has presented considerable barriers to the participation of transgender athletes, who often have faced policies of overt exclusion. However, in response to challenges from transgender athletes and activists, many sporting bodies have begun to adopt policies that appear, at least ostensibly, to be more inclusive of transgender participants. The current chapter serves as an update to previous work (Love 2014) in which I examined this wave of seemingly inclusive policies. In the period of 2014–2016, new policies demonstrating increased inclusion of transgender athletes have been adopted at both the elite and amateur levels. At the same time, an upsurge of anti-trans backlash, both within and outside of sport, has emerged. This chapter addresses these contrasting developments. Ultimately, I build on previous calls for scholars and sporting officials to seek more inclusive, non-sex-binary-based models for organizing sport competition.

A note on the author's standpoint and terminology

In this chapter, I write with the understanding that anatomical, chromosomal, and hormonal complexities involved in differentiating men from women make sex, like gender, a socially and historically-constructed concept (Schultz 2011; Wackwitz 2003). My argument for non-sex-binary-based strategies for organising sport is broadly informed by the ideas of queer feminist scholars, such as Burke (1996) and Fausto-Sterling (2012, 2000), whose deconstruction of sex and gender has highlighted ways in which the two-sex system itself reproduces a hierarchy upon which transphobia specifically, and sexism more generally, are based.

In addition, I should clarify that the term *transgender* is used generally in this chapter to include people who have a gender identity other than that assigned to them at birth as well as those who may not identify with a particular sex entirely. Some transgender persons may desire to seek medical procedures, such as surgery or hormone therapy, to *transition* to a particular sex, while others may not. In contrast to transgender, the term *cisgender* refers to "individuals who have a match between the gender they were assigned at birth, their bodies, and their personal identity" (Schilt and Westbrook 2009, 461). Transgender must also be distinguished from *intersex*, which includes individuals with "atypical combinations of chromosomes, hormones, genitalia, and other physical features" (Buzuvis 2011, 11). Although intersex athletes have often been affected by sporting bodies' exclusionary policies, the primary focus of this chapter is on policy developments as they impact transgender athletes. The analysis in the chapter is limited by my status as a white cisgender man, who has experienced the privilege of not directly suffering the effects of exclusionary policies in sport. With these points in mind, I begin with a brief overview of the history of overt exclusion encountered by many individuals who do not so neatly fit into a static and binary model of sex.

A history of exclusion

The general hostility of sport policymakers to those who transgress the sex binary is vividly illustrated by the history of sex-verification testing in sport. Because the practice has been more rigorously examined by others (e.g., Pieper 2016; Schultz 2011; Sullivan 2011; Wackwitz 2003), I provide only a brief overview of sex testing here as it directly relates to the participation of transgender athletes. The practice of requiring athletes to verify their sex may have roots dating back as far as the original Olympic games in ancient Greece (Wackwitz 2003), but the formalized policy of sex-verification testing in modern elite sport was initiated in the 1960s. This initially consisted of requiring participants in women's events to submit to visual and gynaecological examinations at competitions governed by the International Association of Athletics Federations (IAAF). The introduction of chromosomal testing for competitors in women's events by the International Olympic Committee (IOC) occurred at the 1968 Olympic Games in Mexico City. During the next three decades, the IOC mandated testing to determine who was and was not allowed to compete in women's events, using testing methods designed to identify the presence of a second X chromosome (Barr Body test) or the presence of a Y chromosome (polymerase chain reaction test). However, due in part to the ineffectiveness and ambiguity involved in determining sex through such procedures, mandatory sex testing for women's events was abandoned prior to the 2000 Summer Olympics. Organizations such as the IOC and IAAF still allow for testing on a case-by-case basis, although their ability to do so is currently a matter of legal contention, a point I will return to later in the chapter.

In some instances, sport organizations appear to have implemented sex-verification testing with the specific intent of excluding transgender competitors. The United States Tennis Association (USTA), for example, introduced chromosome-based sex testing in 1977 in response to transitioned woman Renee Richards' attempts to compete in women's events (Birrell and Cole 1990). A decade later, the United States Golf Association responded to the increased success of Charlotte Ann Woods, a transitioned woman, by introducing a policy requiring that competitors in women's events be "female at birth" (Sykes 2006). In some cases, anti-discrimination statutes ostensibly designed to prevent unfair treatment of transgender citizens have specifically exempted sport organisations. For example, the UK's Gender Recognition Act of 2004 allowed sporting organisations to exclude transgender participants to promote "fair competition" or "the safety of competitors" (see McArdle 2008, 47). Sport organisations have also been exempted from a transgender non-discrimination law in New South Wales, Australia (Buzuvis 2011). However, despite this history of exclusion, some sport organisations have begun to adopt policies that are, at least on the surface, inclusive of transgender athletes.

The emergence of policies regarding transgender participants in sport

The "Stockholm Consensus" – a policy approved by the IOC Executive Committee prior to the 2004 Summer Olympic Games – marked an important turn with respect to the potential inclusion of transgender athletes. Prior to the Stockholm Consensus, most sporting bodies either had no policies regarding the participation of transgender athletes or simply relied upon requirements that all competitors in women's events be "female at birth" (Cavanagh and Sykes 2006). However, the Stockholm Consensus only allowed transgender athletes to complete if they had (a) undergone sex reassignment surgery (including external genitalia and gonadectomy), (b) been given legal recognition of their sex by their country of citizenship, and (c) undertaken hormone therapy and lived in their newly-assigned gender for at least two years (Cavanagh and Sykes 2006). The Stockholm Consensus appears to have acted as a model, with numerous sport organisations adopting policies governing the participation of transgender athletes following its implementation. These organisations include the Ladies European Golf Tour, Ladies Golf Union, Ladies Professional Golf Association, USA Hockey, USA Rugby, USA Track and Field, United States Golf Association, and Women's Golf Australia (Buzuvis 2011).

While some have praised the Stockholm Consensus (and subsequent policies modelled on it) for offering a means of inclusion for transgender athletes, many scholars have criticized its restrictive nature. For instance, by relying on the most conservative, medicalized criteria to determine access, these policies excluded many transgender athletes and ignored "all local, economic, cultural, and racial differences in how transsexual athletes have access to sex reassignment surgeries or hormone usage" (Sykes 2006, 11). The access that such policies provide to some transgender athletes is on terms that are gender-conforming rather than gender-transforming (Travers 2006). Ultimately, such policies reassert the notion that there are "two and only two choices when it comes to one's sexual identity, thereby ignoring the range of social and biological possibilities that exist along the continuum between these two seemingly pure categories" (Schultz 2011, 235).

A new wave of inclusion?

While policies such as the Stockholm Consensus worked to exclude many, if not most, people who do not identify with the sex they were assigned at birth, recent developments at both the elite and amateur levels of sport signal the potential for a growing inclusion of transgender athletes. At the elite level, two significant policy developments occurred in 2015 regarding the ways in which gender is governed. First, in July of 2015, the Court of Arbitration for Sport (CAS) suspended the IAAF's policy of "hyperandrogenism" regulation. Shortly thereafter, the IOC Medical and Scientific Commission issued new guidelines concerning "sex reassignment and hyperandrogenism." Below, I discuss both developments in more detail.

In 2011, the IAAF adopted a policy to regulate "hyperandrogenism" – a "condition in which females produce androgens in excess of the range typical for females" (Karkazis et al. 2012, 3). The policy set a ceiling of 10 nanomoles per litre in serum as the amount of naturally-occurring testosterone that was allowable for competitors in women's events; this testosterone level was identified by the IAAF as being "within the normal male range" (Karkazis et al. 2012). If a woman had testosterone in excess of this amount, she would be required to lower her testosterone levels, which would necessitate surgery or use of medication (Karkazis and Jordan-Young 2015). However, as the result of an appeal by Indian sprinter Dutee Chand, who had been banned from competition due to the policy, the CAS suspended the IAAF hyperandrogenism regulations in a ruling issued on July 24, 2015. In the ruling, the court allowed the IAAF two years to submit further evidence demonstrating "the actual degree of athletic performance advantage sustained by hyperandrogenic female athletes as compared to non-hyperandrogenic female athletes by reason of their high levels of testosterone" (Court 2015, 160). If the IAAF is unable to provide such evidence in the two-year window, the hyperandrogenism policy will be declared void. While the IAAF hyperandrogenism policy is not about transgender athletes per se, its focus on regulating sex based upon hormone levels has important implications for the inclusion (or exclusion) of transgender participants. As Karkazis and Jordan-Young (2015) argue, "what looks like a controversy rooted firmly in science is ultimately a social and ethical one concerning how we understand and frame human diversity" (860).

In another important development at the elite level of sport, the IOC adopted new guidelines regarding transgender athletes in November of 2015. Alluding to changes occurring over the past decade, the guidelines state that "there has been a growing recognition of the importance of autonomy of gender identity in society" (International Olympic Committee 2015, 2) since the development of the Stockholm Consensus. In turn, the new guidelines suggest, "it is necessary to ensure insofar as possible that trans athletes are not excluded from the opportunity to participate in sporting competition," but "the overriding sporting objective is and remains the guarantee of fair competition" (International Olympic Committee 2015, 2). As a result, the guidelines declare that female to male trans athletes should be eligible to compete in men's events without restriction, but male to female athletes must demonstrate that their total testosterone level has been below 10 nanomoles per litre for at least 12 months prior to competition (International Olympic Committee 2015). Thus, while the IOC's new guidelines may be less restrictive than those of the Stockholm Consensus, they maintain a reliance on hormones as the ultimate criteria for sorting sex in the context of sport. The focus on hormones is problematic, as there is no evidence showing that athletes with higher testosterone levels perform better than those with lower testosterone levels (Karkazis *et al.* 2012). In addition, rather than being a sexual dimorphism, there is overlap between the testosterone levels of men and women (Karkazis and Jordan-Young 2015). Therefore, while the IOC's guidelines may signal a new level of inclusion for transgender athletes in some ways, they still work to reinforce restrictive assumptions about sex, hormones, and athletic performance.

Given that testosterone is far from a decisive factor in athletic performance, it is promising that some policies without a focus on hormones have emerged. For example, in 2007 the Washington Interscholastic Activities Association (WIAA) became the first interscholastic sport governing body in the United States to adopt a formal policy on participation by transgender athletes (Buzuvis 2011). Specifically, the WIAA policy allows students to participate in sports "in a manner that is consistent with their gender identity, irrespective of the gender listed on a student's records" (Washington 2015–2016, 32). In cases where questions arise about whether a student's gender identity is "bona fide," the policy outlines an appeals process in which the student must appear in front of an eligibility committee composed of such officials as physicians, mental health professionals, administrators, WIAA staff members, and/or advocates "familiar with Gender Identity and Expression issues" (Washington 2015–2016, 32). The committee, rather than requiring medical evidence, considers such documentation as affirmed written statements from the student, a parent/guardian, and/or a health care provider. As of the 2015–2016 academic year, a total of 15 states in the U.S. had "inclusive" policies that did not require surgery or medical hormones as criteria for participation by transgender high school students (transathlete.com).

While policies such as that of the WIAA may be promising, they may be subject to change with relative ease by administrators. In the state of California, however, a law actually exists to guarantee the rights of transgender students in athletic competitions. Specifically, the California School Success and Opportunity Act, which went into effect January 1, 2014, "requires that a pupil be permitted to participate in sex-segregated school programs, activities, including athletic teams and competitions, and use facilities consistent with his or her gender identity, irrespective of the gender listed on the pupil's records" (cited in Mahoney *et al.* 2015, 45). Such a law ensures a level of protection for transgender students that is stronger than that offered by an athletic governing body policy. Overall, the policy developments discussed in this section provide some reason for optimism regarding the increased acceptance of transgender participants in sport. However, accompanying these gains in transgender rights, there has been a simultaneous upsurge of anti-trans backlash, which I discuss in the next section.

Anti-trans backlash

Shortly after the Stockholm Consensus was issued, Cavanaugh and Sykes (2006) suggested that the apparent concern with neutralising alleged masculine advantage in sport is actually more about managing the gender binary at a time when there is growing evidence of its insufficiency and when transgender persons are gaining increased access to basic civil rights in numerous areas of social and cultural life. Similarly, in concurrence with the transgender rights advances noted in the previous section, a new wave of anti-trans legislation has emerged. I specifically discuss some notable developments in the United States below.

One of the primary ways in which legislators have targeted the transgender community recently is in the form of "bathroom bills" that seek to regulate access to single-sex restroom facilities. In March of 2016, the Public Facilities Privacy and Security Act became law in the state of North Carolina. The law bars people from using bathrooms that do not match their birth sex and prohibits local municipalities in the state from establishing anti-discrimination protections for members of the LGBT community (Philipps 2016). As of early 2016, there were more than 100 active anti-LGBT bills being considered by legislative bodies across 22 states in the U.S. (Bendery and Signorile 2016). Some recent policy developments, in fact, have specifically targeted transgender students who wish to participate in school-sponsored sports.

In contrast to the inclusive policies mentioned in the previous section of this chapter, seven states have policies that require trans students to have their sex changed on birth certificates and/or undergo sex reassignment surgery and hormone therapy in order to participate in high school athletics (transathlete.com). For example, school district superintendents and athletic directors in the state of Texas recently voted in favor of a policy that uses the sex listed on one's birth certificate as the sole determinant for student-athlete eligibility (Wright 2016). In order to change the sex listed on a birth certificate, one must obtain a court order, which is likely to be a difficult and expensive process; in Texas, there is no legal standard for gender-marker changes, meaning that decisions about this matter are left up to individual judges (Wright 2016). Given these facts, such a policy presents a barrier that would make sport participation impossible for many transgender students.

Another example of backlash is demonstrated in response to the previously-mentioned California School Success and Opportunity Act. After the law was passed, opponents organized a signature drive to place a veto referendum on the November 2014 election ballot. Opponents narrowly failed to collect the necessary 504,760 signatures to place the veto referendum on the ballot; while they submitted more than 619,000 petition signatures, only 487,484 were declared valid (Egelko 2014). If the referendum were to have qualified for the ballot, it would have required a simple majority of voters to overturn the School Success and Opportunity Act. Overall, the emergence of such backlash demonstrates that recent growth in the acceptance of transgender athletes is tenuous; given the extent of efforts to roll back recent advances, advocates of transgender rights should not view progress as inevitable or irreversible.

Conclusion

In this chapter, I began by highlighting how the history of sex-verification testing illustrates the extent to which many sport governing bodies have operated with a static and binary understanding of sex, creating a hostile environment for transgender athletes. Indeed, some sport organizations seem to have implemented sex-testing policies with the specific intent of excluding transgender participants. However, shortly following the turn of the century, a growing number of sport governing bodies, exemplified by the IOC's 2003 Stockholm Consensus, have adopted policies that provide a limited level of inclusion for transgender athletes. Such policies have been critiqued for their reliance on specific medicalized criteria for inclusion, such as surgery and hormone treatment, and their insensitivity to cultural and economic differences in how transgender persons have access to such procedures. More recently, however, developments such as the CAS's suspension of the IAAF hyperandrogenism policy, the IOC's updated policy, and the existence of interscholastic policies that require neither surgery nor hormone therapy, signal the possible emergence of a new wave of inclusion for transgender athletes in competitive sport.

Despite the possible optimism provided by these developments, I suggest that the potential for greater acceptance and inclusion of transgender athletes is currently tenuous at best. For instance, the CAS decision to suspend the IAAF hyperandrogenism policy is potentially temporary; if the IAAF were to present further evidence prior to the 2017 deadline that the CAS found to be compelling, then the hyperandrogenism policy could be reinstated. Further, the narrowly-failed petition drive to overturn the California School Success and Opportunity Act and the spate of anti-trans legislation that has appeared in numerous U.S. jurisdictions demonstrate that gains made by transgender rights advocates are vulnerable to reversal. Therefore, the future of transgender rights will require continued effort on the part of activists and advocates. While numerous strategies may have potential for success, in this chapter I advocate a strategy of moving away from the sex-segregated model of sport as much as possible in order to advance transgender rights.

Advocates of gender equity should be cautious in supporting the sex-segregated model of sport, given that it often reproduces an ideology of men's superiority and women's inferiority (Love and Kelly 2011; McDonagh and Pappano 2008; Travers 2008). Fortunately, there are a number of alternatives to sex-segregation. One notable example of a sporting activity that has grown with a gender-mixed structure is quidditch, which has developed as a genuine sport adapted from the game in the *Harry Potter* novels. Initiated in the U.S. in 2005, quidditch was founded and remains a non-sex-segregated activity. While the rules dictate that a team may have no more than four players (out of six) who identify as the same gender playing on the field at the same time, there are no other rule adaptations made for men and women. Further, the U.S. Quidditch (USQ) rulebook recognizes that "the gender that a player identifies with is considered to be that player's gender, which may or may not correspond with that person's sex," and "USQ accepts those who don't identify within the binary gender system and acknowledges that not all of our players identify as male or female" (12). Such a strategy creates conditions in which all players can compete together with equal status regardless of gender (Cohen *et al.* 2014).

As another alternative that goes further beyond the two-sex model of sport, Travers and Deri (2011) discuss how some lesbian softball leagues have adopted more radical, non-sex-binary-based policies. These radically-inclusive policies include "transwomen and transmen of all variations and stages of transition (in terms of surgery and hormones) as well as transgender individuals whose gender identities lie between or outside the gender binary" (Travers and Deri 2011, 493). They suggest that the presence of transsexual, transgender and genderqueer players on teams is important because it provides visual evidence of a shift away from dyadic sex boundaries.

There are many potential benefits provided by non-sex-segregated sporting contexts. For example, trans-inclusive teams can serve as valuable sites of support for transgender persons (Travers and Deri 2011). This is particularly important because members of the transgender community suffer disproportionately from mental health problems (Bockting *et al.* 2013) that could perhaps be ameliorated by sport participation in a welcoming environment (McArdle 2008). Additionally, interaction between transgender and cisgender athletes in a supportive context may work to reduce prejudice against members of the transgender community (Buzuvis 2011). Of course, in addition to the direct benefits for transgender athletes, a move away from the segregated two-sex model of sport may help alleviate the damaging effects of orthodox masculinity in sport (Anderson 2008) and disrupt the ideology of natural male superiority that is frequently reproduced in and through sport. Indeed, participants in quidditch have reported gender stereotype reduction and an increased desire for inclusivity and equality due to participation in the sport (Cohen *et al.* 2014).

I wish to emphasize, however, that gender-integrated sport should not be uncritically viewed as a panacea. For example, researchers have reported that an underlying prejudice toward women still exists among many men who participate in quidditch (Cohen *et al.* 2014). Further, there are important issues to be considered in efforts to move away from sex-segregated sport. In the softball leagues studied by Travers and Deri (2011), some lesbian participants feared that transinclusion might take away from the empowering women-only spaces they valued so much. Indeed, support for Renee Richards in her efforts to participate in women's tennis often tended to take an anti-feminist and anti-woman tone (Birrell and Cole 1990). These examples highlight legitimate concerns about advocating integration under broader conditions of deeply-rooted gender inequality. Thus, by advocating that we move toward more inclusive ways of organizing sport, I do not call for a careless elimination of sex-segregation immediately in all contexts. However, I do urge scholars and sport administrators to consider alternatives to sex-segregation as policy is developed in the future. Ultimately, moving away from the segregated two-sex system as much as possible is desirable, not only for the inclusion of transgender athletes but also as a means of promoting gender equity more broadly.

References

Anderson, Eric. 2008. "'I Used to Think Women Were Weak': Orthodox Masculinity, Gender Segregation, and Sport." *Sociological Forum* 23: 257–280. doi:10.1111/j.1573-7861.2008.00058.x

Bendery, Jennifer and Michelangelo Signorile. 2016. "Everything You Need to Know About the Wave of 100+ Anti-LGBT Bills Pending in States." *Huffington Post*, April 15. Accessed June 30, 2016. www.huffingtonpost.com/entry/lgbt-state-bills-discrimination_us_570ff4f2e4b0060ccda2a7a9

Birrell, Susan and Cheryl L. Cole. 1990. "Double Fault: Renee Richards and the Construction and Naturalization of Difference." *Sociology of Sport Journal* 7: 1–21.

Bockting, Walter O., Michael H. Miner, Rebecca E. Swinburne Romine, Autumn Hamilton and Eli Coleman. 2013. "Stigma, Mental Health, and Resilience in an Online Sample of the US Transgender Population." *American Journal of Public Health* 103: 943–951. doi:10.2105/AJPH.2013.301241

Burke, Phyllis. 1996. *Gender Shock: Exploding the Myths of Male and Female.* New York: Anchor Books/Doubleday.

Buzuvis, Erin. 2011. "Transgender Student-Athletes and Sex-Segregated Sport: Developing Policies of Inclusion for Intercollegiate and Interscholastic Athletics." *Seton Hall Journal of Sports and Entertainment Law* 21: 1–59.

Cavanagh, Sheila L. and Heather Sykes. 2006. "Transsexual Bodies at the Olympics: The International Olympic Committee's Policy on Transsexual Athletes at the 2004 Athens Summer Games." *Body & Society* 12: 75–102. doi:10.1177/1357034x06067157

Court of Arbitration for Sport. 2015. *Dutee Chand v. Athletics Federation of India (AFI) and The International Association of Athletics Federations (IAAF)*, CAS 2014/A/3759. Accessed June 30, 2016. www.tas-cas.org/fileadmin/user_upload/award_internet.pdf

Egelko, Bob. 2014. "Transgender Law's Foes Won't Concede Defeat." *San Francisco Gate*, February 25. Accessed June 30, 2016. www.sfgate.com/bayarea/article/Referendum-challenging-transgender-rights-law-5263999.php

Fausto-Sterling, Anne. 2000. *Sexing the Body: Gender Politics and the Construction of Sexuality.* New York: Basic Books.

Fausto-Sterling, Anne. 2012. *Sex/Gender: Biology in a Social World.* New York: Routledge.

International Olympic Committee. 2015. "IOC Consensus Meeting on Sex Reassignment and Hyperandrogenism." Accessed June 30, 2016. https://stillmed.olympic.org/media/Document%20Library/OlympicOrg/IOC/Who-We-Are/Commissions/Medical-and-Scientific-Commission/EN-IOC-Consensus-Meeting-on-Sex-Reassignment-and-Hyperandrogenism.pdf

Kane, Mary J. 1995. "Resistance/Transformation of the Oppositional Binary: Exposing Sport as a Continuum." *Journal of Sport and Social Issues* 19: 191–218. doi:10.1177/019372395019002006

Karkazis, Katrina and Rebecca Jordan-Young. 2015. "Debating a Testosterone 'Sex Gap.'" *Science* 348(6237):858–860. doi:10.1126/science.aab1057

Karkazis, Katrina, Rebecca Jordan-Young, Georgiann Davis and Silvia Camporesi. 2012. "Out of Bounds? A Critique of the New Policies on Hyperandrogenism in

Elite Female Athletes." *The American Journal of Bioethics* 12(7): 3–16. doi:10.1 080/15265161.2012.680533

Love, Adam. 2014. "Transgender Exclusion and Inclusion in Sport," in *Routledge Handbook of Sport, Gender and Sexuality*, edited by Jennifer Hargreaves and Eric Anderson, 376–383. New York: Routledge.

Love, Adam and Kimberly Kelly. 2011. "Equity or Essentialism? U.S. Courts and the Legitimation of Girls' Teams in High School Sport." *Gender & Society* 25: 227–249. doi:10.1177/0891243211398866

Mahoney, Tara Q., Mark A. Dodds and Katherine M. Polasek. 2015. "Progress for Transgender Athletes: Analysis of the School Success and Opportunity Act." *Journal of Physical Education, Recreation & Dance* 86(6): 45–47. doi:10.1080/0 7303084.2015.1054202

McArdle, David. 2008. "Swallows and Amazons, or the Sporting Exception to the Gender Recognition Act." *Social Legal Studies* 17: 39–57. doi:10.1177/ 0964663907086455

McDonagh, Eileen and Laura Pappano. 2008. *Playing with the Boys: Why Separate is Not Equal in Sports*. New York: Oxford University Press.

Philipps, Dave. 2016. "North Carolina Bans Local Anti-Discrimination Policies." *New York Times*, March 23. Accessed June 30, 2016. www.nytimes.com/2016/ 03/24/us/north-carolina-to-limit-bathroom-use-by-birth-gender.html

Pieper, Lindsay P. 2016. *Sex Testing: Gender Policing in Women's Sport*. Urbana, IL: University of Illinois Press.

Schilt, Kristen and Laurel Westbrook. 2009. "Doing Gender, Doing Heteronormativity: 'Gender Normals,' Transgender People, and the Social Maintenance of Heterosexuality." *Gender & Society* 23: 440–464. doi:10.1177/089124320 9340034

Schultz, Jamie. 2011. "Caster Semenya and the 'Question of Too': Sex Testing in Elite Women's Sport and the Issue of Advantage." *Quest* 63: 228–243. doi:10.1 080/00336297.2011.10483678

Sullivan, Claire F. 2011. "Gender Verification and Gender Policies in Elite Sport: Eligibility and 'Fair Play.'" *Journal of Sport and Social Issues* 35: 400–419. doi:10.1177/0193723511426293

Sykes, Heather. 2006. "Transsexual and Transgender Policies in Sport." *Women in Sport and Physical Activity Journal* 15: 3–13.

Travers, Ann. 2006. "Queering Sport: Lesbian Softball Leagues and the Transgender Challenge." *International Review for the Sociology of Sport* 41: 431–446. doi:10.1177/1012690207078070

Travers, Ann. 2008. "The Sport Nexus and Gender Injustice. *Studies in Social Justice* 2: 79–101.

Travers, Ann and Jillian Deri. 2011. "Transgender Inclusion and the Changing Face of Lesbian Softball Leagues." *International Review for the Sociology of Sport* 46: 488–507. doi:10.1177/1012690210384661

U.S. Quidditch. 2016. *US Quidditch Rulebook* (10th ed.). Accessed June 30, 2016. www.usquidditch.org/files/USQ_Rulebook_10.pdf

Wackwitz, Laura A. 2003. "Verifying the Myth: Olympic Sex Testing and the Category 'Woman.'" *Women's Studies International Forum* 26: 553–560.

Washington Interscholastic Activities Association. 2015–2016. *Washington Interscholastic Activities Association Official Handbook, 2015–16*. Accessed June 30, 2016. www.wiaa.com/ConDocs/Con1544/Handbook%20201516.pdf

Wright, John. 2016. "Texas Districts Pass UIL Restriction on Trans Athletes." *Texas Observer*, February 25. Accessed June 30, 2016. www.texasobserver.org/trans-student-athlete-uil-discrimination/

Chapter 16

Queer genes?

The Bio-Amazons project: a response to critics

Claudio Tamburrini

In modern societies, sexual segregation is rejected in most areas of social life. Within sports, however, this practice is seldom questioned, not even by radical feminists.[1]

Together with Tännsjö, I have elsewhere pleaded for eliminating sexual segregation in (elite) sports competitions (Tamburrini and Tännsjö, 2005) so that women and men could compete against each another on equal terms in sport arenas. How could this be achieved? Roughly, the strategy that we favoured was offering women the possibility to genetically modify their physical constitution in order to become as strong as men. The resultant irruption of Bio-Amazons, if such a project ever became scientifically viable, would be desirable as a step towards substantial equality of opportunities in sports. In general, female athletes do not attain equal fame and fortune as male athletes do in professional elite sport. The reason is simple: elite sport is a male-biased activity. Physical attributes historically monopolised by males – strength, muscle volume, speed and height – are much more valued in the sport market than typically female physical traits as balance, rhythm and resistance. This fact renders a situation of sex inequality in elite sports, as women athletes in general get less economic rewards and social recognition than sportsmen.

The traditional (sport) feminist answer to gender inequalities is to keep sex segregation in sports and increase women athletes' share of prizes and rewards (English, 1978). In my view, this is not a rational strategy. First, it would perpetuate the division between male and female sport gender stereotypes and might contribute to cement male chauvinism and power. Second, to increase female athletes' revenues could be perceived by the public as unwarranted positive discrimination. Equal rewards would be overwhelmingly hard to sustain in a situation in which male sport performances are most valued by the market. Instead, we affirmed in our article "the need for women to conquer powerful spaces in male, well-paid sports, not by imposed benefits redistribution, but instead, if necessary, through genetically adapting their physique to market requirements" (Tamburrini and Tännsjö, 2005, p. 183). By offering women the possibility to catch up with men in the most rewarded and popular sports, the Bio-Amazons project might also be expected to generate more appealing female role models for present and future generations of boys and girls, who would experience that women can become physically equally strong, or even stronger, than men.

A discussion on the potential for Bio-Amazons is increasingly necessary as science, particularly sports medicine, is advancing so fast that the prospect of genetically (or by other means) transforming sex-related physiological traits in athletes might become a reality in a relatively near future. Without repeating all the arguments Tännsjö and I already advanced in support of the Bio-Amazons project, I will present the main thrust of our proposal and then proceed to answer the critical reactions to its formulation.

We started from the following assumption ("the conjecture"):

> if, in a certain area, one sex is genetically disadvantaged, then, in this area, it is easier for the disadvantaged sex to catch up with the advantaged one, than it is for the more advantaged one to move further ahead. If this conjecture is borne by realities, it means that genetic enhancement is indeed a feasible means of levelling out differences.
>
> (Tamburrini and Tännsjö, 2005, p. 188)

Furthermore, we provided an answer to the most common objections to the Amazons project.

Against the claim that such a programme would be too risky from a medical point of view, we argued that by the time the genetic modification of women athletes becomes a reality, genetic technology will have been so widely tested as to be relatively safe, at least as safe as any medical technique can be.

Regarding the objection that the programme implies revisiting the Eastern European experiment with women athletes, we underlined that the association often made between genetic enhancement and racial or elitist eugenic programmes disregards the fact that, in the Bio-Amazons' world, it is the individual athletes themselves, not State or sport officials, who decide whether or not to undergo genetic empowerment.

We also provided an answer to the criticism that genetic engineering of women athletes amounts to a misuse of medical expertise and resources, as these women are not sick but rather healthy individuals who wish to enhance their physical traits. In our view, a private, sponsor-supported genetic programme would not burden the State treasury.

Finally, we met the objection that the Bio-Amazons would increase unfairness in competition by pointing out that, on the contrary, the genetic modification of women athletes will contribute to a fairer sport world in two senses: by allowing (at least some) women to compete on more equal terms with men and thereby attain rewards and benefits until now exclusively enjoyed by males, and by equalising competing conditions between them and other female athletes (recall the Caster Semenya's case and intersex female athletes)[2] who, by the work of the genetic lottery, enjoy a more powerful physical condition.[3]

However, it turned out that this defence of the Bio-Amazons proposal was not enough. Further criticism against the project was raised and an intensive discussion started on biologically-induced (not culturally-promoted) gender equality in sports. In this chapter I will try to answer the objections to the Bio-Amazons project.

The best among their class?

In the anthology referred to above, Sherwin and Schwartz argue that the sport public are not merely interested in the most accomplished athletes ('the best male exemplars') but rather in the best athletes among their class. And for this '...separate competitions for men and women are legitimate, as they are for different age groups (and sometimes different weight classes), and for athletes with various types of disability (e.g., the Special Olympics)' (Sherwin and Schwartz, 2005, p. 200).

To begin with, Sherwin and Schwartz' objection is advanced as a factual statement but, to my knowledge, no empirical research has been conducted on the matter. My impression, however, is that their view rests not so much on what sport spectators actually do but instead on what Sherwin and Schwartz hope sport spectators do or what they think they should do. Their assumption that the sport public are not merely interested in the most accomplished athletes but rather in the best athletes among their class is most probably wrong. Our interest in the 'local best' seems to rest on our interest – indeed, our uncritical admiration – for 'the best, period'.[4]

But there is another aspect of sex classes that shows even more clearly that Sherwin and Schwarz' argument does not hit the mark. Sex differences are different in the sense that, unlike age, weight and physical disabilities, they are only indirectly relevant for sport performance. If you are a heavy-weight boxer, then you automatically have a competitive advantage over a fly-weight. If you are a male boxer, however, you might or might not have an advantage over a female competitor: other things being equal (for instance, technical skills), that would ultimately depend on how the two physiques are constituted.

Furthermore, sex is different also in another, ethically and socially more interesting way. While separate competitions between people of different weight and age do not solidify social prejudices against the lower performing group, they certainly do regarding women. As a result of sex-segregated sport, all women are perceived as less powerful ('the weaker sex' was the term used in the past) and therefore separated in order to flourish.

Something similar appears to happen regarding the Paralympics. Segregating physically fully capable and disabled persons probably reinforces negative attitudes towards people with different types of disabilities. Thus, a corollary of our proposal for sex-integrated sport competitions is that the same policy should be advocated regarding disabled sports. I shall return to this issue later in the article.

The objection from male chauvinism

Our proposal has also been charged with being male chauvinistic. John Harris and Simona Giordano, for instance, write that, 'Equality is compatible with both levelling down and levelling up. In order to abolish the distinction between male and female sports, we could make males weaker, rather than women stronger' (Giordano and Harris, 2005, pp. 210–211). Related to this, they also argue that the ideology expressed in our article:

> …presupposes distinctively males attributes as the equivalent of 'health' and 'wholeness' in body. Many disabled groups reject the idea that the non-disabled embody a better paradigm of the good life. [...] The fact that they [Tamburrini and Tännsjö] suggest that women should be allowed (or encouraged?) to make genetic modifications to their body (rather than the other way around) shows that they are implicitly endorsing a male chauvinistic and sexist ideology.
>
> (Ibid., p. 212)

Also Sherwin and Schwartz seem to endorse this criticism when they maintain that equality should not be equated with sameness. According to them, in our proposal the 'best' in sports is defined in terms of male talents. But to require women to become as men is to accept and reinforce this sexist bias. Instead, they advance the view that 'Gender justice sometimes requires that men and women be treated differently precisely in order to ensure that they have equal opportunities' (Sherwin and Schwartz, 2005, p. 201). In a similar vein, Giordano and Harris (2005, p. 212) say that:

> …the moral force of appeals to equality derives not from notions of equal competition or equal opportunity, but rather from the obligation to treat people with equal concern and respect.

So, there seems to be an overwhelming consensus among our critics regarding the sexist and male chauvinistic character of the Bio-Amazons proposal. I will attempt now to answer their criticism.

Are 'levelling down' and 'levelling up' morally equivalent?

To start with the most obvious defence against the charges above, that there is a morally relevant difference between levelling down and levelling up. While the proposal of allowing women to level up to men's level of performance would rest on a voluntary basis, the counter-proposal of levelling down male athletes' performance would obviously have to be implemented by force. How otherwise would male athletes accept to go through genetic modifications that would make them perform at lower levels? It was this difference, rather than a sexist bias, that made us favour increasing women's performance levels instead of decreasing men's. This is compatible with allowing male athletes who might wish to, to transform their genetic make-up with a view to developing physiological characteristics hitherto considered as typically female. But such a radical transformation of the sporting landscape should never be implemented by force.

Is being a woman a disability?

Here our critics might retort that there is an important moral objection to certain forms of 'levelling up'. Maybe raising the strength and level of performance of a fly-weight boxer would not incite social prejudices; but raising women and handicapped athletes to the level of performance of male, full physically-able sport practitioners certainly would do. According to Harris and Giordano, for instance, our proposal presupposes male attributes as equivalent to bodily 'health' and 'wholeness'. But, they object, being a woman cannot qualify as being disabled! By encouraging women to transform their genome in order to acquire male physiological traits we would be sanctioning male standards as superior; and this means telling women that the only way to avoid being discriminated against is to become (at least as strong as) men. Fixing gender discrimination by means of genetics, Harris and Giordano tell us, would be exacerbating the problem as well as insulting to women and this 'would be the equivalent of proposing a remedy for racism which involved a genetic alteration in skin pigmentation rather than a comprehensive assault on prejudice and unfair discrimination' (Giordano and Harris, 2005, p. 216).

I do not think such a comparison is appropriate. A black person who undergoes treatment of whatever kind to get white skin ceases to be black and could be seen as assimilating to the standard values of a predominantly white society. But why should we consider that a woman who develops strong muscles ceases to be a woman or in any way renounces her female condition? Harris and Giordano seem to be equating being a female with having a physically inferior condition. Not only that their sex essentialism renders the unpalatable consequence of depriving women of the right and the possibility of developing the kind of physique they desire: it is contradicted by facts. There are men who are (physically) weaker than the average female as well as women who are stronger than average male exemplars.

Giordano and Harris' argument appears however to be stronger when restricted exclusively to sports. If transforming the female physique is necessary to achieve men's level of performance, being a woman must be seen as a disability in the context of sports. Would that not be an insult to (sports)women?

In the context of sports, excepting a few disciplines which are best adapted to female physiology, I believe that being a woman is a disability. But, unlike Giordano and Harris, I see no insult in this recognition. Historically, sport disciplines were designed to measure typically male physical traits. Thus, most sportswomen are at a disadvantage in relation to most sportsmen, as they compete in disciplines that are better suited to the male physiology. In that regard, the most rewarding and popular sports are male-biased, and the best-performing athletes in absolute terms will almost always be a man. I feel that allowing women the possibility to reduce this performance gap through technology implies annulling the male bias that characterises the sport market in the most rewarding and popular sports.

This technological move might also be effective in speeding up the process of equalizing competitive opportunities between the sexes. As we don't know how much of 'the muscle gap' between the sexes depends on physiological factors, and how much of it originates in culture, we should be open to changes in the physiological status quo (even technologically-induced ones) with the potential to change the public's perception on men's and women's physical prowess.

Harris and Giordano also argue that the Bio-Amazons project seems to imply that we should extend the possibility of bodily transformation (either technologically or genetically) to the disabled or, alternatively, deny women athletes that possibility.

I am convinced that we should let both the disabled and women athletes do what they want with their bodies. As a matter of fact, they already do. In the Special Olympics, disabled athletes try, with the assistance of different technical devices and coping strategies, to overcome their physical handicap in order to achieve sport performances as near as possible to those of non-disabled athletes. And women resort to weight-lifting in order to increase their muscle volume as part of their training programmes. Why should it be different regarding similar, though genetically-induced, enhancements?

The fact that both women and the disabled have always tried to emulate the performance standards of fully physically capable males in elite sports, speaks in favour of extending that possibility to both groups.

'The tyranny of the normal'

It could perhaps also be argued that allowing lower-performing individuals to modify themselves in order to get characteristics (physical, cognitive or of other sort) that belong to the best-situated part of a population implies reinforcing "the tyranny of the normal" and that instead of showing respect for what all individuals do, by letting women become genetically modified we would be indirectly encouraging them to adopt male stand-ards as a condition for admiring and rewarding their sport results. Again, this phenomenon is particularly evident in the disability debate. As it has been explicitly stated in the discussion on deafness culture, many disabled people refuse to emulate, sometimes even to adapt to, 'normal' standards and demand instead to be recognised for what they are (Padden and Humphries, 1988).

I do not think that allowing disabled or female athletes to reach the levels of performance that hitherto have been achieved by male athletes would necessarily imply any form of disrespect for the lower-performers. It is not a question of respect, but rather of securing equal opportunity for all participants in sport competitions. Male and female athletes will not be competing on equal terms in sports as long as we do not equalise men's and women's physiological standards. Respecting lower performances for the effort and sacrifice they no doubt demand should not be confused with considering them as equally good as the best ones. There is no logical incompatibility between showing respect for those who do not reach high standards and allowing them to improve their performances by the means they prefer. From this perspective, it becomes clear that Harris and Giordano are confusing 'respect' with 'equal value'. In physically-demanding sports, we have reason to respect different levels of perform-ance, but this does not mean that the lower ones should be considered as equally valuable. After all, we want sportspersons to reach higher and higher levels of performance. So, even if 'respect' does not require equaliz-ing levels of performance, 'equal opportunity' does. A notion of equality that had no bearing at all on fairness in competition would indeed be a rather empty one.

Fairness in competition

Contributing to fairer competitions is what Sherwin and Schwartz seem to have in mind when they propose treating men and women athletes differ-ently. According to them, gender equality should not be interpreted in terms of making men and women equal, and we should try to abolish sexism in society and treat women athletes differently by giving them the same or more resources than we give men (Sherwin and Schwartz, 2005, p. 203).

Besides, according to Sherwin and Schwartz, there is also a further, global aspect of fairness in competition that might be negatively affected if the Bio-Amazons ever became a reality. They argue that genetic interventions aimed at transgressing biological sex-boundaries will probably be too expensive for the poor as well as for developing countries. Sponsorship, they say, is not a solution to this problem, as genetic alterations would be required before athletes gained recognition from the sport market. In their words:

> Legitimizing expensive interventions for the sake of reducing gender inequality is likely to exacerbate inequality due to income both nationally and internationally. Tamburrini and Tännsjö imply that athletes would pay for these genetic enhancements themselves, rather than relying on the State treasury. They see this as a fair suggestion since lucrative sports sponsorship allows athletes the luxury of paying for elite medical services. We submit that this proposal is confounding since the genetic alterations would likely occur before the athlete had gained international success and secured these sponsorships. […] Currently, success in sports is regarded as a way out of poverty for some underprivileged children who see their poor background reflected in the history of some sports stars. If Tamburrini and Tännsjö's proposal were to become a reality, this avenue of hope may be closed, as successful athletes would increasingly come from families that could afford these expensive technologies. This problem would also be reflected internationally, where it would be unlikely that poor countries would continue to be able to enter athletes in international competition against genetic Amazons.
>
> (Ibid., 2005, pp. 201–202)

This is a very impressive criticism. However, I believe it has less substance than seems to be the case at first sight. To begin with, why would we suppose that only the rich children will be genetically enhanced? Many off-spring of the rich lack the necessary physical endowments required for a successful and meaningful genetic intervention. And, the other way around, why would we assume that no children of the have-nots would be properly supported by sponsors? Sherwin and Schwartz's criticism shows they are unaware of the fact that the sport market, and the enterprises acting in it, is becoming more and more aggressive in discovering young sport talents. Often we read of children/adolescents contracted by a football club for many years to come. No matter what we think and how we feel about talent-spotting, the current tendency of the sport market suggests the objection advanced by Sherwin and Schwartz can be neutralised at national and international level. There is no reason to suppose that sport agents' hunting of young talent will stop at the national boundaries.

Besides, even granting that the Bio-Amazons project might bring about some social inequality, it should be seen in light of the increases in gender equality it might contribute to. Perhaps Sherwin and Schwartz are right in that the rich man's off-spring will get an unfair advantage over the children of the have-nots, but that unfair advantage will also favour the rich man's daughters to the detriment of, certainly both the sons and daughters of the poor, but also the rich man's sons. Why would it be wrong to trade-off some social inequality (related to different social groups' access to a sporting career) for more gender equality (that will probably have positive effects upon the whole social body and not only in the world of sports)?

In relation to fairness in competition, I wish to comment on how Sherwin and Schwartz believe we might come to terms with unequal distribution of the benefits and rewards of elite sports. They argue that 'equality requires equal resources and equal opportunity, not the requirement to change one's genetic makeup to more closely approximate the physical advantages men have for particular sports' (ibid., 2005, pp. 203–204).

Sherwin and Schwartz' proposal has the merit of going further than merely requiring equal concern and respect for male and female athletes' performances.[5] As I argued before, equal opportunity demands more substantial measures than merely adopting a particular mental attitude towards a person or a social group and their achievements. But I think they fail to realise that no matter how much we try to level out resources and opportunities (for instance, coaching and training facilities, sport grants, etc.), there will still be a substantial physiological inequality between the sexes in sports. Short of re-distributing rewards in elite sports, we should instead go for equalising the conditions of competition, biologically. Otherwise, treating women differently by giving them extra rewards (as distinct from resources), we might be risking consolidating general prejudices regarding women's supposed inferiority when it comes to physical performances.

Is the Bio-Amazons project too conservative?

Our proposal has also been charged with being not radical enough. In that regard, Kutte Jönsson has argued that:

> Although their [Tamburrini and Tännsjö's] argument works in favour of the idea of individuals crossing sex/gender barriers, it still entails the acceptance of the concept of gender, and the concept of gender differentiates bodies into certain (gender) norms, and that involves and promotes (gender) discrimination.
>
> (Jönsson, 2009, p. 136)

Thus, in Jönsson's view, it is only in a world of asexual cyborgs that gender discrimination – both in sport and in society – can be successfully neutralised. Rather than trying to abolish sex and gender discrimination by social, cultural and political means (as our critics argue against us) or by biological means (as we propose), he believes that we should abolish sex and gender as normative and discriminating categorisations.

Jönsson's argument is well taken. In the past, there were some sex differences that might have been considered as essential. Mainly they were related to one activity that women, but not men, could perform: child bearing. But things have changed. Some men can today give birth.[6] In the future, ectogenesis (that is, pregnancy outside the womb) might also help women to liberate themselves from 'the tyranny of reproduction' (Firestone, 2002, 185).

The sport world, however, is not evolving so fast. Sex segregation forces sport practitioners into one of two different sex categories, no matter how their physiological constitution looks.[7] Sportspersons are not seen, much less categorised, as asexual cyborgs, either by the public or by sport officials. Starting from this categorisation, men (on average) still jump higher, run faster and lift heavier weights than women (Cheuvront et al., 2005; Holden, 2004). Given this context, the Bio-Amazons project might be a healthy contribution to abolishing sex categorisations in sport and society. Making women stronger than men through genetic modifications is the next step to take at the present stage of our scientific development.

Concluding remarks

The outcome of my discussion seems favourable to the Bio-Amazons project. In the preceding sections I set out to answer the objections raised by our original proposal of allowing female athletes to (genetically) transform their physiques in order to catch up the physiological advantage men have in certain sport disciplines. I will not repeat my arguments here, the critical reader will be the final judge of my defence of the Bio-Amazons project.

However, it might still be asked, why is there resistance against the Bio-Amazons? In my view, part of the explanation rests on our strongly-cemented prejudices that make us perceive any kind of transcending sexual barriers as threatening. This applies even to people who, on behalf of their profession, have devoted themselves to critically scrutinise those very prejudices. In some way or another, we all are sex-blind.

But the Bio-Amazons project is not only part of a sex-equalising programme; it also expresses a secular, science-based libertarian model according to which the deliberate adaptation of our biological nature is the individuals' prerogative, not God's or any other worldly authorities'. Within such a model, moulding our biology implies transcending the limitations imposed upon us by the genetic lottery (some people are born with more or less favourable physiological and intellectual conditions than others) as well as the sex lottery (people are born with physical character-istics that differ from those belonging to the other/s sex/es). We are now entering into an era in which the whimsical limitations imposed upon indi-viduals by these natural lotteries might be modified according to our desires. This prospect will of course add further negative reactions to those expressed against the Bio-Amazons.

I hope this resistance can be overcome.

Notes

1 Exceptions to this are Anderson (2010, particularly chapter, 6 'Sport's use in marginalizing women', pp. 121–134), and McDonagh and Pappano (2008). However, even if other authors have proposed making structural changes in sports in order to promote sex integration, our proposal is, as far as I know, unique in that it purports to attain sex equality by changing women's physiologi-cal condition, rather than the ideological and cultural fundamentals of (elite) sports.
2 The South African middle-distance runner Caster Semenya won the 800 m women's race at the 2009 World Championship in Athletics in Berlin. A few hours after her victory, it was announced that she had been subjected to "gender testing" and was suspended from international competition by the International Association of Athletics Federations (IAAF). After having been examined for more than a year, Semenya was allowed to compete again on 6 July 2010. Her case brought to the light the situation of so called intersex (female) athletes, that is, sportswomen who have higher than average levels of male hormones (mainly testosterone). As a direct consequence of the Semenya's case, new regulations were introduced by the International Olympic Committee and IAAF that set an upper limit to androgen levels for women athletes. Although indirectly, these new regulations imply intersex women should undergo medical treatment (for instance, with oestrogen) in order to be allowed to compete with other women.
3 For a more detailed discussion on these objections, see Tamburrini and Tännsjö, 2005.
4 Being 'the best, period' has to be understood in absolute, not relative, terms. That means that, on average, most men run and swim faster, lift heavier weights, etc., than most women. I will return to this question in the section Is being a woman a disability?
5 In that sense, Harris and Giordano are wrong as well when they refer to 'equal opportunity' as simply requiring 'equal concern and respect'.
6 In 2008, an Oregon couple redefined division of labour in marital life. Thomas Beatie, a man who was born a woman gave birth to a child after undergoing sex change surgery to become a man 10 years earlier, while retaining his female reproductive organs, just in case. His wife Nancy was unable to have children due to a hysterectomy. Thomas – who is legally a man and legally married – stopped taking testosterone injections and started having periods again, allowing him to become pregnant by artificial insemination. After that, Thomas gave birth to two more children (Perth Now, 2010).
7 Recall the decision taken by the IOC and the IAAF that, although indirectly, compels intersex female athletes to undergo oestrogen treatment to be allowed to compete with other women. Intersex athletes illustrate the fact that sex is a continuum with clear-cut females and males on both extremes of the scale, but with many less easily judged cases in between.

References

Anderson, E. (2010) *Sport, Theory and Social Problems – A Critical Introduction.* London and New York: Routledge.

Cheuvront, S. N., Carter, R., Deruisseau, K. C. and Moffatt, R. J. (2005) Running performance differences between men and women. *Sports Medicine* 35: 1017–1024.

English, J. (1978) Sex equality in sports. *Philosophy and Public Affairs* 7 (3): 269–277.

Firestone, S. (2002) *The Dialectic of Sex. In: The Case for Feminist Revolution.* New York: Farrar, Strauss & Giroux (originally published 1970).

Giordano, S. and Harris, J. (2005) What is gender equality in sports? In: Tamburrini, C. and Tännsjö, T. (eds), *Genetic Technology and Sport – Ethical Questions.* London and New York: Routledge, Chapter 18.

Holden, C. (2004) An everlasting gender gap?. *Science* 305: 639–640.

Jönsson, K. (2009) Who's afraid of Stella Walsh? On gender, 'gene cheaters', and the promises of cyborg athletes. In: Tamburrini, C. and Tännsjö, T. (eds), *The Ethics of Sports Medicine.* London and New York: Routledge, Chapter 10.

McDonagh, F. and Pappano, J. (2008) *Playing with the Boys: Why Separate is Not Equal in Sports.* Oxford: Oxford University Press.

Padden, C. and Humphries, T. (1988) *Deaf in America: Voices from a Culture.* Cambridge: Harvard University Press.

Perth Now (2010) First known transgender man to give birth delivers third child. *Perth Now.*

Sherwin, S. and Schwartz, M. (2005) Resisting the emergence of Bio-Amazons. In: Tamburrini, C. and Tännsjö, T. (eds), *Genetic Technology and Sport – Ethical Questions.* London and New York: Routledge, Chapter 16.

Tamburrini, C. and Tännsjö, T. (2005) *Genetic Technology and Sport – Ethical Questions.* London-New York: Routledge.

Tamburrini, C. and Tännsjö, T (2005) The genetic design of a new Amazon. In: Tamburrini, C and Tännsjö, T. (eds), *Genetic Technology and Sport – Ethical Questions.* London and New York: Routledge. Chapter 15.

Tamburrini, C. and Tännsjö, T. (2009) *The Ethics of Sports Medicine.* London and New York: Routledge.

Index

Taylor & Francis eBooks

Helping you to choose the right eBooks for your Library

Add Routledge titles to your library's digital collection today. Taylor and Francis ebooks contains over 50,000 titles in the Humanities, Social Sciences, Behavioural Sciences, Built Environment and Law.

Choose from a range of subject packages or create your own!

Benefits for you

» Free MARC records
» COUNTER-compliant usage statistics
» Flexible purchase and pricing options
» All titles DRM-free.

Free Trials Available
We offer free trials to qualifying academic, corporate and government customers.

Benefits for your user

» Off-site, anytime access via Athens or referring URL
» Print or copy pages or chapters
» Full content search
» Bookmark, highlight and annotate text
» Access to thousands of pages of quality research at the click of a button.

eCollections – Choose from over 30 subject eCollections, including:

Archaeology	Language Learning
Architecture	Law
Asian Studies	Literature
Business & Management	Media & Communication
Classical Studies	Middle East Studies
Construction	Music
Creative & Media Arts	Philosophy
Criminology & Criminal Justice	Planning
Economics	Politics
Education	Psychology & Mental Health
Energy	Religion
Engineering	Security
English Language & Linguistics	Social Work
Environment & Sustainability	Sociology
Geography	Sport
Health Studies	Theatre & Performance
History	Tourism, Hospitality & Events

For more information, pricing enquiries or to order a free trial, please contact your local sales team:
www.tandfebooks.com/page/sales

Routledge
Taylor & Francis Group

The home of
Routledge books

www.tandfebooks.com